UNDERSTANDING PHARMA

A PRIMER ON HOW PHARMACEUTICAL COMPANIES REALLY WORK

JOHN J. CAMPBELL

PHARMACEUTICAL
INSTITUTE

Library of Congress Control Number: 2005906401

ISBN 0-9763096-0-2

To learn more about the full range of off-the-shelf and custom information and training resources offered by the Pharmaceutical Institute, visit us online at www.pharmainstitute.com or call (877) 923-5600.

Pharmaceutical Institute
Raleigh, NC 27615

PHARMACEUTICAL
INSTITUTE

Book design and layout by Susan Wang, www.savantstudio.com

DEDICATION

I want to thank the Campbell Alliance consulting group, both for their invaluable contributions to this work and for proving every day that people who truly understand every aspect of pharmaceutical company operations—and also possess a firm grasp of a very dynamic market environment—can produce truly amazing results for their clients. They justify the premise on which Campbell was built, that the pharmaceutical industry needs not just sophisticated consultants but consultants with a sophisticated, function-specific grasp of their particular problems and challenges. I could not have written, or even have considered writing, this book without them.

Although the book is now complete, I have the continuing privilege of learning daily from my own internal team of experts. Through the Understanding Pharma training modules now available from the Pharmaceutical Institute, I hope to extend that opportunity to others who want to enhance their knowledge of the pharmaceutical industry and, more specifically, of the pharmaceutical company enterprise.

ACKNOWLEDGEMENTS

I could not have completed this book without the help of the Campbell Alliance consulting team and a variety of extremely knowledgeable—and busy—industry executives, who generously shared both their time and expertise. Any errors that remain in the work are not theirs but my own.

For their help with the book's content, I would like to single out Bill Barnett, Kevin Barnett, Ben Bonifant, Horace Cook, Ed Gaffney, Lisa Grimes, Gary Kirby, Susanne Laningham, Tom Luginbill, Michael Luther, Michael Mead, Eva Mitchell, Nader Naeymi-Rad, Darius Naigamwalla, Robert Navarro, Garry O'Grady, John Reddan, George Schmidt, Richard Schuerger, Gary Tyson, and Tim Williams.

For their help with the writing and editorial processes, I would like to thank Puneet Bhargava, Bonnie Hauser, Joshua Kolling-Perin, Rose Mills, and Lisa Pagnani.

And finally, I would also like to thank Dan Blue for helping me execute on this project.

Their contributions and support made this book a reality.

John J. Campbell

Chief Executive Officer

Campbell Alliance

August 2005

FOREWORD

Understanding Pharma is an introduction to how pharmaceutical companies actually work, from both a scientific and business standpoint.

Two years ago, I decided to write a primer on the pharmaceutical industry because I couldn't find the type of book I wanted to share with newcomers to our industry— a good end-to-end overview written in an engaging manner that made an exciting enterprise come alive.

I soon realized that the kind of book I had in mind would be useful to a wide audience. In an industry that is both extremely complex and highly specialized, an understanding of all aspects of the pharmaceutical enterprise is rare even among experienced executives. The need to master their own incredibly sophisticated domains leaves many industry insiders little time to develop a detailed knowledge of other functions and their contribution across the drug discovery, development, and marketing spectrum. Yet the very complexity of the pharmaceutical enterprise makes effective collaboration across functions essential—and such collaboration requires mutual understanding. With this book, I hope to promote that understanding and communicate some of my own excitement about the industry.

It would take an encyclopedia to do full justice to every aspect of the pharmaceutical industry, and I wanted to produce something far briefer that would be accessible to industry newcomers and busy executives alike. To make this undertaking manageable, I limited the scope of this book in some pivotal respects:

- My first decision was to focus upon the US market. The book introduces global product and geographic markets and identifies functions that are managed globally, such as Operations or Drug Development. The overall emphasis, however, remains the US, particularly in discussions of customer-facing functions such as Sales and Managed Markets.

- *Understanding Pharma* derives its basic operational model from leading pharmaceutical companies, rather than biotech and specialty pharmaceutical companies. In many cases, the same practices apply to all three entities. When major operational differences exist, I have attempted to highlight them.

- Companies often tap external resources for assistance with the activities described here. Strategic alliances with other pharmaceutical companies, outsourcing relationships with specialized service vendors, and contracts with suppliers are all enlisted to "round out" functionality and maximize performance. In this book, the focus is on key activities rather than the entities entrusted with executing them, although such relationships are touched upon selectively.

- Regulatory coverage is sharply circumscribed. *Understanding Pharma* introduces the major regulatory bodies and guidelines affecting the industry and explains how regulatory features and controls are integrated with business processes. The work is emphatically not, however, intended as a definitive source for information on an extremely complex and far-reaching regulatory environment.

The book is organized into two major sections: an overview of the industry, its products, and customers, followed by chapters dedicated to major functions within a full-service pharmaceutical company.

Since *Understanding Pharma* is a primer, I introduce and explain common industry terminology. Our publisher, the Pharmaceutical Institute, also offers a more detailed stand-alone ready-reference glossary titled *Lingua Pharma*.

Whether you are a senior executive looking for a way to "put the pieces together" for your team, a mid-level executive assuming new responsibilities, or a professional new to the industry, I believe that *Understanding Pharma* will prove a valuable tool to enhance knowledge and performance.

John J. Campbell

TABLE OF CONTENTS

Chapter 1   Introduction to the Industry
1. The Role of the Pharmaceutical Industry   2
2. Structure of a Full-Service Pharmaceutical Company   8
3. The Worldwide Scope of the Pharmaceutical Industry   14

Chapter 2   What is a Drug?
1. What Makes a Drug a Drug?   18
2. What Are Drugs Made Of?   19
3. How Are Drugs Classified?   23
4. How Do Drugs Enter the US Market?   30
5. The Product Life Cycle   32

Chapter 3   Pharma Customers
1. Overview of Major Customer Groups   38
THE DEMAND DRIVERS
2. Physicians   42
3. Consumers and Patients   47
4. Payers and Pharmacy Benefit Managers   50
THE SUPPLY SIDE
5. Pharmacies   54

Chapter 4   Discovery
1. The Importance of Discovery   62
2. A Closer Look at Discovery   65
3. Operational Model for Discovery   73

Chapter 5   Drug Development
1. The Importance of Drug Development   76
2. A Closer Look at Drug Development   80
3. Operational Model for Drug Development   100

Chapter 6   Business Development
1. The Importance of Business Development   106
2. A Closer Look at Business Development Activities   109
3. Operational Model for Business Development   119

Chapter 7   Marketing and Brand Management
1. The Importance of Marketing and Brand Management   122
2. A Closer Look at Marketing and Brand Management   126
3. Operational Model for Marketing and Brand Management   143

Chapter 8   Sales
1. The Importance of Sales   148
2. A Closer Look at Sales   150
3. Operational Model for Sales   168

Chapter 9   Managed Markets
1. The Importance of Managed Markets   173
2. A Closer Look at Managed Markets   174
3. Operational Model for Managed Markets   183

Chapter 10   Manufacturing Operations
1. The Importance of Manufacturing Operations   186
2. A Closer Look at Manufacturing Operations   189
3. Operational Model for Manufacturing Operations   204

Chapter 11   Distribution
1. The Importance of Distribution   210
2. A Closer Look at Distribution   212
3. Operational Model for Distribution   218

Appendix
1. Overview   224
2. Financial Management and Control   224
3. Human Resources   227
4. Information Technology   230
5. Legal   234
6. Other Corporate Functions   237

Index   238

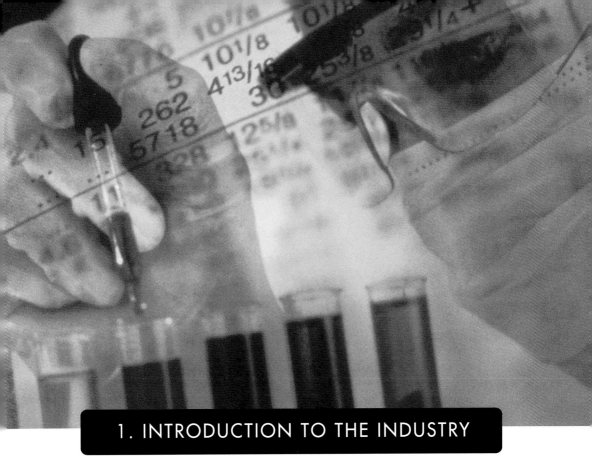

1. INTRODUCTION TO THE INDUSTRY

1. The Role of the Pharmaceutical Industry

2. Structure of a Full-Service Pharmaceutical Company

3. The Worldwide Scope of the Pharmaceutical Industry

1. The Role of the Pharmaceutical Industry

Pharmaceuticals are arguably the most socially important healthcare products. They play an integral role in virtually every facet of the healthcare system and in the life of nearly every person. (See Figure 1.1)

Figure 1.1 The Range of Health Care Products

Products	Description
Pharmaceuticals	• Medicines and vaccines for human and animal use; products may have a trademark (brand) name or be generic, and they may be prescription or over-the-counter
Diagnostics	• Equipment and supplies used in screening, detecting, and monitoring disease; can range from simple home testing kits to sophisticated diagnostic imaging technologies
Medical Devices	• Advanced instrumentation and appliances used for medical therapy, such as joint replacements, implantable defibrillators, and pacemakers; also, drug delivery devices such as syringes, infusion pumps, metered-dose inhalers, and transdermal patches
Medical Supplies	• Commodity, high-volume supplies used in medical settings, such as surgical gowns and gloves
Durable Medical Equipment	• Reusable products for health-related use in the home, such as walkers, wheelchairs, oxygen equipment, prosthetics, and hospital beds

Source: Campbell Alliance.

Role of Pharmaceuticals in Healthcare

In the 20th century, pharmaceutical products have virtually eradicated diseases that had previously killed tens of millions, such as smallpox, and vastly reduced the number of deaths from other pandemic diseases, such as influenza. Other conditions that could not be eliminated, such as cardiovascular disease and asthma, were brought under greater control. In the late 20th century, it became more and more common to use drugs to promote "wellness," disease prevention, and early intervention to control risk factors and stabilize patient health.

Use of drug therapy now spans almost all levels of disease severity and sites of care. (See Figure 1.2) Patients may self-medicate at home using non-prescription products or receive a prescription or medication in a physician office, emergency room, or clinic. Most medicines are taken by the patient at home to treat an acute condition (e.g., an antibiotic for a bacterial infection), a chronic condition (e.g., a heart disease drug), or, in some cases, to prevent a disease from occurring (e.g., cholesterol-lowering medication). Some products, like insulin for diabetes, allow a patient to manage a serious

"Medicine has been transformed by pharmaceutical innovation. We've seen the widespread use of antibiotics, the discovery of agents for cancer, major advances in cardiovascular medicine. We've seen the development of new treatments for depression and the advent of drugs that make organ transplants possible and chemotherapy bearable. Today, we are experiencing the break-throughs of biotechnology and the consequent surge of new therapeutic proteins."

Sidney Taurel (President, Chairman, and CEO of Eli Lilly).
"Hands Off My Industry," The Wall Street Journal, November 3, 2003.

and potentially life-threatening disease for a lifetime. People who require close monitoring due to the severity or instability of their condition are typically treated on an inpatient basis—that is, they stay overnight or for extended stays in hospitals or similar facilities for observation, care, diagnosis, or treatment. The chronically ill and/or elderly residing in skilled nursing facilities are often on complex drug regimens to treat multiple ailments. In addition, terminally ill patients staying in hospices often receive medication to relieve pain.

Fig. 1.2 Role of Pharmaceuticals in Healthcare

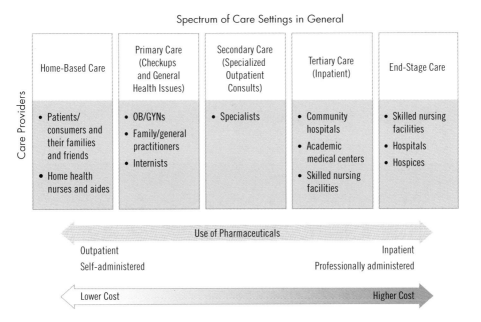

Spectrum of Care Settings in General

Care Providers	Home-Based Care	Primary Care (Checkups and General Health Issues)	Secondary Care (Specialized Outpatient Consults)	Tertiary Care (Inpatient)	End-Stage Care
	• Patients/ consumers and their families and friends • Home health nurses and aides	• OB/GYNs • Family/general practitioners • Internists	• Specialists	• Community hospitals • Academic medical centers • Skilled nursing facilities	• Skilled nursing facilities • Hospitals • Hospices

Use of Pharmaceuticals

Outpatient   Inpatient
Self-administered   Professionally administered

Lower Cost   Higher Cost

Source: Campbell Alliance.

Quality of life and lifestyle enhancement have become more prominent goals of patients, healthcare providers and the pharmaceutical industry in recent years. Better quality of life has always been a consideration in drug development and use, but the meaning of that term was often limited historically, with the focus on freedom from pain and from debility.

Lifestyle enhancement drugs encompass a broader spectrum of quality-of-life considerations today. Drugs are now available to help consumers retard visible signs of aging and maintain sexual function. Some people hail these products as major advances in the promotion of physical and psychological health. Others see them as forms of self-indulgence that, when covered by insurance, unnecessarily inflate the cost of US healthcare.

As a result of the prominent role of pharmaceuticals, the pharmaceutical industry has an enormous impact on the US and the world. The industry reflects a complex, and sometimes controversial, amalgam of science and business. In the US, the pharmaceutical industry is dominated by private, for-profit companies. Even if the profit motive is one driver of innovation, the resulting social contribution is obvious: Significant advances in drug therapy allow people to live longer, healthier lives with fewer restrictions.

A foundational assumption in the industry is that innovators can truly "do well by doing good"—that drugs with compelling social benefits can become products that yield impressive returns to the developers.

The pharmaceutical companies that develop innovative products are in a high-stakes business in which the failure rate is high and the rewards of success commensurately great. Finding that "next big thing"—or even an array of moderately successful products—is not easy. Years of laboratory research, preclinical testing, and clinical testing are involved.

Pharmaceutical development is a high-risk undertaking, in which many promising leads prove disappointing, often after millions of dollars are invested in them. In addition to the huge upfront expenditures for the rigorous testing of a drug during research and development, pharmaceutical companies incur substantial ongoing costs for the sales, marketing, and manufacturing of the product. In the end, the rewards of a successful drug can more than offset the risks: a moderate success can mean several hundred million dollars in annual sales, while blockbuster status translates into sales of over $1 billion annually.

Regulatory Framework

Although pharmaceutical companies operate at considerable business risk, public health and safety is never sacrificed. Pharmaceutical company activities are heavily regulated to ensure drug safety and efficacy—and to prevent misleading product claims and illicit inducements to choose a particular drug. In the US, the primary regulator is the Food and Drug Administration (FDA), part of the Department of Health and Human Services. (See Figure 1.3)

Figure 1.3 Leading Regulatory Bodies

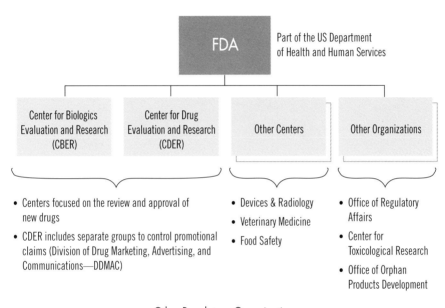

Other Regulatory Organizations

Organization	Description
Office of Inspector General (OIG)	• An arm of the Department of Health and Human Services, which investigates regulatory infractions, provides compliance advice, and brings enforcement actions
Federal Trade Commission (FTC)	• Regulates general business practices to protect consumers against anti-competitive behavior and misleading claims
Drug Enforcement Administration (DEA)	• Regulates the distribution and use of narcotics and other controlled substances

Sources: Food and Drug Administration; Campbell Alliance.

The regulations are designed to protect the public welfare and ensure that critical new therapies reach the market quickly and safely. Selective liberalization of regulations is used to encourage development and expedite patient access to drugs that address urgent medical needs.

The framework that has evolved in the pharmaceutical industry combines active company and industry self-regulation with governmentally enforced standards. (See Figure 1.4)

Figure 1.4 Industry Control Framework

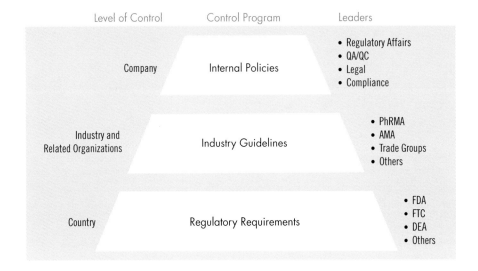

Country-specific regulatory requirements, such as those established by the FDA in the US, establish a baseline standard to which pharmaceutical companies must adhere.

Industry and closely-related non-government groups articulate ethical and process standards that are sometimes more rigorous than regulatory requirements. Most pharmaceutical companies are active participants in the development of industry-wide guidelines that industry associations formulate with input from relevant regulatory bodies. The Pharmaceutical Research and Manufacturers of America (PhRMA) is the most powerful and influential of these groups in the US. Other groups, closely related to but not part of the pharmaceutical industry, also contribute to the ethical and process standards. The American Medical Association (AMA) provides ethical guidelines to physicians about appropriate interactions with pharmaceutical companies (e.g., acceptance of items or services of substantial monetary value). Industry guidelines often shape, or obviate the need for, formal regulatory guidelines.

Companies maintain internal functions that ensure compliance with regulatory and industry requirements by establishing internal policies and organizational controls. In addition, companies monitor changes in regulations on an ongoing basis.

Most, if not all, companies maintain several internal "watchdog" departments, such as Regulatory Affairs and Legal, to oversee compliance of all functions with internal policies and regulatory mandates.

Many companies now employ a compliance officer, often reporting to the chairman or general counsel, with overall responsibility for developing and disseminating business policies and monitoring compliance. The responsibilities of compliance officers often extend beyond adherence to explicit regulatory mandates; these officers grapple with appropriate internal policies to address "gray area" ethical and legal issues.

Managing Costs

In addition to a complex regulatory system, pharmaceutical companies are also subject to utilization controls imposed by the dominant form of health insurance in the US, managed care. After a brief slowdown in the 1990s, growth in healthcare costs has returned to double-digit rates. Insurers and other payers, who absorb most of those costs, view this increase with concern and have responded by tightening controls on the utilization of medications.

In the last 30 years, the American health insurance system has largely transformed from indemnity plans to managed care offerings that emphasize cost control through restricted access to products and services. Escalating drug costs are a particular target of scrutiny. More than 85% of the insured population in the US is under managed care. Managed care payers attempt to limit the range of drugs, particularly expensive branded drugs, for which they will provide reimbursement. Some managed care plans exert a strong influence on prescribing behavior by increasing the out-of-pocket costs of drugs to patients who are prescribed a non-covered medication.

Effective drug therapy can be a cost-effective and highly valuable means of controlling total healthcare expenditures and improving quality of life. In many instances, effective disease management through drug therapy reduces overall healthcare costs by stabilizing patient health and functioning so that costly hospitalization episodes and other forms of intensive treatment (e.g., surgery) can be avoided. Insurers and other payers, however, often view pharmaceutical expenditures in isolation as a cost center rather than a potential source of aggregate savings.

Pharmaceutical companies work hard to overcome negative perception. They map out sophisticated strategies for winning over major payers—offering generous price concessions, presenting compelling data about their products' benefits, and assisting with disease management programs—in order to attain favorable positioning for their products with managed care.

Pharmaceutical Innovation

The current era is one of great clinical promise and great market challenge. The pharmaceutical industry has sometimes come under fire in recent decades for what some call its "incremental" approach to drug development, looking for new drugs that improve slightly upon existing therapies and appear to be driven more by financial than clinical considerations.

Despite the criticism, the pharmaceutical industry now seems poised to make a more significant leap forward than ever before. Sophisticated computer-aided drug design helps researchers match drugs to their intended targets. Advanced technologies allow companies to quickly screen thousands of potential drugs. A vastly improved understanding of the human genetic make-up (genome) and the protein activity through which genetic characteristics are expressed presents opportunities for "tailored" treatment. The industry's previous achievements are likely to pale in comparison to the pharmaceutical breakthroughs of the coming years. (See Figure 1.5)

2. Structure of a Full-Service Pharmaceutical Company

Pharmaceutical companies are generally either research-based or focused on the manufacturing of generic drugs. Some large corporations include both, through research-based and generics subsidiaries.

Research-based companies are the leading-edge innovators. Such pharmaceutical companies develop branded drugs (or brands) that are sufficiently novel to be protected by patent from imitators. These firms are also known as ethical pharmaceutical companies.

When patents expire, other companies are free to market drugs with the same active ingredient and equivalent efficacy, known as generics.

Figure 1.5 Selective Overview of Pharmaceutical Innovation–Past and Projected

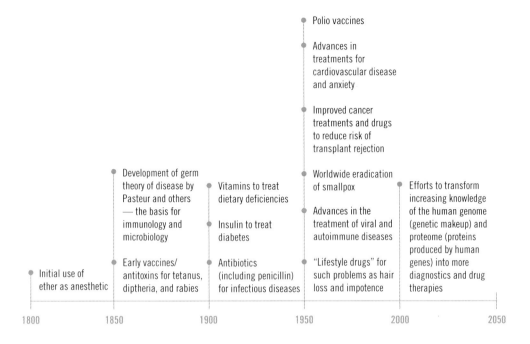

Source: The Pharmaceutical Century: Ten Decades of Drug Discovery, *American Chemical Society, 2000.*

Our focus in this book is on research-based pharmaceutical companies.

Most major activities of full-service pharmaceutical companies can be roughly divided into three functional categories: Research and Development (R&D), Manufacturing and Operations, and Marketing and Sales.

- **Research and Development**, the "engine of innovation," is focused on discovering—or creating—promising new chemicals or molecules and transforming them into safe and effective pharmaceutical products.

- **Manufacturing and Operations** includes the supply chain, manufacturing, and trade and distribution functions of the business. Personnel in this category produce and package the drug product and make it available in markets all over the world.

- **Marketing and Sales** communicates the benefits of the company's pharmaceutical products and creates demand for those products using promotional programs designed to influence physicians, pharmacists, payers, consumers, and other stakeholders in the pharmaceutical decision-making process. Also, in the US, a special Managed Markets group is responsible for outreach to large corporate accounts and managed care organizations.

Business Development (BD) helps the in-house clinical and commercial functions meet the strategic objectives of the company as a whole. To enhance the company's product portfolio and financial performance, BD acquires, sells, and develops partnerships around compounds, technologies, capabilities, and capital based on the needs of the company. By acquiring new molecules and technologies from external sources, BD can fill the company's product pipeline and reduce drug development times. By negotiating co-marketing or co-promotion arrangements, BD can significantly extend a company's reach or market impact during a new product launch.

All of these functions are backed by a highly skilled **corporate and administrative infrastructure**, including Legal, IT, and Finance functions. They also rely on highly specialized experts to help them navigate the complex regulatory environment (Regulatory Affairs, Medical Affairs, and Data Management).

Figures 1.6 and 1.7 provide a highly simplified overview of the structure of a typical pharmaceutical company, including a profile of the key functions that are described in greater detail subsequently in this book.

Figure 1.6 Overview of a Pharmaceutical Company

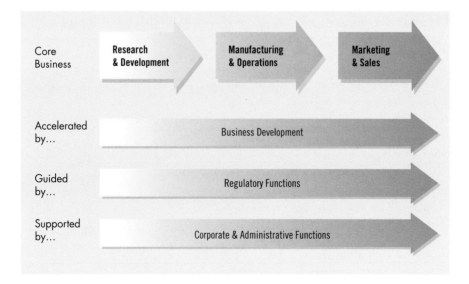

Source: Campbell Alliance.

10

Figure 1.7 Functional Model

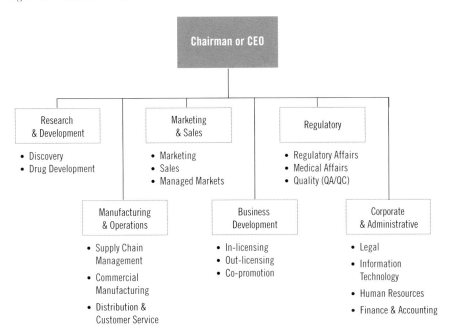

Source: Campbell Alliance.

The largest companies operate global organizations, but customer-facing functions, such as Sales, are usually managed locally to enhance responsiveness to the unique needs of each marketplace. Figure 1.8 presents the geographic leadership model commonly used in global pharmaceutical companies.

Many companies are adopting a therapeutic franchise model, which relies on depth of expertise in separate disease categories to differentiate them in the marketplace. Companies now recognize that deep therapeutic area expertise is often needed to identify and develop products that are truly superior to those of their competitors. In addition, companies want to leverage their relationships with customers and specialists in specific therapeutic categories and take advantage of a corporate image as the leaders in a therapeutic category—an image that can transcend individual product offerings.

Large ethical pharmaceutical companies, collectively nicknamed "Big Pharma," often turn to smaller, more focused innovative companies for new compounds or technologies that accelerate research and development efforts. These companies supplement the internal pipelines of their larger

Figure 1.8 Typical Geographic Leadership Model

Function	Global Control	Global Strategy	Local (Country or Regional) Leadership
Research	●	●	
Development	●	●	
Manufacturing & Operations	●		●
Marketing		●	●
Sales			●
Managed Markets			●
Business Development	●		
Corporate & Administrative Functions	●		●

Source: Campbell Alliance.

partners with promising chemicals and molecules and, to some degree, mitigate the high risks inherent in the drug discovery and development process. In exchange, these innovators, who are often resource-constrained, obtain the funding and expertise to bring a product through development and exploit the product's full market potential. (See Figure 1.9)

Big Pharma often forms mutually beneficial relationships with companies specializing in biotechnology. Biotechnology-focused companies, or biotechs, often begin with a narrow focus—for instance, just a handful of promising biologic or research technologies. Over time, some biotechs have expanded their product portfolios and their range of internal capabilities by adding commercialization functions, until their companies come to closely resemble smaller-scale versions of Big Pharma companies.

Because the requirements and market environment in the industry are so complex, pharmaceutical companies need the support of vendors and suppliers who are dedicated to the industry and are well-versed in its intricacies. These entities are attuned to the unique operations of pharmaceutical companies, regulators, and key customers and are capable of complying with relevant guidelines and restrictions on their activities and service offerings.

Figure 1.9 Pharmaceutical Industry Suppliers and Partners

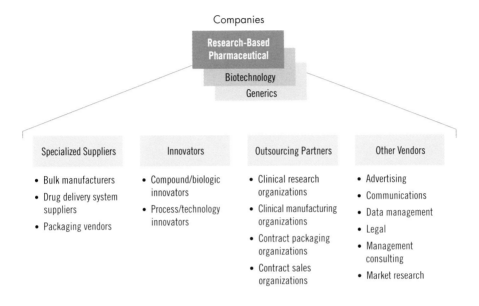

Profile of Pharmaceutical Industry Suppliers and Partners

Segment	Description
Specialized Suppliers	Suppliers of goods or services needed to manufacture a pharmaceutical product or prepare it for distribution
Innovators	Companies that provide products and/or services to accelerate discovery or development
Outsourcing Partners	Companies that offer specific functional services, either in whole or in part
Other Vendors	Suppliers of specialized services for sales, marketing, and other operations (often experts in promotions and regulatory compliance)

Source: Campbell Alliance.

Outsourcing relationships are used to extend functional capabilities, reducing the high fixed-cost burden on pharma companies. It can be cost-effective for even the largest pharmaceutical companies to outsource activities and focus

13

internally upon essential core competencies. It is even more common for pharmaceutical companies to outsource certain activities on an ad hoc basis when extra support is needed for a particular product.

- A clinical research organization (CRO) can coordinate and conduct clinical trials.

- A contract manufacturing organization (CMO) may assume responsibility for specific steps in the manufacturing process or for the entire process.

- A contract packaging organization (CPO) can package drugs into containers (such as bottles, vials, blister packs, or pre-filled syringes) for clinical trials or commercial distribution.

- A contract sales organization (CSO) may extend the ability of a pharmaceutical company to visit physician offices when access is a critical issue.

In some cases, rather than seeking a specialized vendor, a pharmaceutical company will form a partnership with another large pharmaceutical company that is particularly skilled in one of those areas or is renowned in the relevant therapeutic area.

3. The Worldwide Scope of the Pharmaceutical Industry

Although our focus in this book will be on the US, all major pharmaceutical companies have a global reach. The global pharmaceutical industry represents a market that generates nearly $550 billion in annual revenue and employs over 1.7 million people. Pharmaceutical sales are highest in the US, Western Europe, and Japan. (See Figure 1.10)

The US accounts for roughly one-half of the world's pharmaceutical revenues. Here, private insurance—typically obtained through employers—dominates healthcare, and physicians and consumers have high expectations for access to an array of medicines. Most Americans have at least some insurance coverage for pharmaceutical care through managed care organizations, other private health insurance, or government programs such as Medicare or Medicaid.

In Western Europe, the second-largest world market, drug utilization is largely government-controlled. On a per capita basis, sales are considerably lower than in the US. Because prescription drug coverage is primarily government-funded and heavily regulated, access to certain drugs (experimental and non-essential medicines, for example) may be limited.

Fig. 1.10 Profile of World Pharmaceutical Markets

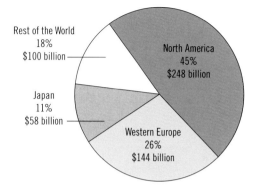

Global Pharmaceutical Sales
2004 Total $550 billion

Rest of the World
18%
$100 billion

North America
45%
$248 billion

Japan
11%
$58 billion

Western Europe
26%
$144 billion

Market	Description
North America	• Dominated by the US ($235 billion in 2004) • Private market system that places great value on access to a variety of healthcare choices • Insurance may cover experimental and lifestyle therapies
Western Europe	• Government-controlled use of pharmaceuticals • Focus on provision of high-quality, medically necessary therapy
Japan	• Second largest individual pharmaceutical market in the world • Low generic penetration, but strong cost containment measures
Rest of World	• Emerging markets in Eastern Europe and Latin America, as well as in large countries such as China and India • Third-world countries in Africa and Asia that frequently receive donations of free medicine • Pharmaceutical use impeded by economic conditions and preference for traditional medical practices

Source: IMS Health, 2005.

Until recently, Japan, the third-largest market, had an unusually restrictive regulatory environment designed to favor Japanese manufacturers. Recent reforms to the Japanese regulatory system have brought it closer in line with the US system.

The worldwide scope of the pharmaceutical marketplace and the lack of standardization within it add a level of complexity to the pharmaceutical enterprise. Companies must overcome a range of regulatory hurdles in order to obtain approval to market their products in each country or region. Although some efforts toward common global standards are under way, regulations today vary by country.

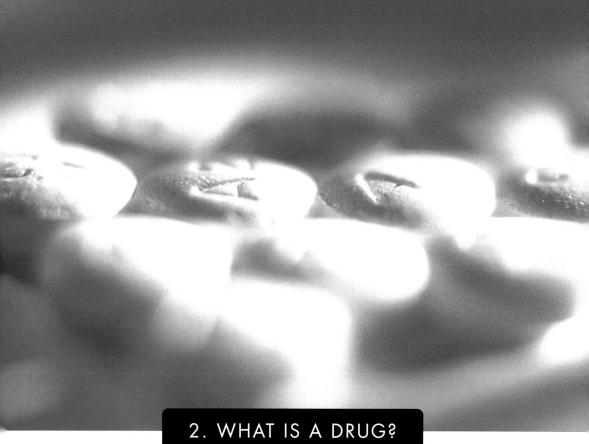

2. WHAT IS A DRUG?

1. What Makes a Drug a Drug?

2. What Are Drugs Made of?

3. How Are Drugs Classified?

4. How Do Drugs Enter the US Market?

5. The Product Life Cycle

1. What Makes a Drug a Drug?

In its broadest definition, a drug is any substance that produces a physical or psychological change in the body. This definition includes products that we consider medicines, such as aspirin or antibiotics, products contained in foods, such as caffeine, and products delivered through other means, such as nicotine or the fluoride in toothpaste. This definition, though, is too inclusive for our purposes.

A more practical definition for the pharmaceutical industry can be found in the Federal Food, Drug and Cosmetic Act (FFDCA). The FFDCA provides different sets of rules and regulations for food products, drugs, devices, and cosmetics. Under the FFDCA, a drug is defined as any substance "intended for use in the diagnosis, cure, mitigation, treatment or prevention of disease," or a substance other than food "intended to affect the structure or function of the body." The first category incorporates drugs intended to address a specific physical or mental condition or set of symptoms, while the second category is broad enough to include products that do not aim to cure or prevent disease, such as oral contraceptives. (See Figure 2.1)

Figure 2.1 Drugs, Devices and Cosmetics

Drugs	Cosmetics	Devices
"Articles intended for use in the diagnosis, cure, mitigation, treatment, or prevention of **disease**" and/or "Articles (other than food) intended to **affect the structure or any function of the body**" FFDCA, Sec. 210(g)(1) Oral contraceptives, for instance, fall into the second category.	"Articles intended to be rubbed, poured, sprinkled, or sprayed on, introduced into, or otherwise applied to the human body... for cleansing, beautifying, promoting attractiveness, or altering the appearance." FFDCA, Sec. 201(i).	In the "pharma" context, medical devices are often the means by which a drug is introduced to the body. Under the FFDCA, the FDA was empowered to regulate these devices. • Hypodermic syringes • Insulin pens and pumps • Transdermal patches • Drug-eluting stents

Products Considered Both Drugs and Cosmetics (Must Comply with Regulations for Both)
• Antidandruff shampoos • Antiperspirants • Fluoride toothpastes • Moisturizers and cosmetics that claim to offer sun protection

Source: Federal Food, Drug and Cosmetic Act.

18

As shown in Figure 2.2, some substances, such as tobacco, are not regulated as drugs, while certain foods or dietary supplements can be regulated as such.

Figure 2.2 Are They Drugs?

NO

Tobacco Products

Although nicotine is addictive and a cigarette is arguably a device for delivering it, the US Supreme Court held in 2000 that the FDA cannot regulate tobacco as a drug. The FDA does, however, regulate smoking cessation products such as nicotine patches.

Dietary Supplements

Dietary supplements that are not intended to treat, cure, or mitigate a disease or affect body structure or function are not regulated as drugs. This category includes products other than tobacco that contain a vitamin, mineral, amino acid, botanical or herbal product, or other dietary substance but are not used as a therapy. Dietary supplements must meet the manufacturing standards established for foods, not drugs.

MAYBE, MAYBE NOT

Nutraceuticals

Nutraceuticals are products that combine traditional food ingredients and active components alleged to affect the structure or function of the body in a way that promotes health, or as the name implies, combinations of nutritionals and pharmaceuticals. They include vitamins and other supplements and so-called "functional foods."

The FDA does not recognize nutraceuticals by that name, but may regulate them as foods, drugs, or dietary supplements, depending on the product's specific attributes and the claims made about them.

Companies developing nutraceutical products are responding to consumer demand for help preventing, managing, and treating disease. If the manufacturer explicitly claims an effect on body structure or function, the FDA is more likely to consider it a drug and regulate it more aggressively than a food or supplement not making such a claim.

Source: Campbell Alliance.

2. What Are Drugs Made Of?

The Active Pharmaceutical Ingredient

The ingredient in drugs that is intended to produce the desired change in the body is known as the active pharmaceutical ingredient (API). APIs fall into two basic categories—chemical and biologic. Chemical or "small molecule" products are developed and manufactured by a chemical process. Biologic or "large molecule" products are derived from living materials, such as humans, animals, plants, and microorganisms. They are called "large molecules" because the proteins or peptides that they typically consist of are larger than those in chemical chains.

Most, but not all, biologics (such as vaccines) work by triggering an immune response. (One major exception is blood and blood products, which are used in transfusions and other therapies.) Compared with chemicals, biologic products are a relatively new area of pharmaceutical inquiry. The first biotech drug was approved by the FDA in 1982. Biologics are the source of vaccines that have virtually eradicated diseases, such as polio, in many countries, as well as insulin to control diabetics. Today, biologic research holds therapeutic promise in such disease states as cancer, hepatitis C, multiple sclerosis, and infertility, to name just a few.

Mechanism of Action

The way in which an API works in the body is referred to as its mechanism of action. Most drugs are either agonists—drugs that attract or bind to cell receptors in order to mimic or enhance healthful activities—or antagonists—drugs that interfere with destructive or undesirable cell functions.

- Insulin, for instance, is an agonist, administered to diabetics who no longer produce it in sufficient quantities.

- Steroids are antagonists; they block cell activities that lead to inflammation.

Some other mechanisms of action include disruption of cell replication (by chemotherapy agents, for example) and stimulation of immune responses (by growth factors). (See Figure 2.3)

Formulation

The API is usually blended with products known as excipients, such as fillers, dyes, and flavors, to create the drug product, which is also known as the formulation. Excipients are sometimes referred to as inactive ingredients, although they may have such effects as increasing the tolerability of the API or speeding its absorption into the blood stream. They also serve such functions as making a drug more stable (so that it can be stored without loss of efficacy over time), easier to administer, or longer-acting through sustained release of the API. (See Figure 2.4)

Formulated products are sometimes offered in various strengths and administered using different delivery methods to aid absorption or enhance convenience. "Strength" refers to the amount of active pharmaceutical ingredient

Figure 2.3 Sample Mechanism of Action

Five Ways That Antimicrobial Drugs Attack Bacteria

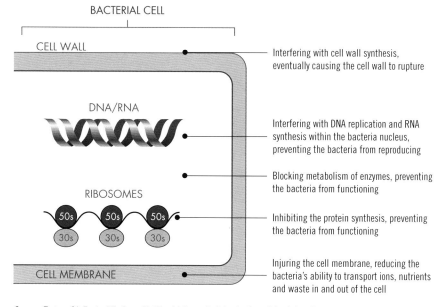

Source: Tortora GJ, Funke BR, Case CL. Microbiology: An Introduction. *8th ed. San Francisco, CA:* Benjamin Cummings; 2003.

in the drug. This delivery method (route of administration) indicates how the drug enters the bloodstream. Common delivery methods are

- Parenteral (intravenous, intra-muscular, subcutaneous)

- Rectal (suppository)

- Oral (tablet, capsule, liquid)

- Transdermal (through the skin via creams or patches)

Pharmacokinetics and Pharmacodynamics

A drug's formulation is designed to optimize the ability of the body to properly use and then rid itself of the drug. Pharmacokinetics uses a process called ADME testing to assess the actions of the body on the drug. ADME testing measures the rate at which the body *absorbs* the drug, *distributes* it to the organs necessary to produce the desired effect, *metabolizes* it into waste material, and then *excretes* it from the body.

Figure 2.4 Excipients

Excipients are the inert ingredients in a drug formulation. They serve such functions as making the manufacturing process easier (e.g., by keeping ingredients from sticking to machinery), enhancing delivery of the active ingredient to the patient, and making the product more attractive or recognizable.

Although all excipients are rigorously tested and most are considered safe enough for use in foods as well as medicines, they sometimes cause side effects. Some experts suggest that excipients are one reason that reactions may differ to brand-name and generic versions of drugs that have the same active ingredients.

Excipient Classes	
Binders cement the active and inert components of tablets together to maintain cohesive portions.	**Disintegrants** help break up tablets in the gastrointestinal tract to ensure full release of the pharmaceutically active material.
Fillers (diluents) are used to make the drug sufficiently large for easy manufacture and patient consumption.	**Lubricants** ease the release of tablets from the dies that stamp them during the manufacturing process.
Glidants (flow enhancers) are added to powdered materials used in pill production to aid movement through tabletting machinery.	**Compression aids** help pills hold their shape when compressed.
Colors include a wide variety of dyes and coloring agents approved by the FDA for pharmaceutical use. Allergic reactions to these compounds are sometimes a problem.	**Sweeteners** (both with sugar and sugar-free) are extremely common in oral medications, particularly in medicines for children.
Flavors, both natural and synthetic, are amendments to improve drug palatability. Flavors can be complex mixtures of compounds and often fall under the rubric of "trade secrets." The manufacturer therefore need not identify the components on its list of ingredients.	**Printing inks** are biologically safe dyes used for printing information or company logos on the exterior of tablets or capsules.
Suspensing/dispersing agents maintain a consistent concentration of the active ingredient throughout a drug product.	**Film formers/coatings** protect against physical breakup during storage and undesirable interactions with substances in which drugs come into contact. They can mask bad taste and allow pills to be swallowed easily.

Source: Lesney MS. More than just the sugar in the pill. Today's Chemist at Work. *2001, 10(1):30-36.*

Pharmacodynamics assesses the biochemical and physiological effects of the drug on the body at various doses, or more specifically, the drug's actions and effects at a molecular level. During development, promising drugs are refined to optimize benefits and to minimize toxicity. Almost all drugs produce some side effects—unintended effects that may be positive or negative. Toxicity refers to the negative or adverse effects of a drug. The level of toxicity that is acceptable in a product depends to some extent on the magnitude of counterbalancing health benefits that it produces. Both toxicity and benefits are likely to be assessed in the context of other available treatments. That is, a product that has serious adverse effects will be considered a viable therapy if other treatments cause yet-more-serious problems and are less effective for the intended use.

The dosage range of a drug that is both safe and produces a beneficial result is known as the therapeutic window. Early in the development process, compounds of varying strengths and dosages are tested in animal models to determine the limits of acceptable toxicity. The formulations and doses adopted for clinical testing are the ones that appear most effective without exceeding an acceptable toxicity threshold. (See Figure 2.5)

Figure 2.5 ADME Testing of Pharmacokinetics: How the Human Body Acts Upon a Drug

Absorption	How does the drug pass from its site of administration into the blood stream?
	• The speed, ease, and degree of absorption are related to the route of administration.
	• More than 80 variations exist, including oral administration via a tablet, gel cap, or syrup. Oral administration is a relatively slow-acting option, in which the drug must be digested before it enters the blood stream.
	• A speedier but less convenient alternative is intravenous, intramuscular, or subcutaneous injection.
	• Other common options include transdermal, topical, inhalation and rectal applications.
Distribution	How is the drug is dispersed among the organs of the body after it is absorbed into the blood stream and how much reaches the target organs?
Metabolism	How is the active part of a drug metabolized into a more water-soluble compound that can be readily excreted by the kidneys?
Excretion	How is the drug eliminated from the body?
	• Usually, drugs are eliminated through urine.
	• Fecal excretion is seen with drugs that are not absorbed through the intestine or have been recovered in the bile.
	• Drugs may also be excreted through the lungs, skin, or in breast milk.

Source: US Department of Health and Human Services. Medicine by Design, 2003. NIH publication no. 03-474.

3. How Are Drugs Classified?

Drugs are classified in a variety of ways for a variety of purposes—including for coverage determinations and payments by insurers, for defining competitive strategy by pharmaceutical companies, and for access control.

Based on Therapeutic Categories

Therapeutic categories, classes, and subclasses are a system of increasingly specific classifications, first by purpose and ultimately by mechanism of action:

- The clinical field or specialty in which the product is used (e.g., cardiovascular, anti-infective)

- The disease or condition that the product is intended to treat (e.g., HIV, anti-hypertension)

- The treatment approach, indication, or mechanism of action that the product employs (e.g., calcium channel blockers for hypertension) (This narrower classification is sometimes called a drug class.)

An illustration of the therapeutic category and drug class concepts appears in Figure 2.6.

Some products span multiple therapeutic categories. For example, certain drugs in the central nervous system (CNS) category are used for a range of conditions: mental illness, seizures, pain, obesity, and other ailments with a psychological or neurological component.

Companies are typically organized by and compete at the level of the therapeutic area. Even the largest pharmaceutical companies do not command significant market share across all therapeutic categories. Small companies with a few highly effective products in a therapeutic area can outperform larger competitors in that category.

The relevant therapeutic category serves as a point of departure for defining a more limited category in which a product will compete. Marketing groups reduce broader therapeutic category classifications to more precise groupings known as "market baskets," which include the product and its important competitors. Marketing and selling strategies are designed to differentiate the product from others in the market basket, and market share performance is typically measured against other products in the market basket.

Based on Target Customer, Duration of Use, and Care Setting

For marketing purposes, pharmaceutical companies need to characterize the target customer base and the nature of product use as well. Three distinctions are commonly made:

Figure 2.6 Examples of Classification by Therapeutic Categories

Therapeutic Category (or Area)	Disease/Risk Factor	Particular Mechanism of Action
Cardiovascular	High Cholesterol	• HMG-CoA reductase inhibitors (also known as statins)
	Hypertension	• Angiotensin-converting enzyme inhibitors (ACEs) • Angiotensin II receptor antagonists (ARBs) • Beta-blockers (BBs) • Calcium channel blockers (CCBs) • Diuretics
Central Nervous System	Depression	• Benzodiazepines • Selective serotonin reuptake inhibitors (SSRIs) • Non-selective serotonin reuptake inhibitors (nSSRIs) • Tricyclic antidepressants
Anti-infectives	Bacterial Infections	• Cephalosporins • Fluoroquinilones • Macrolides • Tetracyclines
Respiratory	Asthma	• Beta-2 agonists • Corticosteroids • Leukotriene receptor antagonists
	Rhinitis	• Antihistamines • Tricyclic antihistamines
Diabetes	Type II diabetes	• Biguanides • Insulin • Sulfonylureas
Gastrointestinal	Gastroesophageal reflux disease (GERD)	• Histamine H2 receptor antagonists • Proton-pump inhibitors

Source: Campbell Alliance.

Primary vs. Specialty Care

This classification is based on the prescribing physician. Primary care products like antihistamines and respiratory products are often prescribed by generalist physicians, such as internists and family practitioners. Specialty products are narrowly indicated and often prescribed by specialists (e.g., anti-psychotics by psychiatrists or HIV drugs by infectious disease specialists). In some cases, a therapy may be initiated by a specialist and monitored and maintained by a primary care physician (e.g., when a cardiologist prescribes statin therapy to lower cholesterol).

Acute vs. Chronic Care

This classification is based on the duration of use. Acute medications, such as antibiotics, are used to address short-term illnesses or symptoms. These medications have a predefined length of therapy (days or weeks), which ends when the symptoms are gone or the prescription is complete. Chronic medications, such as insulin or statins, are used to address long-term conditions and are taken for an indefinite period. Therapy regimens can be fixed (daily, weekly, etc.) or as needed (e.g., inhalers that are used when symptoms are present). Side effects that might be considered merely minor annoyances in acute treatment can be a powerful barrier to adoption in chronic therapies.

Office- vs. Hospital-Based

This classification is based on the principal care setting. Office-based products are typically prescribed in physician offices and dispensed in a retail setting or in the doctor's office (e.g., statin therapy, vaccines). Hospital-based products are prescribed and administered in a hospital or clinic setting. Many hospital-based products, such as IVs or injectibles, require professional administration.

Based on Novelty

As our previous discussion on types of pharmaceutical companies demonstrated, companies that specialize in novel products are very different from those that manufacture equivalent generic versions of once-innovative products whose patents have expired.

Usually the term "branded" refers to a patented product. Generics are typically sold under the chemical name for the drug (e.g., ibuprofen) rather than a brand name (Advil® or Motrin®). It is becoming more common, however, for generics companies to give their products brand names in order to distinguish themselves in the marketplace. Such products are called branded generics.

For purposes of clarity, we will therefore refer to novel branded products as branded prescription products. Branded prescription products are sometimes also called single-source products because only one company (or perhaps a partnership) owns the rights to manufacture and sell it.

By contrast, generics are also known as multisource products because multiple generic products using the same active ingredient can be manufactured once the original maker's patent expires. At that point, no single source owns the manufacturing or marketing rights.

Branded prescription products are novel prescription medications that enjoy or once enjoyed, patent protection or market exclusivity. They are developed through an extensive and expensive process of scientific and clinical development to establish the product's features and formulation. Branded drugs usually are the most innovative and expensive form of drug therapy, but they are often a cost-effective alternative to other forms of treatment (e.g., surgery).

Generic drugs are commodity versions of drugs for which patents or market exclusivity have expired. They use the same active ingredient and rely on safety data from studies of the original product. In order to be approved, generic products must establish bioequivalence, demonstrating that the generic version of the product delivers the same amount of the active ingredient to the patient's bloodstream.

Often the greatest challenge for a generics manufacturer is to replicate drug formulation factors that affect the pharmacokinetic and pharmacodynamic characteristics of the original drug.

Prescription volumes of branded products and generics are roughly comparable, but research-based pharma companies that develop innovative products charge higher prices to recoup their investment. Therefore, the revenue generated by brands is significantly higher that of generics (See Figure 2.7).

Based on Market Potential

A product may be categorized based on the size of its target market and its potential within that market. A "blockbuster" drug, for example, typically generates in excess of $1 billion in sales, generally by treating diseases that are relatively widespread. In contrast, "orphan" drugs, which treat rare diseases, have much lower sales potential.

Based on Access Restrictions

Controlled Substances

Drugs with a high potential for abuse are designated as controlled substances by the Drug Enforcement Administration, which restricts who is allowed to prescribe them and what facilities are allowed to dispense them. There are five controlled-substance categories, known as schedules. Schedule I drugs, the most tightly controlled, have high potential for abuse and no recognized medical use. Heroin is one example. Schedule II, III, IV, and V drugs are

Figure 2.7 Branded Prescription Products vs. Generics

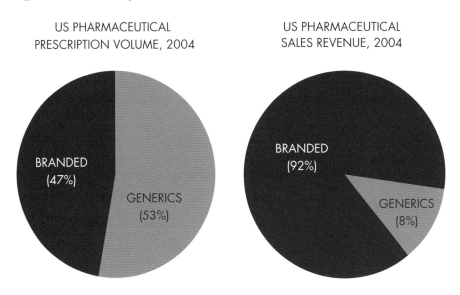

US PHARMACEUTICAL
PRESCRIPTION VOLUME, 2004

BRANDED
(47%)

GENERICS
(53%)

US PHARMACEUTICAL
SALES REVENUE, 2004

BRANDED
(92%)

GENERICS
(8%)

Source: IMS Health, IMS National Sales Perspective™, February, 2005.

generally "prescription drugs" that have accepted medical uses, and, in the case of Schedules III, IV and V, lower potential for abuse. The latter are also subject to less stringent controls. (See Figure 2.8)

Prescription Drugs
Either state or federal law may mandate that a drug be available only with a prescription from a licensed medical professional (physician or other pre-scriber).

Drugs are designated as prescription-only when: (1) a physician is necessary to confirm the diagnosis for which the drug is a therapy; (2) the disease at is-sue is so serious that the patient should be under ongoing physician care; or (3) the drug can be dangerous when used inappropriately (Schedule II and III drugs, for example).

Over-the-Counter
Over-the-counter (OTC) medications share five characteristics: (1) Their benefits outweigh their risks; (2) The potential for misusing or abusing these products is low; (3) The consumer can use them for self-diagnosed conditions;

Fig. 2.8 Schedule of Controlled Substances

Schedule	Description and Examples
I	• The drug or other substance has a high potential for abuse • The drug or other substance has no currently accepted medical use in treatment in the US • There is a lack of accepted safety for use of the drug or other substance under medical supervision • Examples: heroin, marijuana, lysergic acid diethylamide (LSD), and methaqualone
II	• The drug or other substance has a high potential for abuse • The drug or other substance has a currently accepted medical use in treatment in the US or a currently accepted medical use with severe restrictions • Abuse of the drug or other substance may lead to severe psychological or physical dependence • Examples: morphine, methadone, oxycodone, hydrocodone, amphetamine, methylphenidate and pentobarbital
III	• The drug or other substance has a potential for abuse less than the drugs or other substances in Schedules I and II • The drug or other substance has a currently accepted medical use in the US • Abuse of the drug or other substance may lead to moderate or low physical dependence or high psychological dependence • Examples: anabolic steroids, codeine and hydrocodone with aspirin or Tylenol, and some barbiturates
IV	• The drug or other substance has a low potential for abuse relative to the drugs or other substances in Schedule III • The drug or other substance has a currently accepted medical use in treatment in the US • Abuse of the drug or other substance may lead to limited physical dependence or psychological dependence relative to the drugs or other substances in Schedule III • Examples: Darvon, Talwin, Equanil, Valium, and Xanax
V	• The drug or other substance has a low potential for abuse relative to the drugs or other substances in Schedule IV • The drug or other substance has a currently accepted medical use in treatment in the US • Abuse of the drug or other substance may lead to limited physical dependence or psychological dependence relative to the drugs or other substances on Schedule IV • Examples: Over-the-counter cough medicines with codeine

Sources: US Department of Justice; Drug Enforcement Administration; Food and Drug Administration.

(4) The products can be adequately labeled; and (5) The product can be used safely and effectively without the intervention of a physician or nurse. Many OTC products entered the market before the advent of laws that require proof of safety and effectiveness prior to marketing. Others are lower-dosage forms of prescription drugs or full-dosage versions of products that were once prescription but are now considered sufficiently safe for non-prescription use. A prescription drug meeting FDA criteria will often make the shift to OTC at the conclusion of its patent life.

Behind-the-Counter

Behind-the-counter products occupy the middle ground between prescription and OTC. These drugs do not require a prescription but are monitored closely by the pharmacist, who typically keeps them segregated within the dispensary and makes them available upon request. For example, states require pharmacies to store Schedule V drugs, such as cough medicines containing codeine, behind the counter.

4. How Do Drugs Enter the US Market?

To be marketed in the US, a drug must be approved as safe and effective by the FDA. When the FDA grants marketing privileges, it also defines the drug's specific approved indication(s).

Pharmaceuticals are indicated, or proven to be effective for, the treatment of specific diseases (such as hypertension) in specific populations (such as adult females). The FDA approves specific indications for a product based on evidence from clinical trials. This approval is based on demonstrated safety and efficacy, which are balanced against undesirable side effects, also known as adverse events. Pharmaceuticals may be approved for more than one indication, and all approved indications are contained on the FDA-approved drug label.

An approved indication is usually accompanied by a dosing regimen, which specifies how much and how often the drug should be taken. Dosing regimens are specific to the strength and form of a product and are included in the drug label. Uses for other purposes are said to be off-label—because they are not reflected in the FDA-approved labeling for the product.

In exercising their independent medical judgment about patients' best interests, physicians are free to prescribe FDA-approved drugs for off-label purposes, but pharmaceutical companies may not actively promote such uses. However, pharmaceutical companies do have the right to respond to clinical inquiries from prescribers about such potential uses, and they may distribute peer-reviewed journal articles regarding those uses in response to such inquiries. Many companies employ scientists and clinicians to engage in professional discussions with physicians and others to discuss off-label or unapproved uses of their products.

National Drug Codes

During the approval process, the FDA assigns every product a unique National Drug Code (NDC) that identifies its original developer, form, dosage, and package size. The NDC is the tracking code for the product during manufacturing, distribution, administration, and payment. (See Figure 2.9)

Figure 2.9 NDC Labels

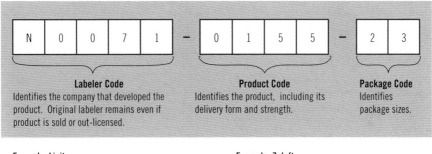

N	0	0	7	1	–	0	1	5	5	–	2	3	

Labeler Code
Identifies the company that developed the product. Original labeler remains even if product is sold or out-licensed.

Product Code
Identifies the product, including its delivery form and strength.

Package Code
Identifies package sizes.

Example: Lipitor
10-mg tablets, bottle of 90:   N0071-0155-23
20-mg tablets, bottle of 5,000: N0071-0156-94

Example: Zoloft
25-mg tablets, bottle of 50:   N0049-4960-50

The labeler code identifies the pharmaceutical company that originally developed the drug. In the examples above, both products are now owned by Pfizer, but Lipitor was originally developed by Parke-Davis and therefore carries the Parke-Davis labeler code.

Source: Campbell Alliance.

The Package Insert

Drugs entering the US marketplace are each packaged with a package insert (PI)—the piece of folded paper stuffed into the cardboard box—that fully describes the proven characteristics of that pharmaceutical product. The PI, which is identical to the FDA–approved label, explains the chemical composition of the product, dosing, side effects, approved indications and uses, and other information that is helpful to the prescribing physician or patient. It also contains precautions and warnings associated with a product. The most severe of these is known as a "black box" warning, which states that a product can cause death in certain circumstances.

The PI, as illustrated in Figure 2.10, is developed as the drug is being formulated and tested during drug development, and it is included in the FDA approval process.

Figure 2.10 Package Inserts

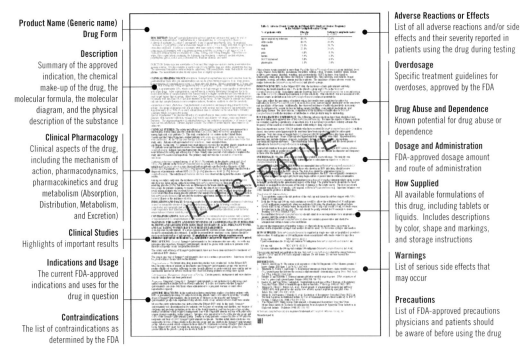

Product Name (Generic name) Drug Form		Adverse Reactions or Effects

Product Name (Generic name) Drug Form

Description
Summary of the approved indication, the chemical make-up of the drug, the molecular formula, the molecular diagram, and the physical description of the substance

Clinical Pharmacology
Clinical aspects of the drug, including the mechanism of action, pharmacodynamics, pharmacokinetics and drug metabolism (Absorption, Distribution, Metabolism, and Excretion)

Clinical Studies
Highlights of important results

Indications and Usage
The current FDA-approved indications and uses for the drug in question

Contraindications
The list of contraindications as determined by the FDA

Adverse Reactions or Effects
List of all adverse reactions and/or side effects and their severity reported in patients using the drug during testing

Overdosage
Specific treatment guidelines for overdoses, approved by the FDA

Drug Abuse and Dependence
Known potential for drug abuse or dependence

Dosage and Administration
FDA-approved dosage amount and route of administration

How Supplied
All available formulations of this drug, including tablets or liquids. Includes descriptions by color, shape and markings, and storage instructions

Warnings
List of serious side effects that may occur

Precautions
List of FDA-approved precautions physicians and patients should be aware of before using the drug

Source: Campbell Alliance.

Pharmaceutical company promotional claims cannot deviate from the approved language. The package insert (label) is the foundation for the product's sales and marketing campaign, because all claims of safety and efficacy must be consistent with the statements there. This requirement affects all promotional literature, advertisements, and even novelty promotional items, such as pens and notepads.

5. The Product Life Cycle

Pharmaceutical products usually follow a predictable life cycle, but to fully understand this life cycle, the role of patents and patent exclusivity must be briefly explained.

The United States Patent and Trademark Office (USPTO) issues patents on breakthrough drugs, and for all practical purposes, these patents grant pharmaceutical companies the sole right to manufacture and sell those drugs in the US for 20 years from the date of patent filing. Similar regulatory bodies issue patents with similar provisions in the other major world markets.

That window of patent protection—beginning with the issue of a patent for a drug and ending with the expiry of that patent—determines the product's "life cycle," as illustrated in Figure 2.11. The company only has a limited period in which to recoup its investment in the R&D of a drug.

Almost every innovative drug obtains patent protection. The FDA also grants market exclusivity under certain circumstances, such as to orphan drugs or breakthrough drugs for pediatric populations.

Figure 2.11 Life Cycle of a Successful Pharmaceutical Product

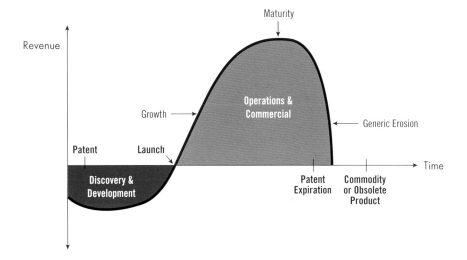

Source: Campbell Alliance.

- Discovery is a drug's infancy, when a compound first comes to light and its medicinal or commercial potential is uncertain. During the discovery or research stage, compounds or molecules are identified and generally patented. It typically takes several years of experimentation to discover and patent a novel compound or molecule.

- Development could be considered the adolescence of a product, when it undergoes increasingly rigorous testing and its qualities become clear. Only a small number of discovered drugs ever show sufficient promise to reach this stage, which includes six to eight years of expensive clinical trials.

- Launch and growth is the coming of age of a product, when the FDA agrees it is ready for the US market. It culminates before the achievement of peak product sales as the product demonstrates its potential in the marketplace. This zenith is usually reached within five to six years of launch.

- Maturity is the period during which a product is at its middle age, reaching and maintaining peak sales. The goal is to maximize current and future profitability of the brand by sustaining revenue and defending against new competitors. Even if share in the market first entered remains stable, sales can grow if the overall market is growing or new indications for the product have been sought and approved by the FDA. The period of peak sales typically lasts less than 10 years.

- Generic erosion is a product's old age, when protective patents expire, lower-cost "copycat" drugs become available, and the drug's market power falls off dramatically. Although the product may continue to be offered as a generic or over-the-counter brand, its commercial heyday is over. After generics enter the market, revenues for the innovator drug drop off steeply.

While the full window of patent exclusivity is 20 years from the date the patent is granted, the effective patent life is even shorter, as discovery and development prior to FDA approval of the drug for marketing can consume many of those years. Studies suggest that the effective patent life for a prescription drug is closer to 11 to 12 years of exclusivity. The peak years in the life cycle of the brand occur during this much narrower window. It is a short span of time in which to recoup investment in a product.

Profit margins vary by company and product portfolio. Margins for vibrant companies tend to be in the range of 10% to 30% of total revenues. Profit margins are generally higher for companies with blockbuster products under patent protection. Margins decline as products approach the end of their life cycle and go off patent, and as competing drugs or therapies enter the market.

A typical cost structure is shown in Figure 2.12.

Companies try to protect their patented products in a number of ways, such as developing alternative formulations that are difficult for generic manufacturers to copy (for instance, time-release versions). Occasionally, a company will create a viable isomer—a new and improved version of an existing drug that is essentially its mirror image. Isomers have the same molecular formula but

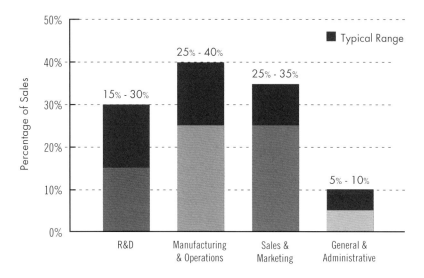

Figure 2.12 Typical Company Cost Structure

Source: Campbell Alliance.

differ in structure (linkages between atoms) or configuration (spatial arrangement of the atoms). An isomer version of an existing product may reduce side effects or have some other beneficial characteristics. Because isomers can be patented separately, they allow pharmaceutical companies with "aging" products to obtain a new period of patent protection.

In some cases, the isomer proves more effective than the original product and displaces it even before patent expiration. For example, AstraZeneca created Nexium®, an isomer of its blockbuster anti-ulcer drug Prilosec®. Nexium is a prescription drug, while Prilosec, and its generic equivalents, are now sold over the counter.

When patent and other exclusivity rights expire, the company must rely on its other products to maintain or enhance its revenue stream. To ensure a continuous revenue stream, every major company must have a relatively full pipeline, with products at different stages in the product life cycle.

Companies must also be prepared to fend off aggressive competition during a product's peak earning years. Today, because of the attraction of high-potential therapeutic markets, most brands face powerful challenges even

2. What is a Drug?

35

if they are patent-protected. Unique branded products may treat the same condition with different active ingredients. An example is Tagamet®, a heartburn therapy that was launched in 1977 and enjoyed market exclusivity for over six years before a major competitor, Zantac®, entered the market. In comparison, Celebrex®, which was launched in 1999 to treat arthritis pain, encountered fierce competition after just six months, when Vioxx entered the market. (Due to safety concerns, Merck voluntarily withdrew Vioxx from the market in late 2004 and Pfizer revised the safetly information for Celebrex in early 2005.) Figure 2.13 illustrates periods of exclusivity for selected products launched between 1965 and 2000.

Figure 2.13 Reduction in New Product Market Exclusivity Periods

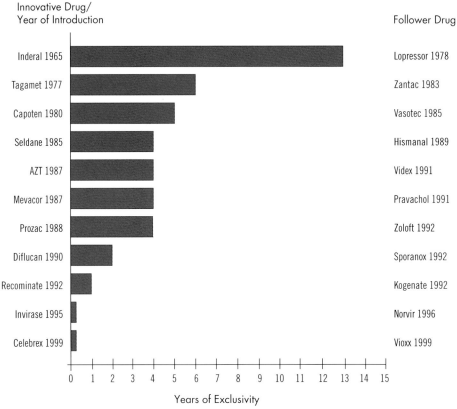

3. PHARMA CUSTOMERS

1. Overview of Major Customer Groups

THE DEMAND DRIVERS

2. Physicians

3. Consumers and Patients

4. Payers and Pharmacy Benefit Managers

THE SUPPLY SIDE

5. Pharmacies

1. Overview of Major Customer Groups

In many industries, a single customer selects, purchases, and uses the product. That's not the case in the pharmaceutical industry, in which one customer group decides which drug to prescribe, another usually bears much of the cost, and a third is the actual user.

Physicians typically initiate drug therapy by writing a prescription for a specific product. Patients then use (or fail to use) the medication. If those patients have health coverage, health insurers usually cover a substantial share of the cost. (See Figure 3.1)

Figure 3.1 What is a Payer?

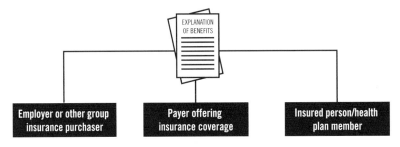

Payers include the insurers, indemnity plans, managed care organizations (MCOs) and pharmacy benefit managers (PBMs) that administer healthcare benefits on behalf of the purchasers of healthcare insurance (often employers) or the government. They are typically very active in efforts to control costs.

Some experts include employers in the payer category. Typically, however, employers are not as involved in decisions about drug coverage and reimbursement as the insurers and PBMs they hire.

Because this chapter emphasizes the most active decision makers and influencers regarding drug choice and reimbursement, our focus in the "payer" category is on insurers.

Source: Campbell Alliance.

The different customer groups influence each other. For instance, variations in payer coverage for different drugs affect patients, who may in turn have a significant impact on the prescribing choices of physicians. And physician demand for a product often encourages payers to cover it.

Most pharmaceutical companies invest significant resources to encourage each of these customer groups—physicians and other prescribers such as nurse practitioners and physician assistants; payers; and patients and their families—to select and use their products.

The strategy for influencing demand is usually developed by Marketing in collaboration with Field Sales and Managed Markets. Each therapeutic area and even each product requires a separate marketing strategy tailored to the most influential customer segments and the concerns driving their product choices.

Those three groups are the demand drivers. The role and interplay of these customer groups is summarized in Figure 3.2.

Figure 3.2 Customers Influencing Demand

Payers attempt to curb drug costs by establishing utilization controls and incentives that encourage consumers and prescribers to choose less-expensive alternatives.

Physicians or other authorized healthcare professionals select and prescribe the most effective drug therapy possible, keeping costs and access in mind.

Consumers initiate requests for treatments and pay a share of the costs (ranging from a modest co-payment to 100% of the price). They may express drug preferences to prescribers, based on favorable product experiences, impressions driven by such factors as direct-to-consumer promotion, and/or cost considerations.

Source: Campbell Alliance.

Another group, trade customers (pharmacies and wholesalers), works with pharmaceutical companies to ensure the supply of product to the marketplace.

Drug wholesalers specialize in distributing pharmaceutical products to pharmacies, hospitals, clinics, and occasionally to physicians' offices. As the primary distribution channel for the industry, wholesalers assume responsibility for ensuring product supply, managing receivables and credit risk, and enforcing regulatory requirements for product handling and distribution. Drug wholesalers and their role in the pharmaceutical supply chain are discussed in Chapter 10, Manufacturing Operations.

Pharmacies and pharmacists are responsible for dispensing drugs in a variety of inpatient and outpatient settings. In addition to this role in the supply chain, pharmacists—particularly those in specialty pharmacies catering to a specific subpopulation, such as oncology patients—may provide ongoing care management and counseling to patients.

The government is a unique customer group that serves special populations and generally receives favorable pricing. At both the state and federal levels, the government provides pharmacy benefits coverage to several important and very large segments of the population—the indigent, the elderly, and the military. Because tax dollars are invested in healthcare for these populations, it is considered in the public interest that pharmaceuticals used by them receive favorable pricing. Sophisticated algorithms and policy guidelines have been developed to ensure that most government customers receive the best pricing in their respective customer classes.

The new, broader Medicare outpatient prescription drug benefit established by the Medicare Prescription Drug, Improvement, and Modernization Act of 2003, which will take effect in January 2006, does not include any "best price" guarantees. Instead, prices will be negotiated ad hoc through routine commercial channels, such as private PBMs.

The major government customers are outlined in Figure 3.3. These customers and the special pricing arrangements available to them are discussed more fully in Chapter 9, Managed Markets.

Pharmaceutical companies attempt to influence the demand for pharmaceuticals at each step in the decision-making process.

Companies work with each customer group to drive the demand for their products. They may try to increase awareness of a disease and available therapies, or they may focus on the differentiating features of their products. Ultimately, they seek to ensure that patients fill their prescriptions promptly and comply with the prescribed regimen. Figure 3.4, below, illustrates the decision-making process for pharmaceuticals. It will be used throughout the chapter as a means of discussing the role of prescribers, consumers, payers, and pharmacists.

Figure 3.3 Federal and Federal-State Customers

Customer	Role	Description	Special Pricing
Medicaid (jointly funded by state and federal governments)	Payer	• State-administered program to provide healthcare benefit for low income populations • Federal statute sets eligibility requirements, but states fine-tune programs to meet state needs	**Medicaid Prescription Drug Rebate Program** • A pricing system created by the Omnibus Budget Reconciliation Act (OBRA) of 1990, designed to leverage Medicaid's purchasing power by requiring the same kind of volume discounts afforded to other large purchasers of prescription drugs. • Pharmaceutical companies that choose to participate in the rebate program obtain Medicaid coverage for most FDA-approved drugs. States, in turn, receive rebate dollars.
Medicare	Payer	• Healthcare benefit for the elderly, disabled, and end-stage renal disease populations • Coverage of inpatient drugs as part of reimbursement for total hospitalization episode • Outpatient prescription coverage was traditionally limited to a few categories of drugs. 2003 legislation, taking full effect in 2006, represents a significant expansion.	• None
Department of Defense (DoD)	Wholesaler (Depot)	• Source of pharmaceuticals for military bases and camps; designated responders with drug supplies for emergency civilian situations	• **Federal Supply Schedule (FSS)** The collection of contracts used by federal agencies to purchase supplies and services from outside vendors. • FSS prices for pharmaceuticals are negotiated by the VA and are based on the prices that manufacturers charge their "most-favored" non-federal customers under comparable terms and conditions.
Veterans Healthcare Administration (VHA)	Pharmacy	• Pharmacies operated in hospitals and clinics dedicated to US veterans	

Source: Campbell Alliance.

3. Pharma Customers

Figure 3.4 Key "Points of Influence" for Pharmaceutical Companies

Identification of Problem Requiring Treatment	Diagnosis	Selection of Treatment (Prescription)	Dispensing of Prescription Order	Adherence to Prescription Regimen

OPPORTUNITY

Encourage consumers to seek out diagnosis and treatment	Increase awareness of disease and of available and emerging drug therapies	Encourage preference for particular product among an array of therapeutic options	Encourage prescription fulfillment	Encourage compliance with prescription regimen and continuance on the prescribed drug for total therapeutic period

MAGNITUDE OF THE OPPORTUNITY

Modest opportunities for products in mature markets. Larger opportunities for undertreated or frequently misdiagnosed conditions/disease states	Critical determinant of product sales potential in many markets, particularly mature ones	Modest opportunity for most products, assuming payer reimbursement policy isn't a major barrier to prescription filling	Substantial issue for products with complex or inconvenient regimens

Source: Campbell Alliance.

2. Physicians and Other Prescribers

Physicians and others with the authority to prescribe drugs are the most important customer base for almost all prescription products. (See Figures 3.5 and 3.6)

These professionals, collectively referred to as prescribers, initiate drug therapy and select the product that best fits the patient's needs and personal situation. Although they rarely purchase or make direct use of the product, they have ultimate authority over the drug chosen.

Prescribers are licensed to prescribe medicines and are professionally liable for the medical appropriateness of their decisions. To avoid undue influence upon those decisions, regulators and professional organizations have established ethical guidelines limiting the fees and other items of value a prescriber can accept from a pharma company. Some of these organizations are listed in Figure 3.7. The FDA, in turn, subjects pharmaceutical companies to restrictions on how they promote products to prescribers and/or attempt to reward them for choosing their products.

Figure 3.5 Role of Prescribers in Driving Product Use

Identification of Problem Requiring Treatment	Diagnosis	Selection of Treatment (Prescription)	Dispensing of Prescription Order	Adherence to Prescription Regimen
Participates in an educational program to build awareness Participates in a screening program	Makes diagnosis	Selects treatment Key opinion leaders (KOLs) in physician community may influence prescribers' treatment choices	Occasionally provides free samples or administers the drug in the office setting	Generally plays a minor role in patient education and monitoring to enhance compliance and persistence

Source: Campbell Alliance.

Figure 3.6 Prescribers and Key Characteristics

Prescribers
- General practitioners and family practitioners
- Specialists
- Nurse practitioners
- Physician assistants

Key Characteristics	Description
Specialty	• The nature of the prescriber's practice. Provides insight into the types of patients that the prescriber treats and the therapeutic areas that he or she is likely to influence.
Prescription Preferences	• The therapeutic areas for which the prescriber writes prescriptions most frequently and the brands or manufacturers he/she prefers.
Attitudes	• Prescriber preferences for therapy or drugs measured in their responses to market research surveys.
Behavior	• Attributes, such as product preferences, demonstrated in prescriptions actually written.
Adoption Pattern	• Willingness to adopt new therapies or to switch to new medications as they become available.
Key Opinion Leader (KOL) Status	• Ability to influence the treatment patterns of other prescribers by leading clinical trials and disseminating favorable messages about new products
Accessibility	• Willingness to speak with pharma sales representatives who make office calls
Managed Care and Group Practice Affiliations	• Health plan affiliations that may affect prescribing choices • Group practice affiliations that may affect prescribing choices

Source: Campbell Alliance.

Figure 3.7 Prescriber Licensing and Professional Guidelines

Organization	Role
American Medical Association (AMA)	• Promotes ethical conduct in medical education, service billing, and interactions with pharmaceutical companies • Assigns medical education numbers to identify physicians who have graduated with an MD or doctorate in osteopathy
State License Boards	• Licenses physicians, physician assistants, and nurse practitioners to practice in their states; licensure is required to prescribe drugs
State Boards of Pharmacy	• Licenses physicians to prescribe controlled substances
Drug Enforcement Agency (DEA)	• Assigns DEA numbers to prescribe and dispense controlled substances

Source: Campbell Alliance.

Prescriptions are typically dispensed in a retail pharmacy. Written prescriptions identify the prescriber and contain his or her instructions for dispensing and using medicines. The prescription identifies the product to be dispensed (including strength and form), how often it is to be used (twice a day, for example), and who the prescription is for (the patient). (See Figure 3.8) It may also include specific dispensing instructions, such as dispense as written

Figure 3.8 Required Elements of a Prescription

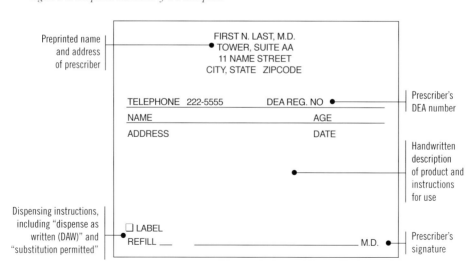

Source: Campbell Alliance.

(DAW), which instructs the pharmacist not to attempt to substitute a generic or a different brand. This information becomes a permanent part of the pharmacy's prescription record. The prescription does not specify the condition that the drug is supposed to treat.

As a promotional tool, pharma companies sometimes make a large investment in providing prescribers free samples of their products to encourage their use among patients. Prescribers are barred from selling these samples; they must distribute them at no charge and be able to account for how the samples were distributed.

In relatively rare instances, a prescriber may stock drugs in his or her office and administer them there. The most common examples are medicines that require professional handling, such as vaccines or other injectibles.

Classifying Prescribers

There are roughly 875,000 physicians in the United States, and they are classified by practice specialty. This figure includes practicing physicians (medical doctors and osteopathic physicians) and does not include nurse practitioners (NPs) and physician assistants (PAs), who are often permitted by state law to write prescriptions.

Select groups of physicians are sought out by companies because of their leadership role in clinical trials and their influence on the adoption of novel medications. These physicians are known as key opinion leaders (KOLs).

General practitioners (GPs) or primary care physicians (PCPs) treat a wide range of conditions; PCPs can be family practitioners, internists, pediatricians, and obstetricians/gynecologists. Specialists, by contrast, concentrate on relatively narrow, often highly complex, medical or surgical categories. They include, for example, neurologists, rheumatologists, psychiatrists, and cardiologists. (See Figure 3.9)

Pharmaceutical companies target prescribers based on practice specialty, prescribing volumes, and demonstrated preferences for specific brands.

Practice specialty is an important indicator of the products that a physician is likely to prescribe, and will often influence the promotional approach of the pharmaceutical company. For example, because specialists often treat patients with more severe or complex conditions, they often receive more detailed product literature and sometimes higher-strength product samples.

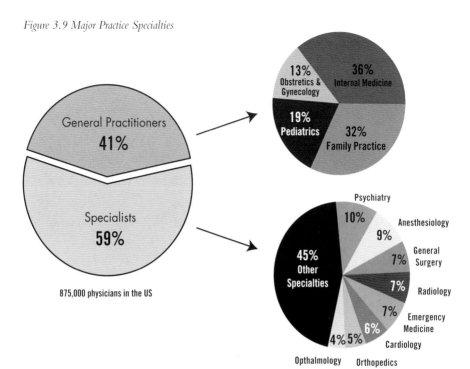

Figure 3.9 Major Practice Specialties

36% Internal Medicine

13% Obstretics & Gynecology

19% Pediatrics

32% Family Practice

General Practitioners 41%

Specialists 59%

875,000 physicians in the US

Psychiatry 10%

Anesthesiology 9%

General Surgery 7%

45% Other Specialties

Radiology 7%

Emergency Medicine 7%

Cardiology 6%

Orthopedics 5%

Opthalmology 4%

Source: Campbell Alliance based on Physician Characteristics and Distribution in the US, American Medical Association, 2005.

Pharmaceutical companies use professional promotion programs and techniques containing hard clinical or scientific evidence to inform prescribers and influence their decision making. Promotions often take the form of substantive clinical information pieces or programs, which are designed to address the prescriber's sophisticated clinical or scientific interests and concerns. These pieces are often delivered by pharmaceutical sales representatives who call on prescribers in their offices and deliver presentations describing specific products. Such one-on-one direct selling efforts are complemented by continuing education programs, speaker programs, journal advertising and professional publications. Prescribers often rely heavily on these programs to stay abreast of developments in pharmaceutical therapy. (See Figure 3.10)

Prescribers are increasingly time-constrained and reluctant to grant time to the large number of sales representatives who want to see them. To gain entry, pharmaceutical companies have to differentiate themselves in terms of the support they offer in areas of critical need, including patient education and assistance in understanding the complexities of the reimbursement environment.

Figure 3.10 Using Clinical Evidence in Promotion

Key Messages are summarized and highlighted.

Science behind the product is explained.

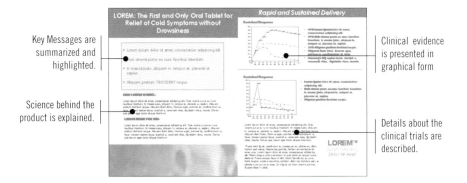

Clinical evidence is presented in graphical form

Details about the clinical trials are described.

Source: Campbell Alliance.

3. Consumers and Patients

Consumers are responsible for initiating treatment by seeking out a healthcare professional, filling the prescription (if prescribed), and adhering to the pre-scribed regimen. They are also increasingly active in suggesting preferences among therapeutic alternatives. An estimated 30% of all drugs prescribed in the US are initiated by a consumer request. (See Figures 3.11 and 3.12)

Traditionally, consumers have not been active partners in their treatment choices. That situation has changed dramatically over the last 30 years. Today, depending on the type of therapy at issue, consumers may be very vocal in attempting to influence the prescribing choices of healthcare professionals. Informed consumers can play a prominent role in selecting routine therapies, such as those for chronic pain, allergies, and gastrointestinal ailments. For complex or difficult therapies, such as oncology treatment, the prescriber of-ten works closely with the patient and caretaker to evaluate options, make tradeoffs, and decide on the most appropriate course of therapy.

Adherence

After a drug regimen is prescribed, patients and the family or friends who care for them have the greatest responsibility for adhering to the treatment. The industry often distinguishes between compliance, which means taking a medicine as prescribed (for example, twice a day), and persistence, which

Figure 3.11 Role of Consumers in Driving Product Use

Identification of Problem Requiring Treatment	Diagnosis	Selection of Treatment (Prescription)	Dispensing of Prescription Order	Adherence to Prescription Regimen
Perceives a health problem and seeks out healthcare services	Must accurately communicate signs and symptoms to obtain a sound diagnosis	May suggest treatment of choice, based on prior experience or response to promotional information	If an outpatient, typically takes prescription to a retail pharmacy	Takes primary responsibility (along with any nonprofessional caregiver) for complying with and remaining on recommended regimen

Source: Campbell Alliance.

Figure 3.12 Consumers and Key Characteristics

Consumers	Key Characteristics	Description
• Information seeker • Patient • Caregiver (family or friend) • Patient with drug coverage • Patient without drug coverage	Age and Sex	• Attributes that frequently correlate with diseases/conditions, treatment preferences, and treatment concerns
	Race	• Attribute that affects incidence of some diseases—and sometimes the nature of treatment preferences and concerns
	Income	• Indication of price sensitivity
	Education and Literacy	• Factors that affect access to healthcare information, likelihood of seeking out treatment, ability to communicate condition to healthcare professionals, and ability to understand and comply with therapy instructions
	Computer/Internet Access	• Factor affecting access to healthcare information
	Nature of Health Need	• Factor affecting likelihood of seeking out and adhering to treatment

Source: Campbell Alliance.

means continuing therapy across a specified time period (including getting refills as directed when prescriptions run out). Together, those two elements make up adherence.

Poor adherence is a challenging issue for the industry because it undermines the effectiveness of drug therapy and may reduce willingness to prescribe a product that, if taken as recommended, can be highly effective. Adherence problems have multiple causes, ranging from characteristics of the individual patient to characteristics of the prescribed drug, such as side effects, costs, or difficulties of administration. (See Figure 3.13)

Figure 3.13 Common Reasons for Non-Adherence

- The patient doesn't understand the therapy regimen.
  Examples: Language barriers or literacy problems

- The patient feels that he or she is fully recovered and discontinues the drug regimen.
  Examples: Cholesterol drugs that reduce lipid levels, antibiotics

- The drug takes time to work (it may take days or even weeks to reach therapeutic absorption levels).
  Example: Antidepressants

- The drug doesn't work at the initial dose (trial and error may be required to find the right product or dose).
  Example: Drugs to treat high blood pressure

- The drug is perceived to be too expensive.
  Example: Almost any chronic-use medications prescribed for uninsured patients or Medicare patients who have no outpatient drug benefit

- The patient or prescriber considers the drug's side effects too dangerous or debilitating.
  Example: Prescription narcotics

- Drug administration is painful or inconvenient.
  Examples: Drugs that must be injected, including insulin for diabetics

Source: Campbell Alliance.

Direct-to-Consumer Advertising

As with all other pharmaceutical promotion, the FDA oversees consumer advertising, controlling promotional claims and how they are delivered. Since the FDA relaxed its restrictions on consumer advertising in 1997, the industry has used consumer advertising techniques, such as television advertising, to reach this customer base. In addition, companies are pursuing one-on-one promotions directed at patients with specific characteristics or diseases. Companies use Web sites, physician referrals, and other techniques to encourage patients to request disease-state information or enter screening programs.

In promotions targeted to consumers, pharmaceutical companies apply segmentation based on characteristics that have an impact on health needs, attitudes toward seeking treatment, and adherence to therapy, including age, education, income, and sex.

4. Payers and Pharmacy Benefit Managers

The term "payer" refers to that broad array of customers that collectively control reimbursement for drug use, which typically includes health insurers, MCOs, self-insured employers, and government programs. From a pharmaceutical company's perspective, these customers are concerned primarily with drug utilization and cost, and they will pay for about 80% of prescription drug costs in the US by 2006. (See Figures 3.14 and 3.15)

Figure 3.14 Role of Payers in Driving Product Selection and Use

Identification of Problem Requiring Treatment	Diagnosis	Selection of Treatment (Prescription)	Dispensing of Prescription Order	Adherence to Prescription Regimen
Sponsor screening programs to encourage earlier, accurate diagnosis of diseases in order to maintain the health of their enrollees and avoid costly illnesses		May establish prior authorization requirements to discourage prescribing of certain drugs In closed-model HMOs (in which the payer employs prescribers or contracts with group practices dedicated to enrollees in its plans), payers can exert more direct influence on prescription patterns	Discourages use of disfavored drugs at point of sale by assigning a high co-payment	Sponsors education programs to encourage adherence and overall disease management Often collaborates with physicians, nurses, and pharmacists on execution of these programs

Source: Campbell Alliance.

Figure 3.15 Payers and Key Characteristics

Payer Classifications

- Private managed care and indemnity insurers
- PBMs
- Employers*
- Government

Key Characteristics	Description
Size	• The number of covered lives—that is, the number of people (members and dependents) to whom benefits are administered
Degree of Management	• The extent of overall control exercised over treatment choices, including drug selection
Formulary and Access	• The extent of efforts to control drug choices through such mechanisms as formulary restrictions and prior authorization
Other Interventions	• The use of other restrictions, such as programs to control drug selection and use

*As noted earlier, our discussion focuses on insurers and PBMs, which are typically more active influencers of pharmaceutical selection than employers.

Source: Campbell Alliance.

Drugs may be covered under a medical or pharmacy benefit. Most routine drugs fall into the outpatient drug category, are dispensed by an open-model retail pharmacy that can be used by any consumer, and are reimbursed via a stand-alone pharmacy benefit. A small portion of drug usage is reimbursed under a medical insurance benefit. This category includes drugs that are dispensed in settings such as hospitals and infusion centers and very expensive biotech drugs dispensed in specialty pharmacies or physician offices. In these cases, the drugs are prescribed and dispensed in the course of providing care.

Pharmacy Benefit Managers

Almost every health plan that offers outpatient drug coverage has established utilization controls and reimbursement restrictions to help keep drug costs down. Payers often work through pharmacy benefit managers (PBMs) to whom they have delegated administration (and sometimes design and management) of the outpatient drug coverage. (See "What are Pharmacy Benefit Managers?" and Figure 3.16 on the next page.)

Fundamentally, payers balance choice against cost, charging more for plans that allow greater selection. When it comes to outpatient drug coverage, they make the patient pay a higher co-payment for drugs that they do not consider to be cost-effective.

The plan design may also include restrictions (also known as interventions), such as generic substitution, to encourage patients to use cheaper generics, or prior authorization, to force physicians to justify the use of a particularly expensive therapy.

Drug Formularies

Drug formularies are lists, organized by therapeutic category, of generic and brand-name drugs that are preferred by health plans, usually for reasons of favorable reimbursement and/or greater clinical effectiveness. Plans use these lists to encourage the use of drugs that they prefer.

Formularies may be open or closed. Closed formularies provide no reimbursement for products that are not on the formulary, while open formularies may require higher co-payments for certain drugs.

The formulary status of products is determined by pharmacy and therapeutics (P&T) committees within the payer organization or the PBM. These

What Are Pharmacy Benefit Managers?

PBMs are organizations that administer pharmacy benefits on behalf of healthcare payers. PBM clients include self-insured employers, MCOs, and insurers. In some cases, PBMs are owned by insurers.

Figure 3.16 PBMs and the Pharmacy Value Chain

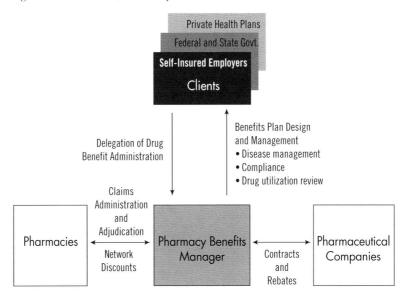

The PBM can leverage the combined clout of all its clients (aggregate membership size) when negotiating with pharmacies and pharmaceutical companies.

Source: Campbell Alliance.

PBMs simplify the administration and management of pharmacy benefits, since they operate large-scale, sophisticated operations and information systems to administer benefit plans and adjudicate (review and approve) claims at the point of service—i.e., when the prescription is filled.

PBMs employ a number of tactics to help the employers and insurers they serve reduce their drug costs:

- They negotiate discounts and rebates with retail pharmacies for brands and generics and then pass all or part of the discount on to their clients.

- They staff call centers that contact patients and physicians and encourage them to choose lower-cost products, particularly generics.

PBMs offer a range of client services, including drug benefit design, formulary

(continued on next page)

(continued from previous page)

management, and the opportunity to participate in rebate programs provided by pharmaceutical companies.

Some clients, such as self-insured employers that lack in-depth pharmacy benefits expertise, allow the PBM to manage their entire pharmacy benefit. In these situations, the PBM will recommend the plan design and co-pay structure, the formulary, and interventions that may be used to improve quality or control cost.

The PBM will also manage the pharmacy network, including the use of mail pharmacies.

Some highly sophisticated clients, such as MCOs, have internal expertise and typically rely on PBMs solely for administrative support in processing and adjudicating claims. Under these arrangements, the MCO designs its own formulary and negotiates its own deals with pharmaceutical companies.

committees typically consist of doctors of pharmacy (PharmDs), physicians, and plan administrators. Figure 3.17 lists common criteria used to evaluate drugs for inclusion on a formulary.

Figure 3.17 Formulary Evaluation Criteria Used by Payers

Formulary Evaluation Criteria Used by Payers

✔ **Clinical safety and efficacy** (in absolute terms and in comparison with other products within the class)

✔ **Approved indications** and off-label use

✔ **Dosage** (therapeutic ranges and route of administration)

✔ **Administration requirements** (need for patient monitoring or administration by a healthcare professional)

✔ **Impact on total care costs and on quality of life**
A pharmaceutical company may supply pharmacoeconomic data regarding the effect of the drug on total pharmacy expenditures and/or on total healthcare expenditures (including medical and surgical interventions and inpatient stays).

✔ **Net cost of the drug**

✔ **Manufacturing reliability**

✔ **Physician demand**

✔ **Employer and consumer demand**

Source: Campbell Alliance.

Tiered co-pays are often used in conjunction with a formulary to encourage the use of formulary products. These systems may, for example, call for a member to pay $5 for a generic, $10 to $20 for preferred brands, and more (e.g., $30, $40, or even $60) for non-formulary brands.

Pharmaceutical companies strive to position their products favorably in the eyes of payers and PBMs to ensure favorable formulary position and avoid barriers such as high co-payments or prior authorization requirements.

Pharmaceutical companies use a number of arguments to convince payers and PBMs to provide favorable positioning for their products. In some cases, a strong argument that a product is substantially more effective or safer than alternative therapies can be used to justify a higher price point. More commonly, companies offer concessionary pricing (rebates) to ensure a position on the formulary.

The size of the rebate is often tied to the expected impact of the payer or PBM on usage of the product, either in terms of sales or of market share.

Managed Markets groups in pharma companies develop long-term relationships with key decision makers at payers and PBMs and "make the case" to them for formulary inclusion and/or the elimination of barriers to use.

Utilization Management Programs

Health plans employ utilization management programs to monitor patterns of drug prescribing. The programs may offer feedback on retrospective drug usage or forward-looking education about drug therapies for specific ailments.

These interventions are most likely to be effective when the payer has considerable leverage over participating physicians and pharmacists. (See Figure 3.18)

The role of the Managed Markets function in a pharmaceutical company is discussed in detail in Chapter 9.

5. Pharmacies and Pharmacists

Pharmacies and pharmacists are typically responsible for dispensing prescriptions. They too have the ability to influence product selection and use, as shown in Figure 3.19

Pharmacies come in many forms, ranging from well-known retail pharmacy chains to those in hospitals and other institutional settings. Generally, pharmacies are classified based on the customer served. For example, a retail

Figure 3.18 Utilization Controls Used by Payers

Immediate Financial Incentives

Formulary
(List of Preferred Drugs, Based on Cost-Efficacy)

Tier I (Generics)	$5
Tier II (Preferred Brands)	$15
Tier III (Non-Preferred Brands)	$25 co-payment

Illustrative Co-Pays

Non-formulary — $40 (open formulary) / No reimbursement (closed formulary)

The implications in terms of patient costs make both physicians and patients more likely to use drugs preferred by the health plan. Often, if a physician knows from experience that a drug is disfavored by large plans and a comparable alternative is available, the physician will change his or her prescribing behavior.

Prior Authorization for Expensive Drugs or Drugs Prone to Be Used Inappropriately
Prior authorization is an inconvenience that provides an administrative disincentive to physicians and (sometimes) a financial disincentive to patients. The prescriber must obtain health plan approval before the prescription is filled. If he/she fails to seek or gain payer approval, the patient must absorb the entire cost of the drug.

Utilization Review and Education

Retrospective Utilization Review and Performance Feedback

Utilization "report cards" provided to physicians, often with comparison of drug costs with those of peers treating patients with similar diagnoses

Letters regarding inappropriate drug use, distributed to patients and physicians

The impact of such performance feedback on physicians is greatest when their financial or job status is at risk—because they are part of a cost-based risk pool, are employed by the payer, or are dependent upon the payer for a large share of their patient population.

Educational Programs

Programs sponsored by payers to teach physicians and/or patients about optimal drug therapies for certain conditions (from the payer's perspective) and the comparative cost-effectiveness of alternative therapies

Such programs may be highly effective in altering physician behavior by providing a compelling rationale to change prescribing practices.

Source: Campbell Alliance.

3. Pharma Customers

55

Figure 3.19 Role of Pharmacists in Driving Product Selection and Use

Identification of Problem Requiring Treatment	Diagnosis	Selection of Treatment (Prescription)	Dispensing of Prescription Order	Adherence to Prescription Regimen
May suggest that a consumer seek medical treatment for symptoms			Explains the co-payment associated with the product	Offers counseling and printed documentation regarding the drug regimen
May run screening programs, such as blood-pressure testing			Under certain circumstances, may substitute a generic so long as the physician does not mark "DAW"— dispense as written	More rarely, may also provide disease management programs and monitor patient status on an ongoing basis
				Such a role is more common in specialty pharmacies

Source: Campbell Alliance.

pharmacy will typically serve any customer with a valid prescription, while a hospital pharmacy will dispense prescriptions to patients being treated within the hospital.

Retail pharmacies fill most of the prescriptions in the US. These pharmacies, including both chain stores and independent pharmacies, sell prescription medicines along with a host of other convenience products. Internet pharmacies and some mail-order pharmacies are variations of the traditional retail model.

Specialty pharmacies cater to narrow patient populations (e.g., patients with diabetes or Crohn's disease). (See Figure 3.20)

Pharmacies that operate within institutions, such as hospitals, specialty clinics, and similar settings, tend to dispense drugs only to patients who are under direct care. In these pharmacies, costs for drugs are generally billed to a third party as a component of overall care expenses. (See Figure 3.21)

Pharmaceutical companies divide pharmacies into units known as classes of trade so that appropriate pricing strategies and marketing priorities can be established. The class of trade indicates the type of pharmacy, such as retail pharmacy vs. hospital or clinic pharmacy. A company that sells oncology products would isolate pharmacies in oncology centers (such as infusion clinics) as a discrete class of trade.

Figure 3.20 Community and Remote Pharmacy Services

Type	Profile
Retail Chains and Independent Pharmacies	• A traditional walk-in pharmacy in which any consumer or patient can have a prescription filled. Examples include RiteAid, Eckerd, and the pharmacies located within such retail stores as Wal-Mart, Target and Kroger. • The examples above are from large regional/national chains, but some chains are much smaller. Single-store "independent" pharmacies remain, although they are becoming far less common. • These pharmacies fill prescriptions for both acute and chronic health problems. They also stock a range of products available over-the-counter (without prescription).
Internet Pharmacies	• Pharmacies that offer a convenient way to obtain "lifestyle" and chronic care drugs remotely. Some Internet pharmacies offer online physician consultation services through which a consumer can obtain and then fill a prescription. • Numerous legal and regulatory concerns have arisen regarding such operations. The National Association of Boards of Pharmacy established VIPPS in 1999, a program for certifying Internet pharmacies that meet its operational standards. • Online pharmacies are sometimes affiliated with a retail chain or independent pharmacy.
Specialty Pharmacies	• Pharmacies that serve relatively small populations with high-cost diseases that require extended or chronic care, such as transplant recipients, diabetics, and patients with HIV/AIDS, end-stage renal disease, multiple sclerosis, and Crohn's disease. • Some specialty pharmacies focus on a chemical or biologic product that requires special handling or distribution (such as hemophilia treatments, which must be administered rapidly when bleeding occurs). • They offer a full range of drugs and medical products to their narrow patient bases. They are extremely active in providing ongoing counseling to their target populations, offering specialized publications, monitoring, and compliance services. Their knowledge of the payer environment for their therapeutic area is invaluable to patients trying to obtain reimbursement. • They also frequently function as compounding pharmacies, preparing customized prescription medications based on instructions provided by prescribers.
Mail-Order Pharmacies (PBM-Owned and Other)	• Pharmacies capable of ensuring continuity of care for people with chronic illnesses, by offering the convenience of multi-month supplies and mailing drugs directly to patient residences. • Some mail-order pharmacies are owned by PBMs and serve only enrollees in plans administered by that PBM. The pharmacies typically operate large call centers to encourage prescribers and patients to switch to less expensive brands or generics. • Many are owned by retail chains or trade associations like the AARP.

Source: Campbell Alliance.

3. Pharma Customers

Figure 3.21 Institutional Pharmacies

Type	Profile
Hospitals and Specialty Clinics	• Pharmacies operated by hospitals and clinics (such as oncology or dialysis centers) for the exclusive use of patients while they are under their direct care—for instance, during a hospital stay. • They often buy products in unit-dose packaging, which simplifies administration. • They typically do not fill prescriptions for chronic medicines.
Staff- or Group-Model HMO Pharmacies	• Onsite, outpatient pharmacies in which enrolled patients may fill prescriptions written by HMO physicians. • They operate as typical retail pharmacies, except that usage is tightly controlled by the HMO and the stock of drugs is generally limited to those on the HMO formulary. • Their tight usage controls mean that they exert great influence on drug choice. As a result, they often receive substantial purchasing discounts and rebates from pharmaceutical companies.
Nursing Homes and Other Institutional Providers	• Consultant pharmacies that package and dispense drugs for institutional settings such as nursing homes and long-term care facilities. • They offer counseling, repackage drugs for administrative simplicity (for instance, organizing each patient's drug regimen by day and time), and handle insurance billing.

Source: Campbell Alliance.

Role of the Pharmacist

All pharmacies employ pharmacists to prepare and dispense medicines. Both the pharmacy and the pharmacist are accountable for dispensing medications correctly and as written by the prescriber. Pharmacy and pharmacist licenses are state-controlled, and each state has specific regulations affecting how drugs are dispensed. Like prescribers, pharmacies and pharmacists are registered with the DEA.

Pharmacists, with their background in chemistry and pharmacology and their involvement in processing insurance requests, commonly offer patients insight into drug use, side effects, drug-drug interactions, coverage and cost, and other areas that affect appropriate and continued use of the product. In certain pharmacy settings, such as the specialty pharmacies that concentrate on narrow therapeutic categories, the pharmacists play a particularly important role in ongoing patient education and counseling. However, pharmacists typically have limited influence on drug selection.

In general, pharmacists are expected to dispense medicines as prescribed, although they do have some leeway to modify prescriptions. In some states, pharmacists are required to substitute a generic product if there is one available (generic substitution), and they may substitute a brand (therapeutic substitution) with permission from the prescriber. Prescribers can prevent generic or therapeutic substitution by noting DAW (dispense as written) on the prescription.

Clinical pharmacists advise practicing physicians, medical directors, and others on effective drug use. Usually PharmDs, they work in institutional pharmacies or on clinical teams within an MCO, PBM, or other payer group. These pharmacists often play a lead role in selecting drugs for the organization's formulary and may advise prescribers on drug therapy for individual patients.

Many pharmacies operate large-scale administration systems, which contain important information about patients and appropriate drug usage. These systems contain extensive profiles of patients (such as age, sex, and drug history) and automatic query systems to avoid errors in drug dispensing (known as concurrent drug utilization review or concurrent DUR). Pharmacy systems are typically connected to patient billing or insurance systems.

Some leading-edge pharmaceutical companies are engaging pharmacists to assist with compliance and educational programs, capitalizing on their strong relationships with both providers and patients to increase adherence to recommended regimens.

4. DISCOVERY

1. The Importance of Discovery

2. A Closer Look at Discovery

3. Operational Model for Discovery

BUSINESS CASE: Herceptin® — A Breakthrough in Disease Targeting

Genentech's Herceptin is considered a groundbreaking step toward personalized medicine. This genetically based therapy targets a particularly aggressive form of metastatic breast cancer in patients with a specific genetic profile.

HER2, or human epidermal growth factor receptor 2, is part of a family of genes that is responsible for the development of malignant tumors in the body. HER2 was found to produce a protein that played an important regulatory role in the growth and development of cells. An overexpression of HER2 would cause a higher-than-normal rate of cell division, which would allow cancerous cells to multiply rapidly. Reseachers isolated HER2 in 1985 and linked it to breast cancer in 1987. Doctors testing for the HER2 gene in cancerous tissue found HER2 overexpression in 25% to 30% of breast cancers. Researchers quickly identified HER2 as a therapeutic target; if a drug could target and prevent HER2 overexpression, it would slow or prevent the growth of cancerous cells.

Using the HER2 gene as a target, scientists from Genentech developed a compound that binds to the excess HER2 proteins responsible for unusually rapid cell division and attracts "killer cells" that destroy these proteins. Herceptin is one of the first products targeting a specific genetic makeup to reach the market. Genetic testing is an essential precursor to such therapy, and Genentech developed a diagnostic to validate the presence of multiple copies of the HER2 gene in patient candidates. Herceptin was approved by the FDA in 1998. For patients with HER2 overexpression, the therapy has proven to be extremely effective. Herceptin works as either a stand-alone therapy or in combination with chemotherapy agents.

Herceptin is an early validation of the potential of genetically based approaches to drug therapy—compelling proof that innovative approaches to disease targeting can save lives.

Sources: "Herceptin: A Novel Approach to the Treatment of Breast Cancer," Healthology 2004; Genentech.

1. The Importance of Discovery

Discovery is the center of innovation within a pharmaceutical company, the place where therapeutic breakthroughs begin. It represents the first stage of a lengthy journey toward introduction of a new product to the marketplace. (See Figure 4.1)

Figure 4.1 Role of Discovery in Pharmaceutical R&D

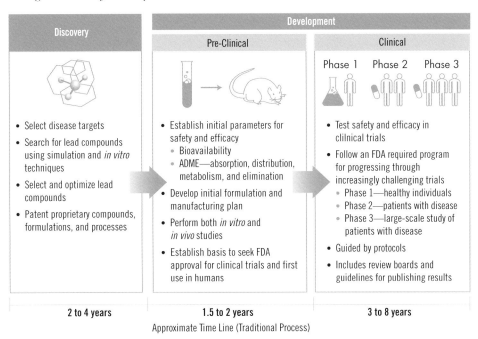

| Discovery | Development | |
| | Pre-Clinical | Clinical |

Discovery
- Select disease targets
- Search for lead compounds using simulation and *in vitro* techniques
- Select and optimize lead compounds
- Patent proprietary compounds, formulations, and processes

Pre-Clinical
- Establish initial parameters for safety and efficacy
  - Bioavailability
  - ADME—absorption, distribution, metabolism, and elimination
- Develop initial formulation and manufacturing plan
- Perform both *in vitro* and *in vivo* studies
- Establish basis to seek FDA approval for clinical trials and first use in humans

Clinical

Phase 1   Phase 2   Phase 3

- Test safety and efficacy in clilnical trials
- Follow an FDA required program for progressing through increasingly challenging trials
  - Phase 1—healthy individuals
  - Phase 2—patients with disease
  - Phase 3—large-scale study of patients with disease
- Guided by protocols
- Includes review boards and guidelines for publishing results

| 2 to 4 years | 1.5 to 2 years | 3 to 8 years |

Approximate Time Line (Traditional Process)

Source: Campbell Alliance.

The mission of discovery in a pharmaceutical or biotech company is to understand the processes associated with a disease and to identify a drug that can intervene in those processes to improve or maintain patient health. It is a "matching game" between disease-related activity and an active ingredient capable of intervening in that activity in a way that is beneficial to patients.

In essence, the journey of discovery begins with the isolation of a "target" (a biochemical entity, such a receptor, associated with a disease or its symptoms) and progresses to perfection of a "lead" compound (a compound that exhibits pharmacological properties which suggest its value as a starting point for drug development. (See Figure 4.2)

The lead compound may be either a chemical agent or a biological agent. During discovery, a group of leads is tested and refined, primarily through modeling of their impact on the intended target. Once one or two leads are identified as the most promising, they undergo preliminary testing for safety and efficacy. Most such testing is *in vitro* testing, or testing of live tissues in a

Figure 4.2 The Evolution of Discovery: From Disease to Lead Compound(s)

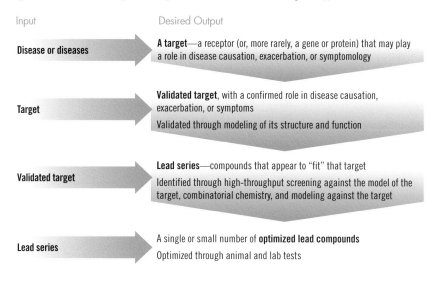

Input

Desired Output

Disease or diseases

A target—a receptor (or, more rarely, a gene or protein) that may play a role in disease causation, exacerbation, or symptomology

Target

Validated target, with a confirmed role in disease causation, exacerbation, or symptoms
Validated through modeling of its structure and function

Validated target

Lead series—compounds that appear to "fit" that target
Identified through high-throughput screening against the model of the target, combinatorial chemistry, and modeling against the target

Lead series

A single or small number of **optimized lead compounds**
Optimized through animal and lab tests

Source: Campbell Alliance.

controlled laboratory environment, such as in a test tube, but some preliminary *in vivo* testing, or testing in live animals, also occurs. (See Figure 4.3)

As a result of its efforts in discovery, the pharmaceutical company hopes to have isolated numerous compounds with sufficient promise to merit development, with the goal of eventual sale.

Because discovery is much less expensive than drug development, it is an economic imperative for pharmaceutical companies to become highly efficient at eliminating less promising compounds/biologics from consideration at the discovery stage.

Researchers are making use of a variety of technological aids to expedite discovery and produce high-potential compounds for development. The roster of available technologies is constantly expanding; some common ones are discussed in this chapter.

For the most part, research is focused in carefully selected areas. Although we sometimes think of research and discovery as the work of scientists operating in isolation from practical goals, their primary research focus is typically based on either a commercial imperative—corporate-level strategic interest

Figure 4.3 Key Considerations Associated with Discovery Process

Exploratory Discovery   Drug Discovery

Selection of a Disease and Disease-Related Target	Identification of Promising Compounds ("Lead Series")	Optimization of Leads and Initiation of Testing

Considerations in selection of disease
- Fit with areas of concentration
- Market size
- Potential for improvement in standard of care through innovation
- Expected improvement in safety and efficacy

Considerations in selection of target
- Relevance to disease
- Ability to create proprietary drugs that affect target

Means of identifying promising compounds
- Compound screening
- Molecular modeling
- Simulation

Time and cost considerations

Selection of lead and backup candidates
- Note that most previous considerations remain relevant and will be revisited at this stage

In vitro and limited in vivo animal testing to show safety and biological activity against the targeted disease
- Results associated with testing

4. Discovery

Source: Campbell Alliance.

in a particular disease or therapeutic area—or a commitment to leveraging previously acquired internal therapeutic or clinical expertise.

More than ever, companies are specializing in discrete therapeutic areas in order to accelerate discovery, focus their resources and manage development risk by building upon prior successes.

2. A Closer Look at Discovery

Disease and Target Selection

Discovery begins with selection of a disease and a target (some biochemical entity in the human body that scientists believe plays a role in causing the disease, exacerbating the disease, or producing symptoms of the disease—such as a malfunctioning protein that may be associated with the onset of a particular chronic illness). The target may be an established one, already addressed by marketed products, or an innovative one based on a novel theory about the disease and its underlying cause.

Once the target is identified, research and commercial leaders develop an ideal profile for a compound addressing that target. They identify desired indications, safety, and other characteristics (such as dosing regimen) that would be of great clinical and/or market value.

The target product profile reflects characteristics needed to differentiate a product in the marketplace. The ideal product profile is one that would make the drug the new gold standard—recognized best therapy—for the disease or symptoms it is meant to treat. (See Figure 4.4)

Fig. 4.4 Example Target Product Profile

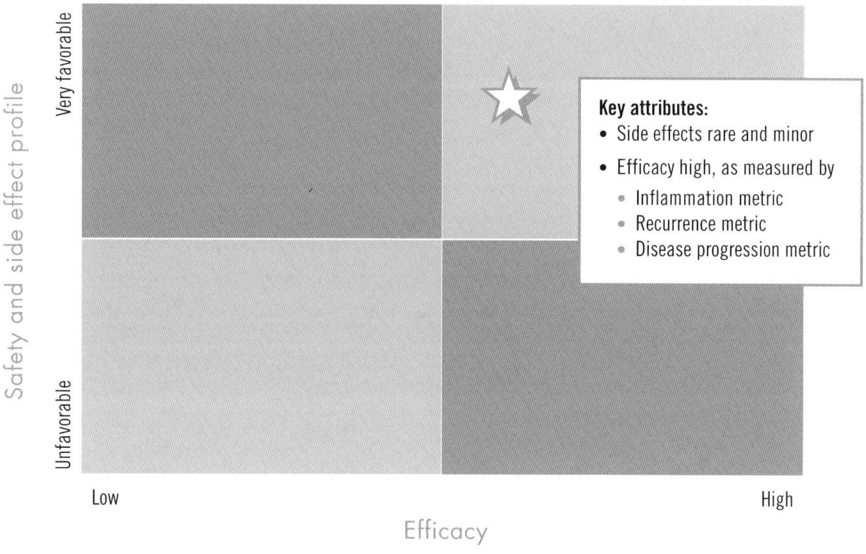

Safety and side effect profile
Very favorable
Unfavorable
Key attributes:
• Side effects rare and minor
• Efficacy high, as measured by
• Inflammation metric
• Recurrence metric
• Disease progression metric
Low
High
Efficacy

Source: Campbell Alliance.

Lead Identification

After the target product profile has been defined, scientists search for compounds that might fit that profile and prove effective against the disease. Frequently, thousands of compounds are analyzed to identify perhaps a few dozen promising ones (lead series).

Like disease targets, potential new therapies emerge from many different sources, including pharma company laboratories, research centers operated in government laboratories, medical centers, and universities. Researchers may examine massive libraries of compounds and data on cell behavior looking for compounds that are likely to affect targets. Additionally, phamaceutical companies pursue a variety of natural products for novel compounds.

Although most discovery is based on matching targets and leads, it is still possible for beneficial connections to be discovered by coincidence. One simple example: an allergy drug that causes drowsiness might become a lead compound for insomnia.

Figure 4.5 suggests the range of sources from which drugs to be tested can be derived.

Figure 4.5 Means of Discovering New Medicines

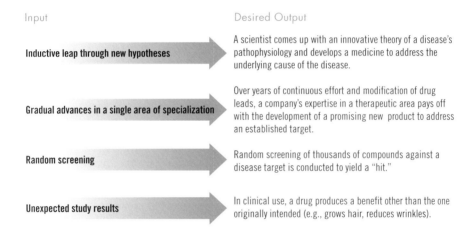

Input	Desired Output
Inductive leap through new hypotheses	A scientist comes up with an innovative theory of a disease's pathophysiology and develops a medicine to address the underlying cause of the disease.
Gradual advances in a single area of specialization	Over years of continuous effort and modification of drug leads, a company's expertise in a therapeutic area pays off with the development of a promising new product to address an established target.
Random screening	Random screening of thousands of compounds against a disease target is conducted to yield a "hit."
Unexpected study results	In clinical use, a drug produces a benefit other than the one originally intended (e.g., grows hair, reduces wrinkles).

Source: Campbell Alliance.

Compound identification has always been a complex and time-consuming process. In the past, each compound had to be individually reviewed and evaluated against a target—an extremely time-consuming process. Today, researchers can use computer-based simulation and analysis to expedite certain facets of the process, including the screening of various leads against a model of the target. For the most part, however, the discovery process remains a lengthy, repetitive one.

Molecular modeling and combinatorial chemistry, the use of chemical methods to generate many possible combinations of a set of similar compounds, can help scientists develop the kind of drug they want more quickly. High-throughput screening, a technique for analyzing large numbers of compounds in biological assays in parallel to identify molecules with specific biological effects, can in some cases process thousands of compounds in a matter of months. Researchers can develop and test many variants on a promising compound and select the one that seems to have the strongest overall profile. Unfortunately, these tools are not always able to capture all the complexities involved in modeling the target and "fitting" a lead to it.

Figure 4.6 illustrates some of the technologies available to facilitate discovery.

Figure 4.6 Emerging Discovery Technologies

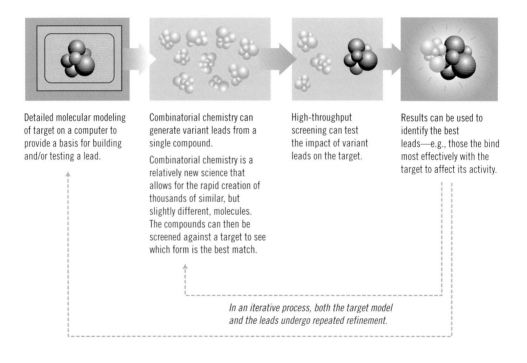

Detailed molecular modeling of target on a computer to provide a basis for building and/or testing a lead.

Combinatorial chemistry can generate variant leads from a single compound.

Combinatorial chemistry is a relatively new science that allows for the rapid creation of thousands of similar, but slightly different, molecules. The compounds can then be screened against a target to see which form is the best match.

High-throughput screening can test the impact of variant leads on the target.

Results can be used to identify the best leads—e.g., those the bind most effectively with the target to affect its activity.

In an iterative process, both the target model and the leads undergo repeated refinement.

Source: Campbell Alliance.

By modeling molecular structure and activities by computer, researchers can predict which compounds are likely to prove effective during preclinical discovery.

In the future, a shift to gene- and protein-based targeting may lead to greater efficiencies. (See Figure 4.7) Pharmacogenomics—the study of genes and their relationship to drug action—offers the promise of drugs tailored to a patient's needs. These more personalized drugs may reduce the focus on the blockbuster model large companies have pursued in the past. Because they will not generate the same huge revenues as successful products of the past, genotype-based drugs may exert pressure to change not only the discovery and drug development processes, but also commercial operations.

Figure 4.7 Rational Approaches to Discovery

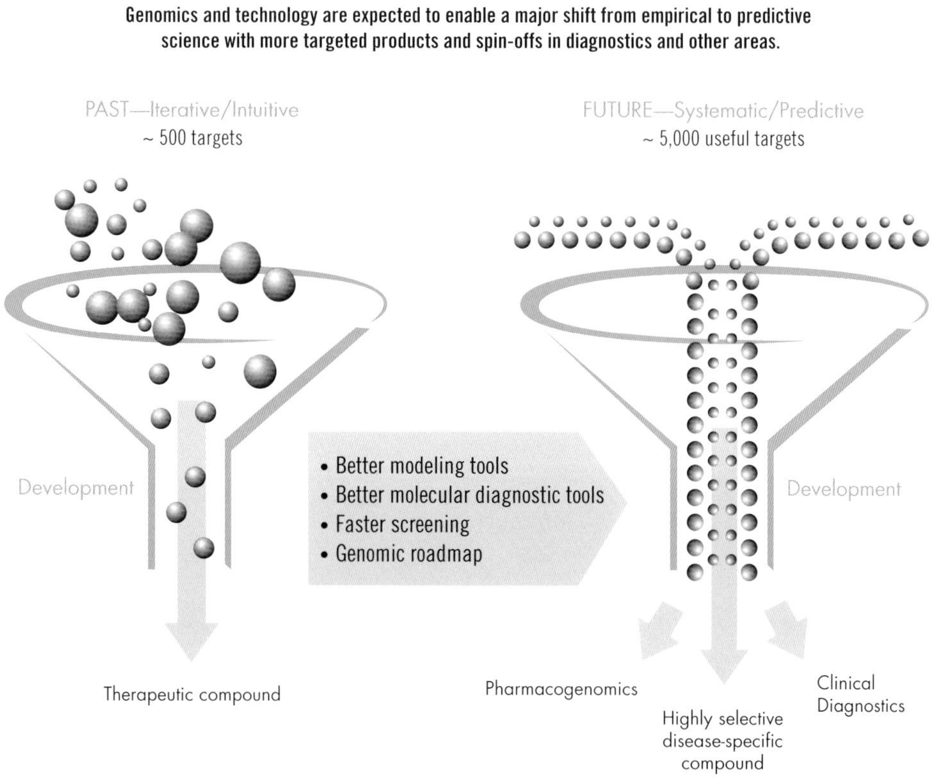

Genomics and technology are expected to enable a major shift from empirical to predictive science with more targeted products and spin-offs in diagnostics and other areas.

PAST—Iterative/Intuitive
~ 500 targets

FUTURE—Systematic/Predictive
~ 5,000 useful targets

Development

- Better modeling tools
- Better molecular diagnostic tools
- Faster screening
- Genomic roadmap

Development

Therapeutic compound

Pharmacogenomics

Highly selective disease-specific compound

Clinical Diagnostics

Source: Campbell Alliance.

Lead Series and Lead Optimization

Later-stage discovery, involves optimization of a set of molecules or compounds that appear to influence the target. This phase requires close collaboration between the company's biologists and chemists, who form a feedback loop. The biologists test the biological properties while the chemists manipulate the chemical structure of these compounds in light of the information provided by the biologists.

Lead optimization is the subsequent effort to select a lead candidate—the compound with the greatest potential for development—from a lead series. One or more backup compounds are also selected. Through this effort, researchers progress from hundreds of compounds to a lead series. Lead optimization typically includes testing of the compounds' physiochemical properties, their pharmacokinetic behavior, and their therapeutic efficacy. These studies are conducted both *in vitro* (e.g., in human or animal organ cells) and *in vivo*, usually in mice or rats.

This phase typically includes testing of preliminary safety, pharmacology, and pharmacokinetics. These tests are conducted in animal tissue and then in live animals, such as mice. At this stage, many companies also undertake studies to help anticipate potential difficulties with the formulation and manufacturing processes for manufacturing it. Typical testing during this phase is outlined in Figure 4.8.

Given the great variety of reactions within animal and human populations and the fact that no drug can be made completely specific to its intended target, every compound or molecule will have some unwanted effects. The optimization phase attempts to identify drugs with high specificity whose action is largely limited to the intended target.

Over time, as more data become available about the compound being tested, the target product profile is revised to align with demonstrated attributes.

As discovery proceeds, it often becomes evident that the compound/molecule will not obtain the "best case" profile defined initially. Many drugs that survive initial discovery do so with scaled-back expectations; they might now be considered incremental improvements on existing therapies and have moderate market potential. Brand managers usually work closely with Discovery leaders to ensure that the product's market potential is sufficiently strong to merit ongoing investment.

Figure 4.8 Lead Optimization: Testing

Laboratory testing

Laboratory Testing (*in vitro*)

1. Tests on live tissues (from human or animal organs) to identify the cellular targets the drug acts on

2. Tests on cell cultures for toxicological effects and other responses to the compound

Animal testing

Animal Testing (*in vivo*)

1. Initial efficacy testing in animals

   a. Within a species (typically mice), animals are selected, bred, infected, or genetically engineered to have the disease scientists want to study

   b. Blood or urine of these animals is analyzed to evaluate relative effectiveness of the compound in terms of ADME

   c. Diagnostics are used to detect the compound's impact on disease.

   d. The toxicological properties of the compound are also tested

Source: Campbell Alliance.

4. Discovery

Patent Protection

Once the Discovery group has identified a truly promising set of lead compounds, it needs to protect those precious assets. The primary means of protection is a patent as a new chemical entity (NCE) or new molecular entity (NME).

Supporting research or manufacturing technologies may also be patented, either during the lead optimization stage or at any other point in discovery.

Companies utilitze sophisticated strategies to secure patents for newly developed compounds, as well as for the technologies that are invented to develop them. And for good reason: If a competitor obtains a patent on a novel compound first, the millions of dollars invested in discovery will be wasted. By patenting a compound or a process for manufacturing a compound, the pharmaceutical company safeguards its rights to sole use for 20 years. The patented entity can then be incorporated as the active pharmaceutical ingredient (API) in a new drug.

71

To ensure that intellectual property is protected adequately, many large companies actually co-locate their patent attorneys with Discovery teams to facilitate close interaction.

The Transition to Development

Once one or more lead compounds have been identified and selected, the pharmaceutical company must make a pivotal decision. The cost of transitioning the compound into development is significant and companies will follow a formal process to evaluate the risks and rewards of pursuing commercialization. Based on its formal evaluation, the company could decide that the compound needs further preclinical investigation and refinement, in which case the compound continues in discovery. Or, the company could decide that the compound, however promising, does not meet its strategic goals, in which case the compound becomes an outlicensing candidate for Business Development. Alternatively, the company could decide to begin the lengthy and expensive process of drug development, at the end of which the NCE or NME may become a marketed product.

Some pharmaceutical companies are striving to make discovery more efficient through a closer alignment with early development. Increasingly, the line of demarcation between discovery and early development is blurring. For the most part, clinical trials have been the exclusive domain of Development. Today, some companies assign a single group responsibility for discovery, all preclinical (animal) testing, and relatively small-scale clinical (human) testing.

Compelling reasons exist for a close alignment. True proof of concept (that is, evidence that the drug is beneficial for the purpose being analyzed) occurs in early phase 2 clinical testing, when the candidate drug is tested for the first time in people with the targeted condition. By establishing an integrated oversight function from discovery through proof of concept, a pharmaceutical company can eliminate delays in communicating problems with a candidate compound to researchers, who can then strive to improve the compound or seek out an entirely new one.

Some Discovery researchers are seeking heightened involvement in clinical trials so that they can learn about the genetic profiles of people with a target disease and search for linkages between specific patient characteristics and the efficacy of different drug treatments. These insights could significantly accelerate the screening and selection of lead candidates that have greater potential to become successful products.

3. Operational Model for Discovery

Discovery functions align with the major process stages (targeting, screening, and testing). Groups involved in discovery efforts are typically organized by scientific specialty (e.g., biology, biochemistry, pharmacology) and then subdivided by therapeutic area.

Discovery activities may be carried out by a company's own laboratories; by outside laboratories in universities, hospitals, or clinics; and in specialized discovery companies. Increasingly, portions of discovery may be outsourced to a strategic alliance partner or another outside company that specializes in selected aspects of the discovery process.

Discovery is typically managed globally and reports to the company-wide head of R&D.

Discovery efforts are supported by professionals from Marketing, Business Development, and Legal.

Marketing works closely with Discovery to identify and select diseases based on such considerations as the company's commercial objectives, and the market potential of therapies for that particular disease.

Business Development (BD) helps to identify and fill innovation gaps. BD seeks outside sources of compounds and technologies in order to accelerate discovery and drug development. BD will also out-license newly discovered compounds or technologies that fall outside the company's target therapeutic areas.

Attorneys and legal staff work closely with Discovery to ensure that patents are put into place for all innovation.

Collectively, these groups work to secure innovation that fits the company's strategic or therapeutic area objectives. Each group is discussed in greater detail in other chapters of this book. (See Figures 4.9 and 4.10)

Figure 4.9 Operational Model for Discovery

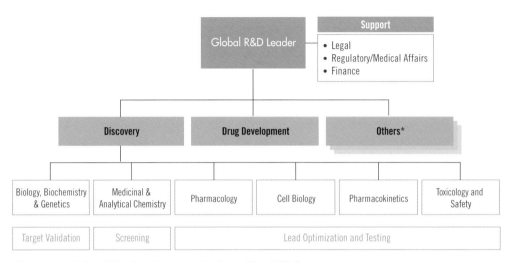

*In various organizations, "Others" may include such functions as BD and R&D IT.

Source: Campbell Alliance.

Figure 4.10 Description of Functions

Function	Description
Biology, Biochemistry, & Genetics	• Identify potential disease targets that may respond to drug therapy
Medicinal & Analytical Chemistry	• Analyze compound libraries and characterize compounds
Pharmacology	• Evaluate compound action on target
Cell Biology	• Evaluate effect on cell functions (such as cell death and enzyme activation)
Pharmacokinetics & Pharmacodynamics	• Evaluate compound activity within the body (such as absorption, distribution, metabolism, and excretion)
Toxicology & Safety Assessment	• Test toxicological effects of compounds on tissue and animals

Source: Campbell Alliance.

5. DRUG DEVELOPMENT

1. The Importance of Drug Development

2. A Closer Look at Drug Development

3. Operational Model for Drug Development

Scientists at Immunex (a company later acquired by Amgen) spent nine years developing Enbrel®, a drug used to treat five chronic inflammatory diseases.

Prior to its development, Immunex's scientists had successfully isolated the gene for the receptor for tumor necrosis factor (TNF), a chemical messenger that helps regulate the inflammation response in the body. After developing a protein from the gene that demonstrated the desired characteristics, scientists began to test the carefully designed molecule in laboratory animals. Tests confirmed that the molecule, named etanercept, had a favorable impact on arthritis and other inflammatory diseases in mice.

After receiving the FDA's permission to conduct tests in humans, Immunex developed a process to produce the molecule, first in quantities sufficient for clinical trials, and then in quantities sufficient for commercialization. The manufactured product, expressed as a mammalian cell and refined, is called Enbrel.

Immunex quickly moved into clinical trials to test Enbrel as a treatment for rheumatoid arthritis (RA). Phase 1 trials evaluated 234 adults with RA, phase 2 trials evaluated 89 adults with RA who were being treated with MTX (another treatment for RA), and phase 3 trials evaluated 632 adults with RA who had never been treated with MTX.

Based on the results of the clinical trials, Immunex submitted a Biologics Licensing Application (BLA), an application requesting permission to commercialize the product, to the FDA. The FDA approved Enbrel as a treatment for RA, and Immunex continued to conduct trials on Enbrel to generate data for additional applications and indications for the product.

Source: Amgen.

1. The Importance of Drug Development

Drug development is by far the most extensive and expensive part of pharmaceutical research. It is the point at which a promising compound is either transformed into a marketable product or shelved.

Development involves preclinical testing to verify that a drug is sufficiently safe and effective to be tested in humans, followed by clinical (human) tests to verify the drug's safety and efficacy for its proposed use.

Preclinical testing is focused on proving that the toxicology profile of the compound is sufficiently favorable to make human testing safe. Preclinical research is necessary to support an Investigational New Drug (IND) application to the FDA requesting permission to begin human trials.

The clinical development process mandated by the FDA involves a series of progressively more challenging tests to demonstrate the product's efficacy, while first and foremost ensuring the safety of the volunteers who elect to participate and consumers who ultimately use the approved drug.

- Phase 1 clinical testing is the first time the product is used in humans and is usually limited to healthy volunteers.

- Phase 2 trials are typically the first studies in people with the target disease or condition.

- Phase 3 trials are larger-scale tests in people with the target disease or condition.

- Phase 4/post-marketing surveillance studies are conducted after the product has obtained FDA approval to market the drug for a specific indication. In most cases, such studies are optional and are pursued primarily for marketing purposes. In other instances, they are FDA-mandated as a condition of approval.

The phases of drug development are summarized in Figure 5.1.

During drug development, the sponsor also establishes a viable drug formulation, and a viable process for manufacturing it consistently. As discussed in greater detail in Chapter 10, that phase of the manufacturing process is called "scale up," because the volume produced is increased as a product approaches commercial launch.

The success rate for drug development is low. Development begins with thousands of potential compounds for each product that ultimately gains FDA approval. The development process, which consists of animal and human (clinical) testing, is laborious, time-consuming, expensive, and often disappointing. Many compounds for which a company has high hopes fail to pass testing hurdles—sometimes after several million dollars have been invested.

According to the Pharmaceutical Research and Manufacturers of America (citing data from the Tufts University Center for the Study of Drug Development), for every 250 compounds that enter preclinical testing, only five go on to clinical development and only one wins FDA approval for marketing.

Figure 5.1 Timeline of Preclinical and Clinical Activities

	Preclinical 1 to 2 years	Phase 1 1 to 2 years	Phase 2 1 to 3 years	Phase 3 and NDA Approval 3 to 6 years	Phase 4 Can last many years
Objectives	• Establish pharmacology and toxicology profiles • Develop drug formulation • Secure authorization to test in humans	• Establish pharmacokinetic profile and dosing regimens • Assess safety issues	• Proof of Concept • Test safety and efficacy (small scale) • Look for side effects	• Confirm safety and efficacy (large scale) • Monitor adverse reactions from long-term use • Expand indications	• Continues to evaulate safety and generate data about how drug affects specific groups of patients (e.g., the elderly)
Population	• Animals	• 20 to 100 volunteers, generally healthy	• Approximately 100 to 500 patients with the disease	• Approximately 1,000 to 5,000 patients with the disease	• Varied size and make-up

On average, it takes between 12 and 15 years to do the discovery research and testing to bring a new medicine to the market.

Sources: Pharmaceutical Research and Manufacturers of America; Campbell Alliance.

Promising compounds may be abandoned because of safety issues/toxicity, poor absorption, manufacturing difficulties, ineffectiveness, or limited market potential. (See Figure 5.2)

Figure 5.2 The Compounds Dwindle Down to a Precious Few...

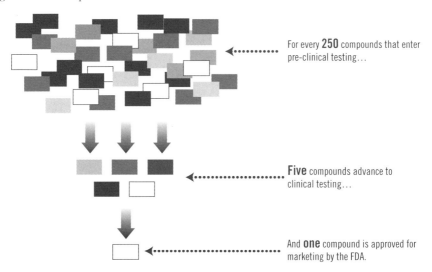

For every **250** compounds that enter pre-clinical testing...

Five compounds advance to clinical testing...

And **one** compound is approved for marketing by the FDA.

Source: Pharmaceutical Research and Manufacturers of America.
    (citing data from the Tufts University Center for the Study of Drug Development)

For the few products that pass successfully through all stages of discovery and development, the process typically takes 10 to 15 years—the vast majority of it clinical development time.

The average number of clinical trials conducted prior to filing an NDA has more than doubled, and the number of patients has tripled in the 20 years ending in 1996. Since then, costs per subject have also been on the rise.

Given the huge investment of time and money involved, the greatest challenges for Development involve managing risk and accelerating time-to-market. Companies need to simultaneously discontinue development of drugs with lower-than-anticipated potential and expedite the development of promising drugs in order to derive maximum value from patent protection. (See Figures 5.3 and 5.4)

Figure 5.3 Duration of Drug Discovery and Development

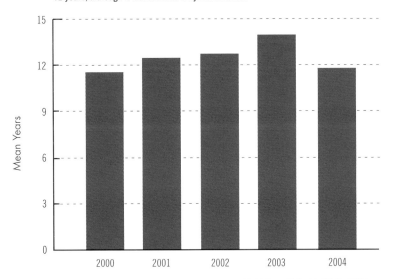

New Molecular Entities (NMEs): From Early Research to FDA Approval

The industry-average discovery and development time is approximately 12 years, although it increased to 14 years in 2003.

Sources: CMR International Institute for Regulatory Science (2000-2001); IMS Health (2002-2004).

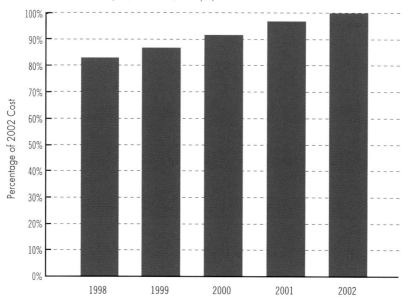

Figure 5.4 Increasing Cost of Clinical Trial

Index of Mean Cost Per Patient in Clinical Trials All Phases 1998–2002 (US, Canada, Europe)

Source: PAREXEL's Pharmaceutical R&D Statistical Sourcebook 2004/2005.

2. A Closer Look at Drug Development

Preclinical Development

Figure 5.5 Summary of Preclinical Development

Summary		
Stage	**Activities**	**Goal**
Preclinical Development	Lab and animal tests to establish pharmacology and toxicology profiles • Studies of pharmacokinetics, or how the body reacts to the drug—typically known as absorption, distribution, metabolism, and excretion (ADME) testing • Pharmacodynamic studies of the drug's positive and adverse effects on the body and the impact of changes in dosing • Toxicology studies to establish the drug's safety, both in high doses and over longer periods of time (for example, 12- to 24-month carcinogenicity studies to determine if the product is likely to cause cancer) • Tests of impact on reproductive health	• Filing an IND application with the FDA • IND will contain evidence that demonstrates that human trials should be allowed

Source: Campbell Alliance.

Drug development begins with a preclinical phase. This testing takes place in the laboratory and builds a base of evidence in models that are progressively more similar to humans, often beginning with tests in human tissue cultures. However, before a drug can be administered to humans, safety concerns dictate that it be tested in animal models (animals, or combinations of animals and diseases, that duplicate human responses to disease and treatment in one or more respects). Mice are commonly used in preclinical tests, as are rabbits, guinea pigs, monkeys, and dogs.

Pharmacological and toxicology testing in the preclinical phase establish practical boundaries for drug strength and dosing by assessing pharmacodynamics—the positive and negative effects of the drug in animal models at various dosing levels. Such testing also clarifies critical features of the product including the lead indication—that is, the most promising use for the product—and likely mechanism of action—a hypothesis about how the drug works in the body to produce its beneficial effects.

Manufacturing begins to get involved during preclinical development. The manufacturing process and quality controls for the product are created and refined during preclinical development. The product is initially formulated in the laboratory to evaluate its stability and assess whether it can be recreated reliably and consistently. Occasionally, a company finds that it is not practical (too expensive or unreliable) to safely produce the product, and the drug development effort is abandoned.

Based on results from animal studies, the drug formulation is refined. If an unusual delivery system or device (such as an inhaler or transdermal patch) is planned, that delivery system will be designed and tested during this period, in parallel with preclinical development.

One last hurdle is a brief commerical review. If probable demand for the drug is sufficient to justify clinical trials, the company attempts to scale up production by designing the manufacturing approach. (See Chapter 10, Manufacturing Operations)

The milestone for preclinical development is the submission of an IND application to the FDA. The IND includes the test results as evidence that the drug is fit for clinical testing in humans. The FDA has 30 days from receipt of the submission to request additional information or deny the IND. If the FDA takes no action during that time, clinical trials can begin. (See Figure 5.6)

Figure 5.6 Major Components of an IND

Component	Description
Cover Sheet	• The sponsor, the phase(s) of clinical investigation to be conducted, and commitments to comply with regulatory requirements (Form 1571)
Introductory Statement and General Investigational Plan	• Overview of the drug, including its active ingredients, pharmacological class, route of administration, previous human experience with the investigational drug, if any, along with a brief description of the overall plan for investigating the drug
Investigator's Brochure	• Overview of drug substance and formulation and/or structural formula, pharmacological and toxicological effects, and pharmacokinetic and biological disposition
Protocols	• Protocols for the conduct of each proposed clinical trial
Chemistry, Manufacturing and Control Information	• Description of the composition, manufacturing, and control of the drug substance and drug products—to ensure proper identification, quality, purity, and strength
Pharmacology and Toxicology Information	• Information about pharmacological and toxicological studies of the drug, based on tests in laboratory animals or in vitro, providing a basis for the sponsor's conclusion that it is reasonably safe to conduct clinical investigations
Previous Human Experiences with the Investigational Drug	• A summary of previous human experience with the investigational drug (e.g., unsuccessful earlier trials or tests of chemically similar products)

Source: 21 CFR 312.

Pharmacology and toxicology studies may continue in animals even after the drug has entered clinical testing. However, these studies are considered "non-clinical" rather than "preclinical."

The Four Phases of Clinical Development

Clinical development is the process of testing a drug in human subjects. A progression of increasingly complex and challenging studies is used to prove that a drug is safe and effective in treating specific conditions in certain patient populations. A successful drug can progress through up to four phases of clinical studies designed to ensure participant safety while demonstrating a drug's efficacy in ever-larger or more varied trial populations. (See Figure 5.7)

Figure 5.7 FDA-Mandated Testing

The FDA requires the most exhaustive testing for new molecular entities (NMEs) or new chemical entities (NCEs), which are the focus of this chapter. Testing for generics and for new indications is abbreviated.

	NCEs or NMEs	New Indication for an FDA-Approved Drug	Generic Version of an FDA-Approved Drug
FDA Testing Requirements	• Preclinical testing • Three phases of clinical testing (phase 4 is generally optional and often pursued for marketing purposes)	• Additional phase 3b trials for the novel indication	• Bioequivalence testing that demonstrates the generic drug is comparable in dosage form, strength, route of administration, quality, performance characteristics, and intended use as the original drug

Source: Campbell Alliance.

Phase 1 Trials

Figure 5.8 Summary of Phase 1 Trials

Summary		
Stage	**Activities**	**Goal**
Phase 1	• Testing on a limited population of healthy volunteers (generally 20–100) to establish pharmacokinetics (how the body absorbs, distributes, metabolizes, and excretes the drug) and a safe dosing range	• To demonstrate that the drug is sufficiently safe to be tested in subjects with the target disease

Source: Campbell Alliance.

Phase 1 trials establish the safety of administration to humans and the range of safe dosing. To minimize the risk to participants, these trials are typically limited to healthy volunteers and take place in a carefully controlled environment.

Phase 1 trials are generally conducted in phase 1 units, where the subjects remain under observation for several hours or days following drug administration.

The trial subjects are most often young, healthy, adult male volunteers. (Male volunteers are preferred to avoid the complication of reproductive health issues.)

Phase 2 Trials

Figure 5.9 Summary of Phase 2 Trials

Summary		
Stage	Activities	Goal
Phase 2	• Small-scale trials on 100-500 patients with the target disease	• To generate proof-of-concept evidence that the drug actually has the intended effect in the target population • To establish safety and effectiveness in treating the disease • To establish minimum and maximum effective dose • To look for side effects

Source: Campbell Alliance.

Phase 2 trials are usually the first tests of the drug in subjects with the disease/condition for which the compound is a potential treatment. These studies are designed to test whether the proposed drug actually works. Demonstrated safety and efficacy during this phase is commonly referred to as proof of concept (POC).

Proof of concept is usually established after dosing, safety, and efficacy testing have been completed and analyses on key endpoints indicate that the product has been beneficial to subjects with the condition. This evidence that the product will be valuable to the target population is the basis upon which the company decides to make the massive investment required for phase 3 development.

Phase 3 Trials and the NDA

Figure 5.10 Summary of Phase 3 Trials and the NDA

Summary		
Stage	**Activities**	**Goal**
Phase 3	• Generally large-scale randomized, blinded, placebo-controlled, trials in approximately 1,000-5,000 subjects with the target disease	• To produce compelling evidence of safety and efficacy in a large population to support submission to the FDA seeking permission to market the product in the US
Phase 3b (optional)	• Generally large-scale randomized, blinded, placebo-controlled, blinded trials in subjects with the target disease	• Often conducted after the FDA filing • To supplement previous trials with additional safety or efficacy data, or to support additional indications or populations

Source: Campbell Alliance.

Phase 3 represents the largest investment of both money and time during clinical development. The drug is tested in hundreds to thousands of subjects with the target disease or condition, in many different sites, and often globally. Although dosing and safety testing continues during phase 3, the primary focus is the collection and analysis of highly specific efficacy endpoint data.

Phase 3b trials, which often begin before approval but after filing, may supplement or complete earlier trials by providing additional safety data or they may test the approved drug for additional conditions for which it may prove useful. Phase 3b trials are optional and are conducted while the FDA reviews the NDA or BLA.

Following completion of phase 3, key data from all three phases are aggregated and analyzed. When a pharmaceutical company judges that phase 3 trials have generated sufficient evidence of safety and efficacy to obtain FDA approval, it will submit an application seeking permission to market the product in the US. For non-biologic drugs, companies submit an NDA to the FDA's Center for Drug Evaluation and Research (CDER). (See Figure 5.11) Some applications for biologic drugs go to CDER as well. For most other biologics, a BLA is submitted to the FDA's Center for Biologic Evaluation and Research (CBER). (See Figure 5.12) Our focus is on CDER's NDA review process.

5. Drug Development

Figure 5.11 Major Components of an NDA

Component	Description
Application	• Formal, signed application that explains the nature of the marketing permission sought (prescription or over-the-counter) and cross-references any related or prior submissions
Index	• Comprehensive index of all NDA volumes (there are frequently 50 to 100) and sections
Summary	• Integrated summary of efficacy and integrated summary of safety. Usually contains labeling, marketing, and pharmacology information along with the expected risk-benefit profile
Chemistry, Manufacturing, and Controls Section	• The composition, manufacturing process, and controls for the drug substance (API) and the drug product (formulation)
Non-Clinical Pharmacology and Toxicology Section	• Description of animal and in vitro (test tube) studies of the drug
Human Pharmacokinetics and Bioavailability Section	• Description of the human pharmacokinetic and bioavailabilty data, including the analytical and statistical methods used to assess these characteristics in each study
Microbiology Section (for Anti-Microbials Only)	• The biochemical basis for the drug (how it acts in the body), including known mechanisms of resistance
Clinical Data Section	• Description of the clinical trials of the drug, including a summation regarding evidence of effectiveness and safety for the claimed indications, dosage, and administration
Statistical Section	• Explanation of the statistical analyses for each study, which may require samples and product labeling to allow the FDA to test the compound, including copies of case report forms and tabulations of aggregate data from those forms
Other Administrative Information	• Other administrative information, including patent information (for drug and proprietary processes), licensing agreements, and other information that may affect the approval of the drug

Source: 21 CFR 314.

Once the application is filed, the FDA will review the submission. Figure 5.13 illustrates the review process.

One critical component of the submission is the highly detailed draft package insert, which is usually developed by Regulatory Affairs, Clinical Development, and Marketing using information gathered during all phases of clinical

Figure 5.12 Allocation of FDA Responsibility for Biologic Products

Center for Drug Evaluation and Research	Center for Biologics Evaluation and Research
• Proteins intended for therapeutic use, including cytokines (e.g., interferons), enzymes (e.g., thrombolytics), and other novel proteins, except for those that are specifically assigned to CBER (e.g., vaccines and blood products)	• Cellular products, including products composed of human, bacterial or animal cells, or from physical parts of those cells
• Therapeutic proteins derived from plants, animals, or microorganisms, and recombinant versions of these products	• Vaccines
• Nonvaccine and nonallergenic products intended to treat disease by inhibiting or modifying a preexisting immune response	• Allergenic extracts used for the diagnosis and treatment of allergic diseases and allergen patch tests
• Certain growth factors, cytokines, and monoclonal antibodies	• Antitoxins, antivenins, and venoms
	• Blood, blood components, and plasma derived products

Source: 70 Fed.Reg. 14378 (2005).

trials. The insert specifies indications for the new medicine; explains dosage and administration guidelines; and provides key statements regarding safety, risks, mechanism of action, and other characteristics. Ideally, the draft package insert is consistent with the target product profile established during discovery, with minor changes to reflect the results of drug development.

The importance of the package insert, introduced in Chapter 2, cannot be overemphasized. The pharmaceutical company's promotional claims for the product are limited to statements that the FDA approves for inclusion in the package insert, which is therefore the foundation for the product's marketing strategy.

During the NDA approval process, the FDA may dictate changes to the package insert and the product's label. One required modification may be highlighted health warnings involving drug safety or side effects. The warning may be highlighted in bold text, or in the most extreme cases, a black box indicating that the drug can potentially be fatal (this is known, appropriately, as a black box warning). Of course, any of these limitations to the product label (package insert) are likely to have a severe negative impact on product adoption.

5. Drug Development

Figure 5.13 NDA Review Process

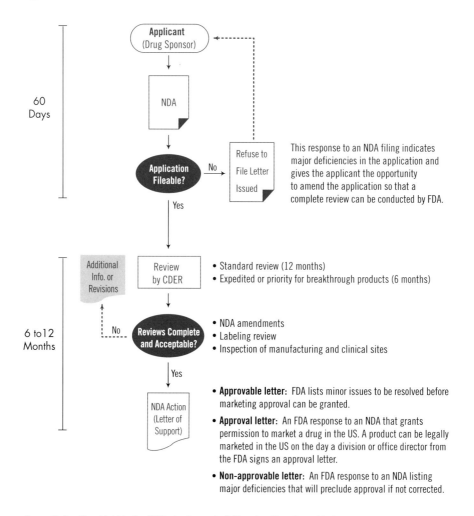

60 Days

6 to 12 Months

Applicant (Drug Sponsor)

NDA

Application Fileable?

No → Refuse to File Letter Issued

This response to an NDA filing indicates major deficiencies in the application and gives the applicant the opportunity to amend the application so that a complete review can be conducted by FDA.

Yes

Additional Info. or Revisions

Review by CDER

- Standard review (12 months)
- Expedited or priority for breakthrough products (6 months)

No ◄--- Reviews Complete and Acceptable?

- NDA amendments
- Labeling review
- Inspection of manufacturing and clinical sites

Yes

NDA Action (Letter of Support)

- **Approvable letter:** FDA lists minor issues to be resolved before marketing approval can be granted.
- **Approval letter:** An FDA response to an NDA that grants permission to market a drug in the US. A product can be legally marketed in the US on the day a division or office director from the FDA signs an approval letter.
- **Non-approvable letter:** An FDA response to an NDA listing major deficiencies that will preclude approval if not corrected.

Source: Food and Drug Administration. NDA Review Process. Available at: http://www.fda.gov/cder/handbook/nda.htm. Accessed June 15, 2005.

The FDA classifies NDAs on two criteria: novelty of the active ingredient and clinical improvement. The FDA committed to reducing the time frame for NDA review as part of the Prescription Drug User Fee Act (PDUFA) in 1997. Under PDUFA, the FDA's normal timetable for NDA approval is 12 months. If the product satisfies an unmet medical need or represents a significant advance compared with available therapies, the FDA may grant priority review, which takes six months. (See Figure 5.14)

Figure 5.14 NDA Classification

By Novelty of Active Ingredient	
Classification	**Description**
New Chemical Entity (NCE) or New Molecular Entity (NME)	• A product whose active ingredient has never before been approved by the FDA
New Salt of a Previously Approved Drug	• A new salt or derivative of a drug previously approved drug (but not a new entity)
New Formulation	• New formulation of a previously approved drug (but not a new entity or new salt)
New Combination	• New combination of two or more previously marketed drugs
Already Marketed Drug	• A duplicate of an already marketed drug (typically with a new manufacturer)
New Indication	• A new indication for an already marketed drug, including switches in marketing status from prescription to OTC
Already Marketed Drug with No Previously Approved NDA	• A drug, typically OTC, that is already marketed but has no previously approved NDA on file • For example, the FDA reviews specific categories of OTC drugs, such as antacids and laxatives, based upon their active ingredients rather than reviewing individual products

By Probable Impact on Treatment Options	
Classification	**Description**
Priority Review	• A potentially breakthrough drug—one that is the first treatment available for a particular purpose or represents a significant advance in efficacy, safety, side effects, or probable compliance • These benefits qualify the drug for review by the FDA within 6 months of NDA submission
Standard Review	• All other drugs are subject to the standard 12-month review process

Source: Food and Drug Administration. New Drug Application. Available at: http://www.fda.gov/cder/handbook/ndabox.htm. Accessed June 15, 2005.

Limitations found during drug development—such as unforeseen side effects, toxicity, or poor efficacy—may lead the pharmaceutical company or the FDA to halt trials. Marketing and Drug Development leaders acting in concert may also decide to abandon the product.

5. Drug Development

Abandoned compounds do not simply disappear, however. Some are out-licensed to other companies. (See Chapter 6, Business Development) Others are archived in the company's compound library and may be resuscitated later if new applications come to light.

Some compounds that proved ineffective for their initial planned use have been found years later to be effective to treat another condition. One well known example is Viagra®, which was originally developed for the treatment of hypertension but was found instead to be an effective treatment for erectile dysfunction.

Phase 4 Trials

Figure 5.15 Summary of Phase 4 Trials

Summary		
Stage	**Activities**	**Goal**
Phase 4 (Post-Marketing Surveillance)	• Additional marketing studies following FDA approval for US marketing or • Additional safety studies required by the FDA as a condition of NDA approval	• To introduce the product to a large pool of target subjects and physicians and/or generate additional compelling data to support current indications and/or confirm safety

Source: Campbell Alliance.

Even after a drug has FDA approval for an indication, phase 4 studies may be undertaken. These studies, known as post marketing surveillance or "post-approval" studies, are a means of introducing the drug to a broader population as well as gathering additional information about product safety and efficacy for that particular indication. In some cases, the FDA makes phase 4 safety studies a condition of NDA approval.

Unlike many other clinical trials, these studies are not typically randomized or placebo-controlled. Instead, these trials are "open label"—all subjects are given the newly approved product, and they and their caregivers know what that product is.

Phase 4 studies may include new populations (e.g., lower-severity cases), new formulations, or adjusted dosing regimens.

Medical Affairs teams in concert with Marketing often conduct these studies.

Anatomy of a Clinical Trial: What Is a Study Protocol?

The protocol describes in detail how the study should be performed, including subject, investigator, and site selection; data collection and analysis; adverse event reporting; and study termination procedures. It also defines the target endpoint(s) for the study— the metrics of the drug's effectiveness.

Study protocols must be approved by institutional review boards (IRBs), which assess the ethical soundness of the planned study (that is, whether it complies with Good Clinical Practice and safeguards subject safety). When a study is to be executed at multiple sites, each site must have an IRB review the protocol and grant its approval.

Figure 5.16 Major Components of a Clinical Trial Protocol

Component	Description
General Information	• Identification of the protocol, sponsor, and types of investigators
Background Information	• Explanation of the investigational product, results of non-clinical studies, and references to related literature
Trial Objectives and Purpose	• The rationale for conducting the trial (including the primary endpoint by which performance will be measured)
Trial Design	• Characteristics such as number of participating sites, desired endpoints, protections against bias (e.g., randomization and double blinding), criteria for each study visit, data to be collected, and planned treatment regimens and duration
Selection and Withdrawal of Subjects	• Inclusion/exclusion criteria used in choosing study participants (e.g., age, sex, ethnicity, presence and severity of disease/condition being assessed, co-morbidities, concomitant drugs)
Treatment of Subjects	• Specific instruction on the frequency of drug administration and return visits to the investigative site
Assessment of Efficacy	• Parameters and process used to record and measure efficacy
Assessment of Safety	• Parameters and process used to record and measure safety, including adverse event (AE) and severe adverse event (SAE) reporting
Statistics	• Explanation of statistical analyses to be used and sample size/composition
Direct Access to Source Data/Docs	• Processes to ensure study documentation is readily available for review by clinical research associates (CRAs) and regulators
Quality Control/ Quality Assurance	• Process to verify protocol is followed and results are accurately recorded
Ethics	• Ethical considerations, such as informed consent by trial participants
Data Handling and Record Keeping	• Processes for data collection and retention

Source: 62 Fed.Reg. 25692 (1997).

5. Drug Development

Anatomy of a Clinical Trial

Clinical Development must be seen as more than a series of discrete steps or phases. We will therefore step back to look at how the entire process unfolds. The heart of clinical development is the clinical trial or study, which is a complex, carefully regulated activity. Each study is executed in compliance with a detailed study protocol that serves as a roadmap for every stage of the trial, from investigator and patient recruitment through data analysis.

The protocol must be approved by the institutional review board (IRB) affiliated with each participating site. The IRBs are composed of representatives from the local community, including scientists, physicians, ethicists, and religious leaders. Their charge is to make certain that the proposed study will protect the rights and safety of trial subjects.

The study protocol includes mechanisms for avoiding bias in assigning subjects to treatment groups. Specifically, three techniques are frequently used to protect the integrity of study results: randomization, placebo and control groups, and double blinding. (See Figure 5.17)

Figure 5.17 Anatomy of a Clinical Trial: Protections Against Bias

Protections Against Bias

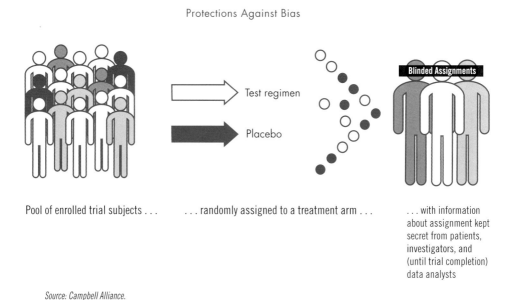

Pool of enrolled trial subjects . . .   . . . randomly assigned to a treatment arm . . .   . . . with information about assignment kept secret from patients, investigators, and (until trial completion) data analysts

Source: Campbell Alliance.

Several protections are typically incorporated to correct for an unconscious tendency of both study subjects and trial investigators to exaggerate the benefits of the drug being tested:

- A placebo group allows analysts to assess the difference in the reported outcomes of subjects who are taking an inactive substance (a "sugar pill") and those taking the drug formulation being assessed.

- Randomization means that the assignment of a subject to a placebo (control) or test group is truly by chance—that, for instance, less severe subjects aren't all assigned to the test group, skewing resultant findings.

- Single blinding means that the study subject does not know the treatment arm to which he/she has been assigned, but the investigator does. In double blinding, which is more common, neither the study subject nor the trial investigator knows whether the subject has been assigned to the test group or a control group.

If a clearly beneficial treatment, or "standard of care," exists for a disease, particularly a life-threatening disease, most researchers agree that it cannot ethically be withheld from the study participants. In such cases, people in the control group receive the drug considered the standard of care, and researchers compare the safety and efficacy of the new drug with that of the standard treatment. (See Figure 5.18)

Figure 5.18 Anatomy of a Clinical Trial: Controls

Controls Typically Employed, by Study Phase

Phase	Placebo Control	Blinding of Assignments	Randomization of Assignments
1	No	No	No
2	Yes*	Yes*	Yes*
3	Yes*	Yes*	Yes*
4	No	No	No

*Exception: Cases of life-threatening disease for which there is no viable alternative treatment or a current standard of care is available.

Source: Campbell Alliance.

5. Drug Development

Regulations concerning the conduct of clinical investigations are very demanding. The FDA has developed a body of regulatory guidance on good clinical practice (GCP) to which pharmaceutical companies and the contract research organizations (CROs) to which trials are sometimes outsourced must adhere.

Drug development phases and processes are designed to comply with the FDA's requirements for how trials are conducted and documented, which are known as Good Clinical Practices (GCP). Their rigorous study design and documentation requirements are meant to safeguard the health of participating trial subjects while allowing a pharmaceutical company to generate reliable data about the efficacy and safety of its new product.

Clinical studies require close collaboration between the sponsoring pharma company (or the CRO to which it delegates study oversight) and the sites that conduct the research. On the sponsor/CRO side, key personnel include medical directors, project managers, and clinical research associates (CRAs). The study leaders based at each site are principal investigators (PIs) and study coordinators. (See Figure 5.19)

Before patient recruitment begins, the medical director and project managers who lead the study for the sponsor organization provide training on the study protocol for all participating PIs and study coordinators. Timely recruitment of study participants who satisfy the inclusion/exclusion criteria in the study protocol often poses a considerable challenge and can delay the study. Estimates suggest that nearly 94% of study delays are triggered by recruitment problems.

Across the study time frame, subjects are expected to visit the trial site at specified intervals so that investigators can monitor their health status and response to the assigned study treatment.

Conduct of the Study

Subjects are expected to follow specific instructions for taking the drug and returning to the site for follow-up visits. During each follow-up visit, the PI checks vital signs, drug levels in the blood, and other indicators of health status as dictated by the protocol. If the product being tested is an injectable, the PI may also administer the treatment.

The PI or study coordinator records data in source documents—the original record made of information about the subject, both at the time of enrollment

Figure 5.19 Anatomy of a Clinical Trial: Key Personnel

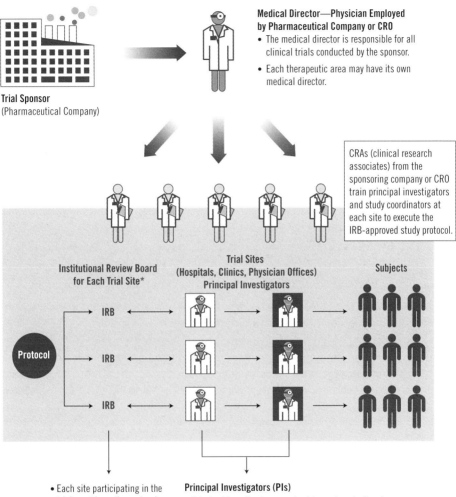

Medical Director—Physician Employed by Pharmaceutical Company or CRO
- The medical director is responsible for all clinical trials conducted by the sponsor.
- Each therapeutic area may have its own medical director.

Trial Sponsor
(Pharmaceutical Company)

CRAs (clinical research associates) from the sponsoring company or CRO train principal investigators and study coordinators at each site to execute the IRB-approved study protocol.

Institutional Review Board for Each Trial Site*

Trial Sites
(Hospitals, Clinics, Physician Offices)
Principal Investigators

Subjects

Protocol

IRB

IRB

IRB

- Each site participating in the trial must have the protocol approved by an IRB.*
- The IRBs approve the trial protocol and oversee trial conduct to protect patient rights.

*Some sites will have an affiliated IRB. Other IRBs serve sites in their area that need assistance.

Principal Investigators (PIs)
- Principal investigators are physicians at each site who oversee trial activities. PIs are selected based on reputation/specialty and ability to recruit subjects.
  - Spearhead efforts to recruit trial participants
  - Educate potential participants about the nature and risks of the trial
  - Treat study subjects and personally handle the most pivotal, intensive subject visits during the trial
- Study coordinators at each site—typically nurses—work with the PIs and are responsible for the administrative aspects of such key trial activities as recruiting and data collection.

Source: Campbell Alliance.

5. Drug Development

Anatomy of a Clinical Trial:
Recruitment Process

The recruitment process involves:

- Searches of investigator databases for appropriate subjects
- Outreach to potential participants via their physicians and various forms of advertisement
- Screening of potential trial subjects—including taking a health history and conducting medical tests to assess whether they satisfy inclusion criteria
- Explanation to the potential subjects of the purpose, structure, and risks of the study
- Signing by each candidate of an informed consent form stating that he/she understands the risks and is willing to participate

Figure 5.20 Recruitment Problems Yield Substantial Delays

Recruitment-Related Delays in 2003

- 72% of trials were delayed more than one month due to recruitment issues.
- Only 6% experienced no enrollment delays.
- These figures exclude trials for which enrollment was never completed.

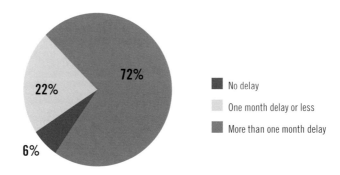

Source: PAREXEL's Pharmaceutical R&D Statistical Sourcebook 2004/2005.

and on an ongoing basis throughout the trial. These source documents remain at each trial site. (See Figure 5.21)

Figure 5.21 Anatomy of a Clinical Trial: Conduct of the Study

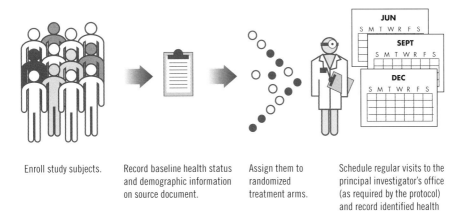

| Enroll study subjects. | Record baseline health status and demographic information on source document. | Assign them to randomized treatment arms. | Schedule regular visits to the principal investigator's office (as required by the protocol) and record identified health |

Source: Campbell Alliance.

The subject's case report form (CRF), in which all subject information from various source documents is gathered, is collected by the sponsor. Data from the CRFs of all subjects are then aggregated and analyzed in preparation for inclusion in the NDA filing. (See Figure 5.22)

Figure 5.22 Anatomy of a Clinical Trial: Typical Contents of a Case Report Form

Typical Contents of a Case Report Form

- **Patient Identifiers:** The patient's age, sex, assigned study arm (Group A or B), and trial site

- **Baseline Measures:** Vital signs at the start of the study (such as weight, blood pressure, underlying disease)

- **Data Collection Dictated by the Protocol:** Data to be collected at specified times in the trial, to gauge treatment safety and efficacy

- **Adverse Events (AEs):** Injuries or health problems arising during the study, which may or may not be related to the treatment being administered

- **Serious Adverse Events (SAEs):** Serious health problems that arise during the treatment and follow-up periods

Source: Campbell Alliance.

Review of Data

As a study progresses, the CRAs regularly visit sites for audit purposes. Their review includes cross-checking data in the CRF against source documents, such as patient charts, in order to ensure accuracy. They record the results of their audits and provide reports to the sponsoring pharmaceutical company.

The pharmaceutical company has an ethical and practical obligation to ensure that the protocol is being adhered to at each site and that the data are being collected in a high-quality and consistent manner. CRAs from the sponsor organization or CRO—often nurses trained on both GCP and the specific study protocol—visit the sites to audit performance. The CRAs compare the CRFs with source documents to identify discrepancies and monitor protocol compliance. Any discrepancies found between a source document and the CRF result in a query that must be resolved by site personnel.

Adverse events (AEs), also sometimes known as adverse drug reactions (ADRs), are carefully monitored by both the PI for each site and the medical director for the study as a whole. The FDA has established specific time frames for reporting serious adverse events (SAEs) that occur during a drug's development.

AEs include any unpleasant experience that the subject has while receiving the drug. These events must be reported to the FDA during drug development as information is gathered about subjects undergoing the therapy. The Medical Officer (often within Medical Affairs), Safety and Surveillance Departments, and Regulatory Affairs generally monitor adverse events. (See Figures 5.23 and 5.24)

Figure 5.23 Anatomy of a Clinical Trial: Adverse Events

What Is An Adverse Event?
• The term is defined as "any adverse event associated with the use of a drug in humans, whether or not considered drug related."
• Adverse events may be serious or non-serious and expected or unexpected.
• Adverse events are reported both for drugs under clinical investigation and products that have been launched. An adverse event is considered to be serious if the result is: • Death or a life-threatening episode   • Initial or prolonged hospitalization   • Significant disability and/or incapacity   • Increased risk of congenital abnormalities   • An intervention to prevent permanent impairment or damage
• The event is unexpected if it does not appear on the drug's label.

Sources: 21 CFR 310; 21 CFR 314.

Figure 5.24 Anatomy of a Clinical Trial: Adverse Event Reporting

Patient Information
Section for entering age, sex, weight, and identification code.

Adverse event or product problem Details of the adverse event or product problem, including relevant history and laboratory data.

Initial Reporter
Contact information for the person reporting the adverse event, which will allow the FDA to follow up if needed.

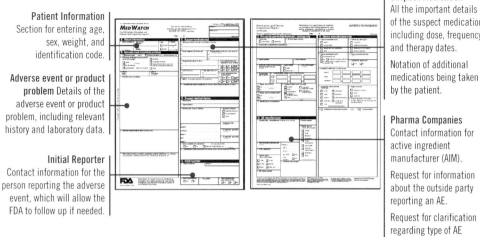

Suspect Medication
All the important details of the suspect medication, including dose, frequency, and therapy dates.

Notation of additional medications being taken by the patient.

Pharma Companies
Contact information for active ingredient manufacturer (AIM).

Request for information about the outside party reporting an AE.

Request for clarification regarding type of AE (e.g., a serious or unexpected one requiring 15-day notice).

Source: Food and Drug Administration.

Pharmaceutical companies are required to report each AE, both serious and unexpected (i.e., not in the product's labeling) of which they are aware, to the FDA. Any post–marketing surveillance program depends on health professionals to report SAEs to the FDA. Except for AEs associated with specified vaccines, reporting by an individual health professional is voluntary.

At the conclusion of the study, CRF data are aggregated and analyzed by data management staff in the pharmaceutical company or CRO to assess the drug's safety and efficacy. (See Figure 5.25)

The increased complexity of clinical trials combined with the increasing difficulty of recruiting study participants are extending clinical development time frames and increasing costs.

Today, pharmaceutical companies face a growing number of challenges when they embark on large phase 3 trials: multiple trials in the same therapeutic area compete for the same sites, investigators, and patients; patient enrollment criteria are becoming increasingly difficult to satisfy; and the FDA has made demands for more participants. All these factors make late-stage clinical trials more difficult to conduct.

5. Drug Development

Figure 5.25 Anatomy of a Clinical Trial: Data Collection and Analysis

Data Collection and Analysis

- The sponsor generates a New Drug
  Application (NDA) or a Biologic License
- Data are aggregated and analyzed   Application (BLA)—the formal application
  by biostatisticians employed by the   to the FDA for a license to market a new
  pharma company or CRO.   drug or biologic in the US.

- Various reports regarding safety   - The application is often accompanied by
  and efficacy are generated.   more than 100,000 pages of study results.

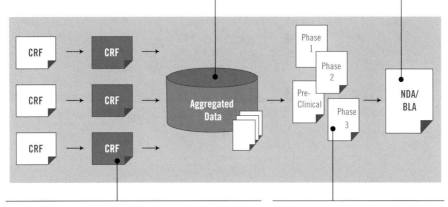

- Periodically during the study and at the end of the trial, completed   - Data from all pre-clinical and clinical studies
  CRFs are collected by the sponsor or CRO.   and from manufacturing runs are collected
                                                                              by the pharma company or CRO.
- The data undergo a thorough "cleaning" process to ensure accuracy.
                                                                            - All studies are combined to form the
  - A data manager reviews the data. If a particular piece of   Integrated Summary of Safety and Integrated
    data appears to be incorrect (e.g., out of expected range,   Summary of Efficacy reports which are the
    wrong type of answer), a query is generated.   basis of the FDA's evaluation of the drug.

  - Following query resolution by the site (in which the reason
    for the inconsistency is identified), the CRF data may be
    revised to reflect the information in the source document.

  - Identification and resolution of discrepancies is often
    referred to as data cleaning or data scrubbing.

Source: Campbell Alliance.

3. Operational Model for Development

Like the Discovery leader, the Development leader typically reports to the global head of R&D. Development usually has separate preclinical and clinical organizations. (See Figures 5.26 and 5.27)

Figure 5.26 Operational Model for Drug Development

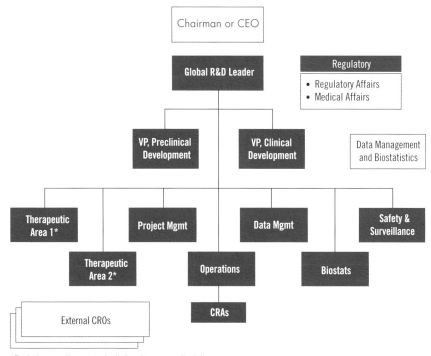

*Each therapeutic area typically has its own medical director.

Source: Campbell Alliance.

Clinical development represents the shift from laboratory science to the project management responsibilities needed to manage human trials. Clinical development groups are typically organized by therapeutic area or product and include professionals responsible for designing study protocols, recruiting subjects and investigators, and overseeing clinical trials that are under way—including those that are outsourced to CROs. Clinical Development often has a dedicated function focused on managing relationships with CROs.

Most companies also maintain teams of biostatisticians who work closely with clinical development teams to establish sample/population sizes, geographic coverage, dropout rates, and other factors that can affect the statistical significance of trial results.

Figure 5.27 *Description of Functions*

Function	Description
Preclinical Development	• Pharmacologists and toxicologists focused on formulating products and testing them on live tissues and animals
Clinical Development	• Clinical and project management resources responsible for managing trials in humans
Therapeutic Area	• Group of professionals responsible for management of study conduct in a specific therapeutic area
Project Management	• Project management support team
Operations	• Variable responsibilities, but typically consists of CRAs and field personnel
Data Management	• Analytic support resource that compiles data and reviews its accuracy
Biostatistics	• Analytic support resource that determines the number and the size of a statistically significant patient sample and analyzes study results
Safety and Surveillance	• Clinical group responsible for monitoring side effects and adverse events associated with clinical trials
Regulatory Affairs	• Group responsible for preparing submissions to the FDA (the IND and NDA) and ensuring compliance with Good Lab Practice (GLP) and GCP
Medical Affairs	• Group responsible for clinical and medical surveillance activities after a product is launched

Source: Campbell Alliance.

Pivotal Relationships with Other Internal Functions

Marketing, and occasionally Legal and Business Development professionals, participate in a drug's development, as they do in discovery, to ensure that data are gathered on characteristics pivotal to realizing the product's full market potential—and that development investment ceases as early as possible for products that clearly have a weak commercial profile.

Regulatory Affairs

Most companies have a separate Regulatory Affairs function that serves as the company's liaison with the FDA during the clinical trial process. Regulatory Affairs works with Clinical Development to prepare submissions and ensure that studies and reporting are compliant with FDA requirements. On the commercial side, Regulatory Affairs also collaborates with Sales and

Marketing teams to ensure their compliance with FDA promotional regulations. Regulatory Affairs sometimes includes a Quality Assurance group, which is, among other things, responsible for the periodic audit and review of drug development activities and adherence to GCP and GLP guidelines within the pharma company. Regulatory Affairs may report to the global R&D leader or to an independent senior executive. In some companies, Regulatory Affairs may report directly to the CEO.

Medical Affairs

Medical Affairs is focused primarily on approved and launched drugs. Its responsibilities generally include medical and safety surveillance—the process for reporting adverse events for marketed products. Medical Affairs also usually manages phase 4 studies and sometimes oversees inbound call centers that field product inquiries from prescribers and patients. Occasionally a sales representative will call Medical Affairs to get clarifying information about a product.

Medical science liaisons (MSLs) within Medical Affairs are professionals who work closely with key opinion leaders in the relevant therapeutic area to share preliminary findings from ongoing clinical trials, information about planned phase 4 studies, and data on off-label drug use with interested prescribers, as allowed under guidelines set forth by the FDA. To avoid any taint of sales bias in presenting such product information or impropriety with respect to promoting products, Medical Affairs does not report to Sales.

Outsourcing Practices

Many companies find it necessary to outsource some preclinical and clinical trials to CROs. Leaders within the Development function then manage the CROs they have hired.

The expansion in CROs reflects the efforts of pharma companies to balance the need for control our development efforts against the desire to limit fixed investment in a development function that is prone to large fluctuations in workload based on the pipeline of compounds and biologics.

Some companies outsource all preclinical and clinical activities. Under this "virtual" development model, the in-house development function is a small team of managers who oversee the CROs hired to conduct development. Other companies maintain an extensive in-house development capability but utilize CROs on an as-needed basis to supplement their internal capacity and expertise.

Industry wide, CROs conduct approximately 25% to 30% of clinical development studies. Outsourcing of preclinical research occurs on a more modest scale, but is on the rise.

Some vendors are full-service CROs. (See Figure 5.28) Their array of capabilities mirrors that of pharmaceutical company development organizations, and they can assist a pharmaceutical company with any aspect of clinical and preclinical trials, including protocol design, site selection, patient enrollment, data management, and FDA interactions. Other vendors are known as niche CROs. They focus on just a few aspects of drug development (sometimes only one aspect), such as patient recruitment, monitoring, data entry and management, and/or report writing. Some CROs are known for expertise in a particular therapeutic area, such as oncology or cardiology.

In addition to CROs, some pharma companies enlist the help of site management organizations (SMOs) that specialize in lining up experienced sites to participate in studies.

Figure 5.28 CRO Structure

The structure of a full-service CRO typically resembles the pharma company development function it serves.

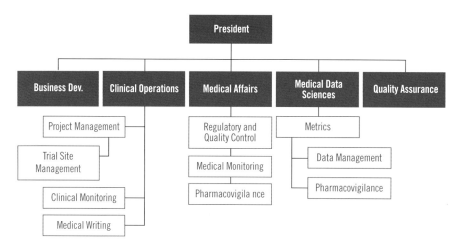

Source: Campbell Alliance.

6. BUSINESS DEVELOPMENT

1. The Importance of Business Development

2. A Closer Look at Business Development
   Activities

3. Operational Model for Business Development

BUSINESS CASE: Lipitor® — Effective Partnering Leads to Blockbuster Sales

The anti-cholesterol drug Lipitor, one of the best-selling products ever, was launched as a co-promotion alliance between Pfizer and Warner-Lambert. This strategic relationship was the prelude to one of the largest acquisitions in the industry and highlights the importance of effective partnering.

In 1997, Warner-Lambert was seeking a co-promotion partner for Lipitor, which at launch would be the fifth marketed drug in its class (statins). The company lacked the size and scale to effectively promote Lipitor and, therefore, wanted a commercial partner with a strong presence in the cardiovascular and primary care markets but with no competitive offering. Pfizer, a sales and marketing powerhouse, fit the bill.

From Pfizer's perspective, Lipitor was an attractive opportunity. Lipitor was the best therapy in its class, and with Pfizer's sales and marketing muscle, it had blockbuster potential. Peak sales were projected at $9 billion per year by analysts. Pfizer and Warner-Lambert shared financial risk in the initial co-promotion deal.

Lipitor quickly became one of the dominant new products in the market. When Pfizer began experiencing problems within its development pipeline, Lipitor became one of the most important products in its portfolio. Buoyed by Lipitor's success, Warner-Lambert soon became an attractive acquisition target. Faced with the threat of losing Lipitor to a competitor, Pfizer purchased Warner-Lambert in 1999 for an unprecedented $90 billion.

By 2002, Lipitor was experiencing over 20% annual growth, fueled by an impressive safety profile and continued expansion of the market and potential uses of Lipitor. Analysts project sales of $10 billion for 2005, and it is likely that there will continue to be significant revenue from this product for a number of years, as the patents on this product protect it until 2009.

Sources: Pfizer; Campbell Alliance.

1. The Importance of Business Development

Today few pharma companies, even the largest ones, realize their strategic vision solely through compounds and capabilities developed in-house. As competition intensifies and companies increasingly focus their R&D in therapeutic areas and functional competencies, they are realizing that internal resources may not be able to deliver results fast enough to meet their commercial objectives.

Many companies rely on other pharmaceutical and biotech firms as a source of intellectual property (compounds, tools, and technologies), expert support, and capital. Large pharmaceutical companies often form alliances with smaller, research-driven companies (including many biotechs) to capitalize on their complementary strengths. Typically, the larger company provides funding, infrastructure (such as clinical development and commerical capabilities), and other assets of scale in exchange for access to innovative intellectual property from the smaller company, usually in the form of a new chemical or molecular entity or a product under development. (See Figure 6.1)

Figure 6.1 Common Benefits of Partnerships and Alliances

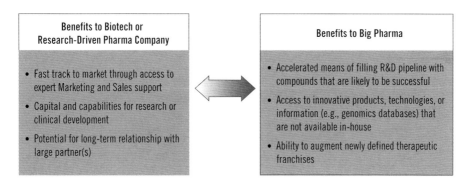

Source: Campbell Alliance.

Without the diversity in "bench strength" such relationships can offer, pharmaceutical companies are vulnerable to sudden declines in revenue due to patent expirations and/or a limited development pipeline.

The business development (BD) function is charged with finding opportunities and negotiating alliances and partnerships to secure strategic assets that can accelerate the achievement of corporate goals and objectives. BD may also become involved in identifying new revenue opportunities, out-licensing, or divestiture of assets of less strategic importance to the company.

The BD function is playing an increasingly prominent role in stocking the product pipelines of pharmaceutical companies. As a result, a growing share of revenues and overall corporate value are based on in-licensing or co-promotion deals.

Example Business Development Procedure

BD, particularly the scientific evaluation arm, works closely with R&D to identify gaps or opportunities in the product pipeline or portfolio. There may even be a licensing sub-team within a therapeutic team that does this. BD could be on that team or could lead it. The commercial team, including Marketing and Sales, is usually also active in recommending opportunities. Additionally, BD may work in concert with the CEO or COO to generate opportunities.

Once a deal passes a very preliminary review on its commercial and scientific merits, the other party is contacted or, if the other party initiated the contact, it is informed of the company's interest. Usually a non-confidential package is exchanged followed by a confidential package for additional and more extensive assessment and valuation. In almost every instance, more than one group within each company is involved in the process.

When the extensive evaluation is undertaken, patent attorneys are brought in immediately to perform due diligence on the intellectual property estate surrounding the products. Additional scientific support is sometimes brought in to carefully analyze the product, and a commercial team is formed to construct forecasts and profiles of the product and competitive products. At this time, initial deal terms are either delivered or negotiated.

If both parties are still interested in the deal, more extensive due diligence is planned. The patent work continues, and depending on the phase of the asset, scientific, clinical, pharmacology, regulatory, and manufacturing personnel become involved and prepare reports that are approved through their line management and then assembled in a document by BD.

Management is provided with recommendations and acceptable deal parameters before the final deal terms are negotiated and encapsulated in a contract. The contract then needs senior management or board approval, depending on the company's corporate governance structure. At this time, HSR filings may be necessary for FTC approval.

Most leading companies in the industry are engaged in both in- and out-licensing and are concerned about positioning themselves as attractive and effective partners. A strong reputation as an effective licensing partner is considered a strategic imperative. Small companies that have discovered potential blockbuster compounds are in great demand as alliance partners—and their agreement to such an alliance is more likely to be won by entities that have a reputation as a good partner.

Partnership reputation is based on such criteria as ability to forge BD contracts and creative payment strategies, as well as fulfillment of commitments throughout the life of the partnership.

BD deals typically involve alliances or partnerships with another company to commercialize a product or to acquire or divest a particular asset. Unlike mergers, these deals are not usually purchases of an entire company, although they may involve taking an equity position as part of a deal. Many industry mergers, like the acquisition of Warner–Lambert by Pfizer, were preceded by a BD deal.

2. A Closer Look at BD Activities

The BD function identifies, negotiates, and often implements deals that align with corporate strategy. Figure 6.2 provides an overview of the process.

Figure 6.2 Overview of Business Development Process

| Defining Strategy | Identifying Opportunities | Assessing Opportunities | Negotiating Deals | Monitoring Deals |

Gaining Approval

Source: Campbell Alliance.

Defining Strategy

The first step for BD is defining a strategy that will help the company achieve its corporate goals and objectives. It is essential that the BD group understand the overall corporate strategy and its implications for the brand portfolio. The company's financial goals, therapeutic area priorities, and competitive situation shape criteria for seeking out and evaluating deals.

BD typically works closely with Marketing, Clinical Development, and Discovery leaders both inside and outside of the company to identify gaps and opportunities in the product portfolio and the product pipeline. It also seeks to identify the services, tools, and technologies that can be filled through partnerships with outside companies. For example, a company may seek to mitigate the development risk of products within its product pipeline by licensing or acquiring similar early-stage products. A company may also realize that it can better leverage its sales and marketing infrastructure by promoting products that are complementary to one of its blockbuster products. BD also works with Marketing, Clinical Development, and Discovery to identify "misfit" assets or other assets that should be licensed or divested to optimize their value to the company.

Identifying Opportunities

Once the strategy for BD has been established, BD professionals make a global survey of organizations and innovations to find opportunities to license or sell financial assets, physical assets or intellectual property. The survey is conducted using personal networks combined with commercially available databases. These resources provide insight into products under development and licenses that may be available. Opportunities can come from anywhere within the company, but they are processed through the BD function for a first-pass screening.

Once an array of opportunities is identified, each opportunity is qualified—that is, it undergoes a preliminary analysis of value in terms of potential fit with the portfolio and capacity to fill strategic gaps. The potential benefits are profiled, including ability to accelerate product development, increase revenue, and improve competitive positioning. If the deal will require close ongoing collaboration with the other party, cultural fit is assessed as well. Figure 6.3 lists some of the criteria used to qualify BD opportunities.

Gaining Approval to Further Assess the Opportunity

In most companies, once an opportunity passes its initial screening, BD often advances the opportunity to an internal committee for review and approval. This committee is typically a standing committee that includes representatives from across the company, and its function is to determine which opportuni-

Figure 6.3 Opportunity Qualification Criteria

Criteria	Initial Analysis
Rationale	• Does the deal have a clear and credible business rationale in the context of company strategy? • Does the potential partner have a real commitment to pursuing this deal and the expertise to do so?
Market/ Product Sales Performance	• What are the market forecasts for annual sales (by cash and volume) in the target market? • For currently marketed products, what has sales performance been (by cash and volume) for the last five years?
Product Promotional Needs	• For currently marketed products, what sales support has been available across the last three years (number of sales reps and priority given the product during sales details)? • What was the total promotional expenditure on the product during the previous three years?
Customer Base	• Who are the key customers for the product (e.g., prescribers or stakeholders that influence prescribers)?
Patent Scenario	• Will the product be covered by patent protection during any part of the deal period? If so, for how long during the deal period?
Scope of the Deal	• What services and responsibilities will each partner be required to provide under the deal (e.g., marketing, medical affairs, regulatory affairs, manufacturing, distribution)?
Financials	• What is the cost of manufacturing, marketing and selling the product? • What are the investment and the projected return on investment?

Cultural Fit	• If the deal will require ongoing collaboration with the other organization, is there a cultural fit?
	   • Commitment to quality standards?
	   • Common ethical standards?
	   • Collegial working relationship?
	   • Other tensions or synergies?

Source: Campbell Alliance.

6. Business Development

ties warrant additional evaluation. Qualified opportunities—that is, those that pass the initial screen and are approved by the committee for further consideration—are subjected to a second, more in-depth evaluation. The standing committee may then commit resources to further assess these opportunities.

Assessing the Opportunity

As part of the assessment process, the entire opportunity, including the potential partner company, is profiled in detail. Due diligence is conducted to identify problems and risks associated with the opportunity. In a potential acquisition or in-licensing deal, due diligence efforts can include detailed reviews of intellectual property, analysis of clinical data, and an analysis of the partner's ability to perform on a deal. In a divestiture or out-licensing deal, due diligence efforts typically focus on the potential partner's ability to perform its obligations under the agreement.

The results of the due diligence are combined with detailed financial and scientific analyses to conclude the overall assessment of the opportunity. Pro forma financials are prepared to show how the product might fare financially. Discounted cash flow techniques showing the net present value of the licensed product are typically the basis for evaluating deal potential. Additional statistical analyses are often included to provide a better understanding of the risk and value of an opportunity.

Gaining Approval to Negotiate a Deal

Based on the analysis conducted during due diligence, BD refines its estimates on the value of the opportunity and identifies the key risks involved. BD reports the more detailed findings back to the standing committee. If the opportunity is still worthwhile, the committee will give BD permission to negotiate the deal, provided the deal falls within specified parameters.

Negotiating Deals

For opportunities that survive in-depth analysis, a team usually comprising BD, Legal, and Finance sits down at the negotiating table to finalize the deal, addressing the needs and interests of both parties.

BD begins intensive negotiations with the other party regarding deal terms. Key terms to be agreed upon include the structure of the deal, rights to assets and intellectual property, commitments of key resources (both financial and personnel), and the payment terms and conditions. Typically, BD deals have many moving parts, including price, which allows both sides to make valuable tradeoffs to reach their objectives.

The Three Basic Kinds of Deals Handled within BD

While BD deals may involve any of a variety of complex structures, they tend to fall into one of three general categories: rights are purchased from a third party (through in-licensing and acquisitions), rights are effectively shared between companies (through cooperative development and commercialization), or rights are sold to another company (through out-licensing and divestitures). The actual structures devised to support these basic forms can include partnerships, joint ventures, equity investment, strategic alliances, or relatively simple acquisitions and divestitures of particular assets. (See Figures 6.4 and 6.5)

Figure 6.4 The Three Basic Deals

Deal Type	Definition

In-Licensing and Acquisitions	• Securing the ownership or rights to use assets or intellectual property (IP)
	  • IP may be in the form of new compounds or molecules, drug discovery or development technologies, or manufacturing technologies.
	  • The value of IP may rely on the availability of critical personnel who are instrumental in developing or using these assets.

Cooperative Development and Commercialization	• Entering agreements to pursue development jointly (with the larger entity typically providing funding to the company that discovered a promising compound) • Entering agreements to commercialize the same product under the same or different brand names (co-marketing) • Entering agreements to commercialize the same product under the same or different brand names but to different customer segments or in different markets

Out-Licensing and Divestiture	• Selling or disposing of assets (discrete products and services), usually because they do not fit within:
	  • The company's area(s) of therapeutic focus or
	  • The company's revenue-potential criteria

Source: Campbell Alliance.

Deals Occurring in Different Life-Cycle Stages

Although deals may be struck throughout the product life cycle, the nature of such deals and the support which BD lends tends to vary with the life-cycle stage.

• Discovery and Early Development

Rather than pursuing discrete compounds that are still in discovery or very early development and whose promise is far from clear, BD generally tries to jump-start innovation through the acquisition of enabling tools, technologies, and libraries (of compounds, targets, or genetic material).

Figure 6.5 Common Business Development Deals

Type of Deal	Description
Co-Marketing	• Marketing of the same product under different brand names in the same territory
Co-Promotion	• Marketing of the same product under the same trademark in the same territory by different companies
Joint Venture	• Establishment of a new corporate entity to commercialize a product that is jointly owned by the partners
Manufacturing or Supply	• Licensing by one contract partner of manufacturing rights to the other's product; deals typically negotiated and implemented by the Manufacturing Operations function due to their technical complexity
Marketing-Licensing	• Licensing by one contract partner of sales and marketing rights to the other's product in a specified geography
Product Acquisition	• Outright purchase by one contract partner of all rights to another's product (the seller will no longer possess any legal rights to or ownership stake in the product)
R&D and Marketing Licensing	• Licensing of limited commercial rights by one contract partner to the other partner's product in exchange for development funding and/or assistance

Source: Campbell Alliance.

- Late-Stage Development (Phases 2 and 3)
  Deals for molecules or compounds are most prevalent during phases 2 and 3 of clinical development, when the product is beyond the proof-of-concept stage (See Chapter 5, Drug Development). Out-licensing efforts are also more common at these stages.

- Marketed Products
  Products that are on the market are another focus of out-licensing efforts, usually because the company that owns them decides that these brands no longer align with their business objectives or therapeutic focus.

Co-commercialization deals are often made to intensify contacts with target customers.

Figure 6.6 illustrates the relationship between deal types and life-cycle stage in a typical large pharmaceutical company.

Contractual Terms

The deal team spends considerable time working out the contractual terms of the relationship. The contract includes terms that address payment, the

Figure 6.6 Business Development Deals Aligned to the Product Life Cycle

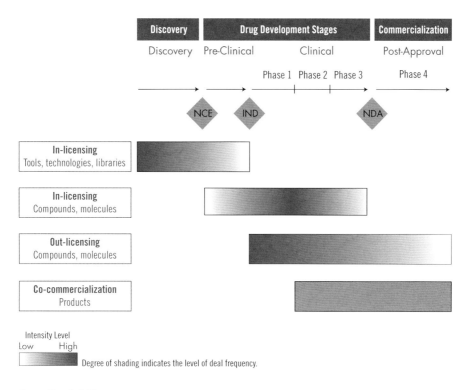

Source: Campbell Alliance.

ownership rights assigned to each party, the roles and responsibilities of each party across the product's life cycle (or a specified portion of it), and the governance of the alliance.

While all terms of the contract are important, the description of the business relationship and schedule of payments usually receive the most attention. Those sections allocate responsibilities between the parties and reflect the value of the deal.

- Description of the Business Relationship

  The description of the business relationship is spread across multiple sections of the contract, and much of the description allocates responsibilities between the parties.

Some contracts call for a shift in responsibilities across the product life cycle. For example, a deal to in-license a compound under development may include a collaborative manufacturing or a co-promotion component. (See Figure 6.7)

Figure 6.7 A Sampling of Key Terms in BD Contracts

Payment Type	Description
Allocation of Functional and Life Cycle Responsibilities	• Clinical development strategy and execution • Product registration (developing NDAs and handling FDA interactions) • Manufacturing and product specifications • Supply/production forecasting and logistics • Commercial strategy and execution • Geographic/territory inclusions and exclusions • Operational dependencies (e.g., functioning call centers)
Allocation of Intellectual Property Ownership and Defense Responsibilities	• Defense of patents • Treatment of new or derivative IP • Registration, ownership, and defense of trademarks
Governance and Dedicated Human Resources	• Overall governance for alliance • Assignment of full-time personnel

Source: Campbell Alliance.

Deals may cover multiple products and/or involve complementary services. For instance, a small company that is out-licensing rights to a product in development, Compound A, may want to build a stronger internal sales force. A larger company that is eager to in-license Compound A has a first-rate sales force. To make its licensing offer more attractive, the large company may offer co-promotion rights to one of its other products (Product B) so that the small pharma company can gain sales experience.

Alternatively, the two parties may want to "test the waters" with one product, while securing an option to collaborate on others. Such a contract could be structured so that the success of the initial product triggers mutual obligations with respect to other products.

• Deal Value
Deal value ranges widely depending on the asset and its role or stage in the life cycle. Deal value is driven by risks associated with the development of the asset and the anticipated sales revenues of the asset. Early-stage products

in which the potential value is speculative and the risk of failure high are generally less valuable. Later-stage products that are closer to commercialization are generally more valuable because the risk of failure is lower.

• Payments

BD often mitigates risk by structuring deals to include up-front payments, milestone payments paid when identified hurdles are attained, and some form of revenue sharing. Deals usually include a guaranteed up-front payment followed by the possibility of further, more generous "milestone" payments if development and commercial goals are satisfied.

The up-front payment is typically tied to the immediate value of the asset and its phase in development. Milestone payments are contingent on the achievement of certain development or commercialization goals (such as FDA approval). Royalty payments may also be part of the deal, and they are usually based on sales performance. Companies will often manage their commercial risk by setting higher milestone payments in exchange for lower royalty payments (or vice versa depending upon the nature of the risk being managed). (See Figure 6.8)

Figure 6.8 Common Payment Types

Type of Deal	Description
Up-Front Payment	• Initial payment for product rights • Cash or equity investment • Often the only guaranteed return on an agreement
Research Payments	• Funding for research
Milestone Payments and Marketing Expense Slips	• Rewards for pre- or post-commercialization performance • Cash or equity investment • Share of launch/post-launch expenses if both companies are involved
Royalties/Profit Splits	• Rates sometimes vary with product indications or geography • Typical structure a series of sales thresholds at which various royalty rates kick in
Other Payments	• Payments often contingent on success of the initial product around which the deal was formed • Cash or equity investment

Source: Campbell Alliance.

Seeking Approval to Close the Deal

Once both parties have agreed upon the terms of the contract, the contract is signed and executed. However, most contracts are subject to approval by internal bodies (such as a board of directors) and external regulatory bodies (such as the FDA, in cases where the contract calls for a change in manufacturing facilities). Certain mergers or acquisitions are subject to antitrust review, as described in the callout. (See Hart–Scott–Rodino Review)

Hart-Scott-Rodino Review

Under the Hart-Scott-Rodino Antitrust Improvements Act of 1976, parties to certain mergers or acquisitions are required to notify the Federal Trade Commission (FTC) and the Department of Justice (DOJ) (the enforcement agencies) before consummating the proposed acquisition. The parties are required to wait a specific period of time (usually 30 days or 15 days in case of a cash tender offer or bankruptcy) while the enforcement agencies review the proposed transaction. This process is referred to as the Premerger Notification Program. Prior review enables the FTC and the DOJ to determine which acquisitions are likely to be anticompetitive and to challenge them before they occur.

When pharmaceutical companies propose a merger, the FTC often requires the divestment of products that would likely have an anticompetitive effect in those product markets and, therefore, violate antitrust laws. For example, Pfizer and Pharmacia were required to divest products in nine separate markets in order to win FTC approval of their merger in 2003.

Under Section 1112 of the Medicare Prescription Drug, Improvement, and Modernization Act, effective Jan. 7, 2004, agreements between pharmaceutical companies regarding the manufacture, marketing, and sale of generic versions of brand-name products must be filed with the FTC and DOJ. In addition, generic drug manufacturers that have filed Paragraph IV certification containing abbreviated new drug applications (ANDAs) for the same brand-name drug and that enter into an agreement related to the 180-day exclusivity period for that drug must file the agreement with the FTC and DOJ. The agreement must be filed prior to the date of the first commercial marketing of either of the generic drugs for which those filings were submitted. There are similar approvals required in the European Union and elsewhere in the world.

Monitoring Deals

Once a contract has been negotiated and internal and governmental approvals have been attained, a team is put into place to manage the implementation and ongoing progress. This may or may not include BD involvement.

During this step, the deal is implemented. These often complex arrangements require the establishment of sophisticated communication and project management processes. Ideally, the implementation is co-managed by the deal partners rather than delegated to one of them. Results, including issues for resolution, are reported back to management from both companies. Depending on the nature of the deal and its partners, some companies may elect to assign responsibility for implementation to their line operations. Others assign oversight to more senior line managers, perhaps with the help of Finance experts.

The management of all aspects of the deal is very often critical to the success or failure of the objectives defined at the initiation process.

3. Operational Model for Business Development

The BD function is typically a small organization of specialists. Core competencies of the department may include opportunity prospecting, deal evaluation and closure (which includes scientific evaluation, financial evaluation, contract negotiation, and matrix team management), and alliance management.

These competencies may be organized by or based on the product life cycle (i.e., discovery, development, and commercialization), therapeutic area, geography, or even at times by company relationships. (See Figure 6.9)

Occasionally, the BD function reports directly to the CEO. Overall, the reporting relationship can vary widely based on corporate strategy and the overall needs of the organization, as well as on the company's structure and processes. It is not uncommon for BD to report to R&D, nor is it uncommon for it to report to the leader of strategic marketing or commercial activities. BD can also report directly to Corporate (COO, CFO, or CEO). (See Figure 6.10)

To bring a deal to fruition, the BD group must work closely with champions within the therapeutic area discovery or development teams and/or regional commercial operation heads. On every deal, BD is supported by legal and finance professionals, as well as functional or technical specialists that provide expertise on the nature of the assets being secured.

Figure 6.9 Business Development Compentencies

Competency	Description
Opportunity Prospecting	• Continuing surveillance of the marketplace in order to monitor developments and identify opportunities for alliances, partnerships, and acquisitions
Deal Evaluation and Closure	• Analysis of the potential of a particular deal, followed by negotiations specifying the business and financial terms in a formal contract
Alliance Management	• Implementation of the terms of the contract, followed by ongoing monitoring and resolution of operational, cultural, and communication issues that arise • In some cases, ongoing responsibility for ensuring that the terms of the deal are being carried out and that value is being created as planned

Source: Campbell Alliance.

Figure 6.10 Operational Model for Business Development

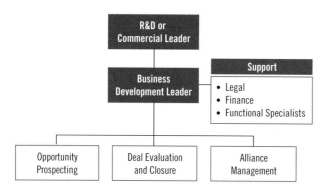

Source: Campbell Alliance.

7. MARKETING AND BRAND MANAGEMENT

1. The Importance of Marketing and Brand Management

2. A Closer Look at Marketing and Brand Management

3. Operational Model for Marketing and Brand Management

1. The Importance of Marketing and Brand Management

Marketing is the commercial command center of a pharmaceutical company; its role is to differentiate the company's products in the marketplace in order to maximize revenues while maintaining a target level of profitability. In many companies, Marketing is considered the general manager for the product or brand.

Ideally, Marketing is involved and provides a commercial perspective early in the discovery and development process. In this context, its mission is to guide the identification of innovative products that will be highly valued in the marketplace—and to spotlight commercially important product characteristics and differentiated attributes that should be evaluated during trials. At this point, Marketing is responsible for forecasting the opportunity and developing strategies to bring the product to market and realize the opportunity.

The highest-profile role of Marketing, however, comes later in the life cycle, with drugs that are near launch or have been launched. At this time, Marketing translates overarching commercial strategies into promotional and other outreach strategies designed to highlight the brand's distinctive advantages and maximize product uptake.

Marketing Priorities

Lay a foundation for product success
Assess commercial opportunities
Develop value proposition
Forecast revenue
Outline commercialization strategy

Extend brand life cycle in the face of evolving competitive, regulatory, and reimbursement environments

Accelerate product adoption and peak sales
Differentiate from competitive products among:
- prescribers
- payers
- pharmacies and distribution
- consumers (often)

Encourage consumers to pursue diagnosis and treatment

The promotional strategy includes a number of components.

- **Positioning**: A succinct statement or series of statements designed to help the brand "occupy" a certain space in the minds of customers

- **Message Platform**: A series of messages specifically crafted to support positioning by highlighting and addressing the key brand attributes and the concerns of discrete customer segments (e.g., physicians, consumers, and payers) and specific subgroups within those categories that are high-priority targets

- **Techniques and Channels**: The delivery methods to be used with each key customer segment

- **Promotional Mix**: The allocation of total promotional investment among various techniques and channels

Promotional efforts typically include advertising (patient and professional), patient screening and counseling, point-of-sale brochures, sales calls to physicians (detailing), and free product samples (sampling). Figure 7.1 shows an industry breakdown of promotional spending by category; overall, detailing and sampling account for over 75% of the marketing budget. The fastest-growing segment is direct-to-consumer promotion (DTC), which—while not appropriate or used for all products—represents approximately 13% of the total US promotional spend.

Figure 7.1 Total US Promotional Spending by Category 2003 ($ billions)

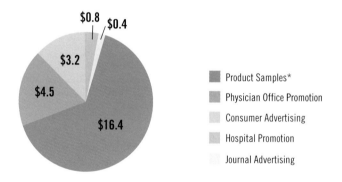

* The product sample figure represents the value of free product samples given to doctors as if purchased at retail prices.

Source: IMS Health, Integrated Promotional Services™, and CMR, June 2004.

Besides directing and managing promotions, Marketing provides input into the long-term data generation plan for the product. It is rare that a product launches with all the data and evidence needed to support the long-term strategy; in other cases, a sudden change in the market (such as a new competitive entrant) may warrant a change in the message platform. Marketing takes the lead in identifying and prioritizing data gaps and works with Drug Development to address those gaps with additional studies.

Marketing is responsible for developing sales forecasts, projections of marketing and sales expenditures, and profit and loss (P&L) statements. Once these have been approved, Marketing directors often control the budget for sales force activities, as well as for all other promotional efforts; this budget is quite substantial—millions, tens of millions, or even hundreds of millions of dollars.

In addition, the overall sales forecast provides the foundation for planning in other commercial functions within the company, including field sales, managed markets sales, manufacturing and operations, and distribution.

Finally, Marketing will monitor product performance after launch and will refine or adapt both strategy and programs as needed to maximize performance. (See Figure 7.2)

Figure 7.2 Overview of Marketing Activities

Define Brand and Promotional Strategies

- Define the current market
  - Disease treated
  - Competitive products
  - Segment the customer base and identify targets
- Profile the target customers
- Identify the product profile and how it should be positioned in the market
- Contribute to the data generation plan
- Develop sales forecasts
- Define promotional strategy ("mix")
  - Programs and messages
  - Channels (means of dissemination such as sales force details and TV ads)
  - Reach and frequency
- Allocate promotional budget

Develop and Deploy Promotional Programs

- Develop appropriate promotional programs
- Assist with development of materials to train sales force on key messages
- Deploy those programs in collaboration with stakeholders such as Sales and Managed Markets
- Manage promotional budget

Monitor Performance and Make Necessary Strategic/Tactical Adjustments

- Evaluate overall performance
  - Revenue/market share
  - Profitability
- Refine or adapt strategy and programs as needed to maximize performance

Source: Campbell Alliance.

7. Marketing

2. A Closer Look at Marketing

Marketing strives to ensure that all compounds added to the company portfolio realize maximum commercial potential and support the company's business goals. Marketing's role spans the entire product life cycle, from discovery through product maturation. (See Figure 7.3)

Figure 7.3 Marketing Objectives by Stage in Product Life Cycle

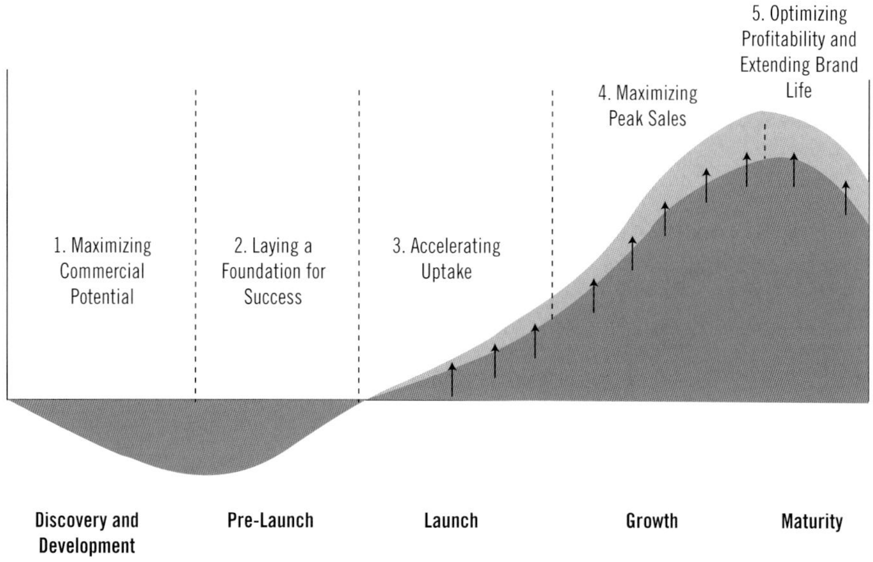

Source: Campbell Alliance.

Maximizing Commercial Potential—Discovery and Development

Even during discovery, when winning FDA approval for a compound is only a distant hope, Marketing offers a valuable commercial perspective to help focus research investment on diseases, indications, and uses with the widest market potential and largest unmet needs. Ideally, Marketing collaborates closely with Discovery and Development, ensuring that products with commercially desirable characteristics are being developed. In addition, Marketing helps ensure that developing new candidates fit with the overall corporate strategy. If the internal discovery pipeline looks weak, Marketing can also work with Business Development to help assess the commercial potential of in-licensing opportunities.

Although there are a large number of questions to be addressed by Marketing, these questions can be broken down into five general categories. The five general questions—and specific associated questions—are shown in Figure 7.4.

Figure 7.4 Comprehensive Commercial Plan

General Question	Specific Questions
What is the current and future market?	• How is the disease state currently managed and by whom? • What is the extent of the unmet medical need? • What is the current and future competitive situation? • How do healthcare professionals and patients make treatment decisions and what motivates those decisions?
Who are the target patients?	• What are the key customer segments? • What are the capabilities of target prescribers? • What are the primary barriers to use of the product? • What are the primary barriers to adopting the product as the preferred therapy?
What is the value proposition?	• What is our ideal and minimally acceptable target product profile? • What is the clinical rationale for treatment? • How should our product be positioned?
How big is the opportunity?	• What are the price boundaries? • What is the revenue forecast under a variety of scenarios?
How can the company successfully commercialize the product?	• How do we translate barriers and opportunities into strategic imperatives? • What are our strategies for commercialization, including the desired promotional mix? • What else must we understand to fully capitalize on the opportunity?

Source: Campbell Alliance.

7. Marketing

Development attempts to find products that satisfy the requirements of the target profile (at least the minimum requirements). As more trial data about the product's actual characteristics are gathered, the product profile (as discussed in Chapter 4, Discovery) is updated and utilized in primary market research with physicians to: (1) better understand the optimal positioning for the product; (2) develop supporting communications strategy; and, (3) forecast potential revenue.

Sales forecasts are based on extensive market research with assumptions about a number of key variables, such as price and demand, market growth and market penetration, the typical therapy regimen, compliance with the recommended regimen, and product pricing. Many of these assumptions are influenced by the strength of the product profile.

Laying a Foundation for Success—Pre-Launch

When it becomes evident that a product is likely to win FDA approval, the comprehensive commercial plan developed earlier is translated into a promotional strategy that defines the following:

- Message Platform

- Key Communication Channels

- Sales Targeting (customer segments)

- Promotional Mix

- Financial Projections (forecast, budget, and P&L statement)

Each of these individual components will be introduced in more detail.

Message Plan
Marketing will develop the product positioning and supporting message platform, including both branded and unbranded messages.

Unbranded messages are disease state messages designed to illustrate the unmet medical need currently existing in the market. These messages can be delivered prior to official FDA approval of the product. Unbranded message campaigns typically start prior to launch.

Branded messages are product-specific messages which will form the core of the overall promotional strategy. Product messages are designed to accelerate uptake and maximize adoption by differentiating the product based on safety, efficacy, and convenience. In addition to communicating product characteristics, branded messages may provide other information essential to facilitating product use, such as the availability of reimbursement. These types of brand messages are essential to overcoming barriers to adoption.

Both branded and unbranded messages can be communicated to various customer segments (including prescribers, payers, and patients) through a number of channels (including advertising and person-to-person encounters).

In order to support the person-to-person encounters, Marketing is responsible for developing a variety of promotional materials. The FDA monitors promotional claims, and companies can only promote a product for indications and uses that are in the FDA-approved product label. The FDA does not require that promotional materials be submitted for advance review. However, the FDA's Division of Drug Marketing Advertising and Communications (DDMAC) advises the pharmaceutical industry on proposed advertising and promotional labeling. DDMAC has requested in guidance to industry that launch campaigns be submitted voluntarily to DDMAC for comment prior to dissemination.

The particular wording used to express brand messages must be consistent with the FDA-approved indications and uses of the product. In virtually all pharmaceutical companies, such language is first reviewed by the company's Medical, Legal and Regulatory Affairs groups.

The FDA can and often does mandate the retraction of promotional claims that are not in compliance with its regulations (which means, in essence, consistent with the approved label). One mechanism of retraction is a "Dear Doctor" letter from the pharmaceutical company to all physicians to whom the non-compliant promotion may have been communicated, correcting the erroneous messages.

Key Communication Channels

Once branded and unbranded messages are defined, Marketing needs to determine the optimal means to disseminate these messages to target audiences.

Promotional channels are the means of communicating information to the universe of customers—patients, prescribers, and payers. As shown in Figure 7.5, the promotional channels and tactics vary based on the target customer.

7. Marketing

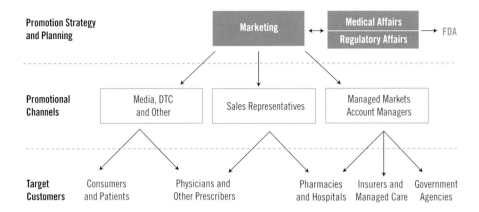

Figure 7.5 Use of Promotional Channels

Promotion Strategy and Planning

Marketing ←→ Medical Affairs / Regulatory Affairs → FDA

Promotional Channels

Media, DTC and Other | Sales Representatives | Managed Markets Account Managers

Target Customers

Consumers and Patients | Physicians and Other Prescribers | Pharmacies and Hospitals | Insurers and Managed Care | Government Agencies

Source: Campbell Alliance.

There are typically two types of promotion: professional and non-professional. Professional promotion is designed to appeal to physicians and other healthcare practitioners and often includes technical or scientific pieces that detail a product's pharmacology or track record in clinical use. Professional promotion occasionally extends beyond clinical information to such topics as coding and reimbursement, dosage and administration, and other factors that can affect prescriber acceptance and use of the product. Marketing prefers to reach prescribers and payers through person-to-person contact from sales representatives or Managed Markets account managers. The methods employed include sales details, informal lunches, and conversations at conferences or symposia. Marketing will also target physicians and other prescribers through Web sites and media ads as a secondary channel.

In contrast, non-professional promotion, which is directed towards patients, potential patients, and their families, typically includes DTC advertising as its primary channel, product-specific and disease state Web sites, and media ads. These promotions are designed to drive consumer awareness of possible symptoms or conditions in order to encourage diagnosis, treatment, and sometimes a preference for a specific therapy. (See Figure 7.6)

Figure 7.6 Commonly Used Promotional Tactics

Tactic	Description	Primary Target	Common Delivery Channels			
			Sales	Managed Markets	Print/Mass Media	Internet
Direct Tactics						
Details	• Product information and supplemental materials	Prescribers	X			X
Samples	• Trial sizes of products	Prescribers	X			X
Speaker Programs	• Scientific or medical seminars led by key opinion leaders and others	Prescribers	X			
Media Programs (for Healthcare Professionals)						
Journal Ads	• Product advertising in professional journals	Prescribers			X	
Monographs or Articles	• Sponsored research or publications about a disease or therapy	Prescribers, Managed Care	X	X	X	X
Continuing Medical Education	• Information about products or therapies delivered through medical education programs	Prescribers, Pharmacies and Hospitals	X			X
Patient Education Programs	• Programs designed to educate patients or physicians on appropriate product use	All	X	X		X
Media Programs (for Consumers and Patients)						
Direct-to-Consumer Advertising	• Mass media advertising directed toward consumers and patients	Consumers			X	X
Pricing Programs						
Pricing Incentives and Rebates	• Off-invoice discounts and rebates offered in exchange for access and market share	Insurers and Managed Care Government		X		
Coupons and Retail Incentives	• Price incentives offered to consumers	Agencies Consumers	X		X	X

Source: Campbell Alliance.

7. Marketing

Sales Targeting

To maximize limited resources, Marketing must identify the target segments within each customer group (e.g., specific prescriber specialties) that are best positioned to influence use of the company's product. Promotional targeting is based upon segmentation analysis that allows the brand team to define key customer targets and the drivers of adoption behavior among those targets. The Sales team then directs its selling efforts at these key customer targets. Typically, the prescriber population is a top priority for segmentation. The segmentation process is described in depth in Chapter 8, Sales.

Prescriber Targeting

Prescribers are typically segmented into groups based upon their ability to generate prescription volume.

Prescribers typically are segmented based on (1) opportunity and (2) behavior. Opportunity segmentation seeks to identify the doctors with the greatest opportunity to prescribe a particular product. For example, cardiologists practicing in a hospital setting would have the opportunity to prescribe a relatively high number of antihypertensive medications. Once opportunity segments have been identified, Marketing further analyzes the most promising segments to identify discrete behavioral sub-segments, such as cardiologists who are early adopters of new antihypertensive treatments. The results of the segmentation analyses are used to fine-tune product messages and sales forecasts.

Opportunity segmentation is typically supported though the analysis of secondary data on retail prescription volume in various therapeutic categories. Information about each physician's specialty and prescribing behavior is readily available from well-established data vendors such as IMS, NDC, and Verispan, which purchase prescription information from retail pharmacies, wholesalers, and other entities (e.g., hospitals and specialty pharmacies), aggregate it, and sell it to pharmaceutical companies.

Data sources are stronger for prescriptions filled in retail pharmacies; information about drug usage in hospitals and other inpatient institutions is comparatively limited. Companies may purchase information about hospital purchases from wholesalers (this is known as outlet data) but have to rely on audits of hospital medical charts (known as chart audits) and other niche sources to find out about prescriber behavior in hospitals, clinics, and other environments in which prescriptions are filled by the treating institution's own pharmacy.

Behavioral segmentation is almost always supported by primary market research specially commissioned by the brand team. While syndicated studies and secondary data reveal past physician prescribing behavior, a brand team often wants to delve deeper into adoption drivers and barriers for its product and specific behavioral attributes that distinguish one segment from another. For example:

- Solo practitioners may be unlikely to adopt an IV product that requires them to develop in-office IV capabilities because the office economics (e.g., the number of patients) do not support it. The physician may be more likely to refer the patient to a specialty practice that has IV capabilities established.

- A core group of prescribers may be early adopters of new therapies, while others are more conservative in prescribing new treatment.

- Physicians may vary their prescribing habits based on the severity of the disease state (mild, moderate, or severe) or on the age of the patient (under 65 or older than 65).

Such information can be gleaned from highly specific attitudinal research conducted via physician interviews and surveys. Such research efforts are customized to the particular brand being supported.

It is important to note that market research in support of segmentation is a highly iterative process with each market research study leading to insights and additional questions that may require further research to validate or address. Brand teams repeat this process until they believe they are receiving a consistent read on the market.

In addition to segmentation based on prescription volume and prescribing behavior, Marketing will identify key opinion leaders (KOLs) in the therapeutic area of interest. These KOLs typically are regarded as the leading practioners or thought leaders in their fields; as such, they carry a great deal of influence over prescription choices of other physicians. (See Figure 7.7)

Patient Targeting

Marketing will also segment the patient population to identify patient groups for targeting. Using the patient description established in the Comprehensive Commercial Plan ("Who are the target patients?" from Figure 7.4),

7. Marketing

Figure 7.7 Physician Universe

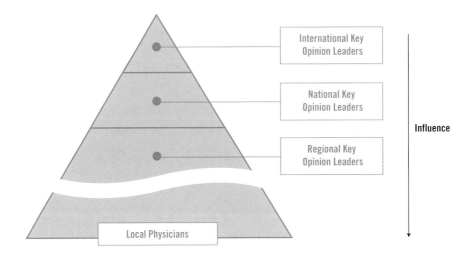

International Key
Opinion Leaders

National Key
Opinion Leaders

Regional Key
Opinion Leaders

Local Physicians

Influence

Source: Campbell Alliance.

Marketing segments the patient population based on population size, age, disease severity and other factors. First, all variables with an impact on a physician's willingness to prescribe—or a patient's willingness to use a product—are identified. Next, the team analyzes each variable and prioritizes it based on its impact on adoption. Based on this analysis, Marketing devises strategies to use channels, messages, and programs of particular interest to the targeted consumer/patient population. For instance, if a condition is particularly common among young adults, Web-based programs might be highly effective; in a condition with a high prevalence among seniors, who tend to be less comfortable with the new technology, investment in Web-based promotions might not be cost-effective.

Privacy considerations make it difficult for pharma companies to find and reach out directly to people who have or are at risk for the target disease or condition. Many companies ask pharmacists and prescribers to encourage interested patients to contact the pharmaceutical company for information. They may also use Web sites and other mechanisms, including mass mailings, as a means of reaching at-risk consumers and their families. If these consumers contact the company and provide identifying information and the appropriate permissions, the pharmaceutical company can then follow up with product discount coupons and information to encourage diagnosis and treatment.

Payer Targeting

In collaboration with the Managed Markets group, Marketing will often craft a promotional strategy for large accounts, including payers, the headquarters operations of retail pharmacy chains, and drug wholesalers. As discussed in Chapter 3, payers in particular play an important role in influencing prescription drug selection. To achieve favorable reimbursement status among important payers, pharmaceutical companies may offer pricing programs, patient counseling and education, and compliance programs, among other options. Retail pharmacy chains and wholesalers, known collectively as "Trade," ensure supply of prescription drugs rather than driving demand. Managed Markets or the Trade function usually handles the segmentation of these customers, collaborating with Marketing to define attractive product features and compelling messages. (See Chapter 9, Managed Markets)

In the end, the segmentation analyses are combined to develop a market map which allows both Marketing and Sales to better understand the market and barriers to adoption. As Figure 7.8 demonstrates, the completed segmentation analysis shows the company where to derive the most value from its sales and marketing investment.

Financial Projections

At this point, P&L statements are finalized and the promotional budget is defined. In addition to creating the product sales forecast, Marketing must create the promotional budget that it hopes will generate those sales. Many factors affect the size and allocation of expenditures within the annual promotional budget, including key customer segments, desired promotional mix, and the overall corporate budget. This budget must accommodate such large line items as calls on physician offices by the sales force and free samples. Marketing is often accountable for all expenses related to the promotional effort—even costs incurred by another department (e.g., Sales). Budget requests are based on detailed promotion plans for each target customer segment.

Promotional Mix

Once the budget has been finalized, it is Marketing's responsibility to supervise development of the promotional program and prepare for the logistics of deployment.

Figure 7.8 Segmentation Analysis/Illustrative Example

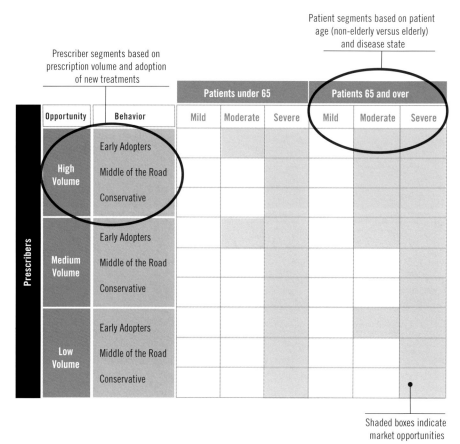

Source: Campbell Alliance.

The right promotional mix—the optimal combination of promotional programs or techniques and channels for delivering messages—is considered a pivotal factor in successful marketing. Success at launch depends on expert planning and management.

The Marketing group establishes both the appropriate promotional mix for the product and the desired reach and frequency for each promotion (i.e., which customer groups should be contacted via each channel and how often they should be contacted using those means). The promotional mix and intensity depends largely on the nature of the product and the marketplace in which it will compete. In an extremely competitive market, such as hypertension, the adoption of products is often found to be responsive to product sampling. As a result, the promotional mix for such products would, therefore, include a large investment in free samples for Field Sales to distribute to prescribers. In comparison, a large investment is not needed for an injectable biologic product with no competition.

Accelerating Uptake — Launch

The most intensive promotional effort and the greatest promotional funding are reserved for the product launch and the years immediately thereafter. After the FDA has approved a drug, Marketing can begin its branded promotional efforts.

Successful product launch is considered a make-or-break step in realizing a brand's potential. A successful launch will differentiate a new product from its competitors and set a course for market leadership. As a result, launch is the period of greatest promotional intensity. First, Marketing deploys its promotional programs and then, Marketing monitors and updates the programs to maximize commercial value.

Deployment

Once promotional plans are in place, Marketing supervises promotional program development and the logistics of deployment.

Marketing works with Sales, Managed Markets, and vendors such as advertising agencies and medical communications companies that specialize in promotions and marketing collateral to develop specific programs for deployment. Once the target audience and specific program goals are clarified, program materials and advertising copy are drafted. The promotional materials are then usually reviewed for compliance by internal departments, including Marketing, Regulatory Affairs, Legal, and Medical Affairs. If the program is to be disseminated by the sales force or Managed Markets account managers, a training module will be developed to prepare them to communicate the program and share tools with customers effectively. The complete roadmap for sales force activities, which is developed in collaboration with Sales management, is called a Plan of Action and is discussed in greater detail in Chapter 8, Sales.

7. Marketing

Introduction to Product Pricing

Pricing is typically controlled by senior management in the company, with key recommendations coming from Marketing, based on guidance provided by a committee that also includes Sales, Reimbursement and Pricing, Managed Markets, Legal, Public Affairs, and Finance leaders. The price for any product reflects an effort to achieve high sales volume without sacrificing margin.

The price is based, in part, on the innate competitive strength of the product—that is, how innovative it is and the degree to which that innovation satisfies the needs of target customers. Highly innovative products are generally sold at a higher price than generics or branded products that are very similar to that of competitors ("me-too" products).

Another consideration is pharmaceutical companies' need to recoup research, development, and marketing costs and earn a profit.

Wholesalers purchasing drugs from pharmaceutical manufacturers pay the wholesale acquisition cost (WAC). WAC is the listed price a company charges to wholesalers purchasing the product, before any rebates, discounts, or other price concessions offered.

Pharmacies purchasing from wholesalers pay WAC plus a small service fee. Pharmacies are reimbursed by payers based on average wholesale price (AWP), a figure set by industry vendors such as First Data Bank rather than by pharmaceutical companies. AWP is often 20% to 30% higher than WAC.

Two customer groups receive special price breaks:

- Large, influential private payers that can deliver high market share are offered contracts with special pricing terms.

- Some government programs, such as the Veterans Health Administration (VHA) and Medicaid, have the right to preferred pricing as a result of legislation or regulations.

These price breaks often come to the private or public payer in the form of a rebate. The rebate is paid by the pharmaceutical company upon demonstrated evidence of product utilization by the payer.

Other customers who have not negotiated special contracts may negotiate pricing directly with drug wholesalers. (See Figure 7.9)

Figure 7.9 Pharmaceutical Customers and Pricing

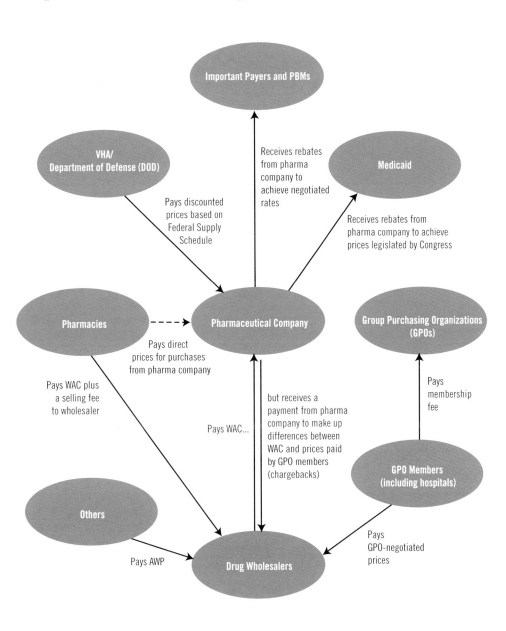

7. Marketing

As discussed earlier in this chapter (and in Chapter 8), promotional materials ranging from highly developed scientific pieces to inexpensive pens, pads and other novelty items, must adhere strictly to the content of the FDA-approved product label.

Figure 7.10 illustrates how Marketing collaborates with other departments and outside organizations to develop promotional programs.

Figure 7.10 Marketing Collaboration in Program Development

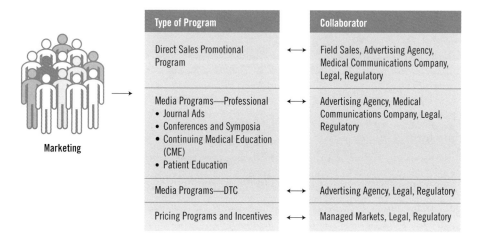

Source: Campbell Alliance.

Depending on the company, Marketing may also guide the distribution strategy to ensure that patients have access to products and that there is sufficient supply in the marketplace. The distribution strategy will vary for different products and therapeutic categories.

Monitoring
In addition to pursuing promotional efforts, Marketing continually monitors product performance and makes adjustments accordingly. Revenue and market share are two important measures, along with profitability (which is calculated by factoring in discounts and the direct costs of promotion).

- **Revenue** measures direct sales of the product to wholesalers and other direct customers. Although such sales drive the revenue performance of the company, they are not an entirely reliable measure of demand. Wholesalers generally buy based on anticipated market or inventory needs, but can also engage in buying practices that can misrepresent the demand in any given period. Also, wholesalers can typically return unused product to the company at the company's expense, so until product is purchased by the patient, the company cannot count on it as a solid sale.

- **Market share performance**, which is obtained from outside data vendors such as IMS, NDC, and VeriSpan, reflects actual prescriptions written or filled, and more accurately represents the market demand.

In addition to monitoring these overall indicators, Marketing analyzes performance in specific customer and geographic segments in order to understand variations in program efficacy and identify further opportunities to improve promotions.

Such quantitative metrics are always a bit "behind the times," because it takes time for the impact of a successful promotion to affect sales or market share. For more "real-time" feedback, Marketing relies upon its direct selling channels—Sales and Managed Markets—for insight into how well customers are receiving the promotional programs. For example, Sales personnel might report that materials are difficult to use or that customers are not responding positively to select messages, necessitating a change by Marketing.

Maximizing Peak Sales—Growth

Following launch, Marketing faces continuous challenges to differentiate products and to maximize profits and market share, often in crowded or competitive markets. Operating in an increasingly complex environment typically amid an array of alternative therapies, Marketing faces daunting challenges:

- Successfully differentiating their products from "the pack"

- Gaining access to target physicians, who are overwhelmed by the number of sales reps competing to reach them and, beset by managed care paperwork, increasingly reluctant to spare the time for sales details

- Understanding differences in customer responsiveness to each piece of an increasingly varied array of promotion techniques and channels

- Securing the sales and market share needed to justify the company's investment in R&D and promotion. With promotional spending at an all-time high, Marketing teams are under increasing pressure to justify investments by demonstrating their value in driving sales and/or market share.

The commercial success of the product is determined by product attributes determined and proven during development combined with the quality of the commercial strategy (e.g., targeting, messaging, and distribution). During the launch period and throughout the product life cycle, Marketing works with Sales and other functional areas to evaluate market reactions to the product's effectiveness and the product's promotion effectiveness, in order to refine the commercial strategy to realize maximum value.

An important responsibility of Marketing is to make timely course corrections to address market or competitive changes and to overcome barriers to adoption. Even when an initial strategy is highly effective, it must be adjusted on an ongoing basis (e.g., in reaction to changes in the business or reimbursement environment). Post-launch, the promotion strategy is updated periodically (usually every quarter or trimester) to integrate new clinical findings into existing promotional programs. For example, the results of a phase 4 study offer additional evidence that is an an extremely valuable addition to the promotional message for all customer segments, or a particular segment only. Marketing also works with Sales to determine whether a change in size, structure, or alignment of the sales force is needed.

Optimizing Profitability and Extending Brand Life—Maturity

Effective brand managers craft winning strategies during each stage of the product life cycle, from the initial indication through the late-in-life-cycle transition for brands whose patents are expiring.

As a product reaches maturity, Marketing's primary focus shifts from achieving growth to maximizing profit potential by seeking new indications, staving off generic competition, and adjusting the promotional investment. Marketing has three major approaches at its disposal to accomplish its objectives. The best approaches depend on the nature of the product.

- Marketing can work with Business Development to identify potential out-licensing opportunities or other arrangements with third parties. (For a discussion of out-licensing, see Chapter 6, Business Development.)

- Marketing can extend the product life through reformulations and line extensions or through new indications.

  - Reformulations typically refers to changes in the delivery system of a drug that is already being marketed. For example, a tablet-based drug may be reformulated as a liquid. Reformulations can be patented.

  - Line extensions are new formulations or new means of delivering drugs that are already being marketed. Line extensions can include new strengths and dosage forms. Line extensions undergo clinical testing and often demonstrate substantial benefits in terms of efficacy, ease of administration, and patient compliance. Line extensions can be patented.

  - A drug's life can be extended by adding to its list of approved indications. A new indication can be approved for changes in the symptoms, risk factors, conditions, diseases, or target population for which the FDA originally approved the drug for use. Drug companies that want to add an indication for an already-marketed drug (to the product label and to advertising) must file a new application with the FDA.

  - In order to provide an incentive to pharmaceutical companies to test drugs for pediatric use, a special incentive was put in place extending overall patent life for six months.

- Marketing can develop conversion strategies to switch physicians and patients from mature products to newer replacement products.

3. Operational Model for Marketing and Brand Management

Brand teams fall within the umbrella of the Marketing function. In many companies, Brand teams operate at two levels—global and regional/local (market-specific). A market might be a single country (the US or Japan) or group of countries with similar characteristics (e.g., Western Europe).

Global Marketing

Early in a product's life cycle, Global Marketing plays a lead role, with local markets collaborating in setting the overall strategy for the therapeutic area or brand prior to product launch preparation in individual markets.

Global Marketing may report to the CEO or the VP of Commercial Operations. Global leadership is necessary to define consistent messages for use in all markets, coordinate activities with cross-market implications (e.g., pricing approaches), and determine the value of entry into various markets. As in a local market, a global brand leader might handle one high-volume brand or several smaller ones.

After the product is submitted for regulatory approval, local Marketing then takes responsibility and Global Marketing's function shifts to coordinating across regions and undertaking major initiatives.

Regional/Local Marketing

The regional Marketing unit in a major market like Western Europe works with local Sales, local Marketing, and other local functions to achieve optimal results across all countries under its supervision. Regional teams focus primarily on coordinating promotion across regional markets and may participate in phase 4 activity and other expanded uses of the product. Recognizing that each local market is often affected by the market environment in neighboring countries (e.g., low pricing in Italy and France can affect brand performance in the UK), regional teams work to maximize overall financial performance for the region.

Local leadership is necessary because the competitive and regulatory environments—including restrictions on both product approval and product promotion—often vary from market to market. Even the nature of the approved indication may differ. The local brand team can adapt pricing and promotional approaches as necessary to each marketplace.

The product manager or brand director who heads the brand team in each geographic market has overall responsibility for the brand and is expected to have in-depth familiarity with the product's clinical and scientific characteristics, as well as the customer groups exerting the greatest influence on demand. (See Figures 7.11 and 7.12)

Figure 7.11 Operational Model for Marketing and Brand Management

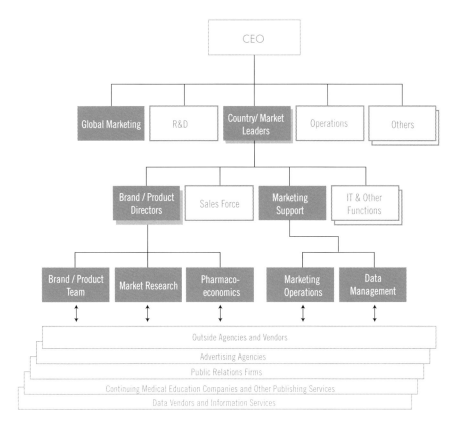

Source: Campbell Alliance.

Therapeutic Model

Many companies are adopting a therapeutic class or franchise model, in which Marketing, Development, and other parts of the company are organized by therapeutic area. This model encourages greater cross-functional cooperation and deep therapeutic market expertise. Using this model, companies are successfully capturing the benefits of this expertise in their product or brand strategies and exploiting it at every stage of the product life cycle.

Figure 7.12 Descriptions of Functions

Function	Description
Global Marketing	• Leads in setting an overall strategy for the therapeutic area or brand • Supports regional and local Marketing to execute strategy in individual markets
Brand / Product Teams	• Responsible for adapting brand strategy to local markets • Work with Sales and others to develop promotional programs • Possess in-depth product and market knowledge
Market Research	• Provides data and analytical research to support market analyses
Pharmacoeconomics	• Responsible for health economics and outcomes analyses
Marketing Operations	• Usually responsible for a wide range of marketing support functions, such as coordinating conventions and symposia and advertising production • May coordinate vendor activities
Data Management	• Responsible for securing and communicating secondary data from outside vendors

Source: Campbell Alliance.

Collaboration with Internal and External Functions

To be effective, Marketing must work in close collaboration with other internal functions—not only Sales and Managed Markets, but also Discovery, Development, BD, and Operations. Even the development of brand strategies and promotional programs are cross-functional endeavors. After a product has been approved, Marketing works with Sales, Managed Markets, and Medical Affairs to launch and promote them. It continues to collaborate with those groups and with Development to secure expanded indications and uses.

Each brand team is extremely reliant on informational support functions such as Market Research and Pharmacoeconomics. Market Research is typically the interface between various departments within the company and external vendors that conduct market research on the company's behalf or publish syndicated market research materials. The Pharmacoeconomics (sometimes known as Health Outcomes) department is focused on the evaluation of the company's drugs from the perspective of issues related to cost-effectiveness, quality of life, health outcomes, or drug utilization.

The brand team also needs internal and external support to develop promotional materials and monitor customer behavior. Typically, the team will work with a range of advertising agencies, public relations firms, and medical communication companies to execute the brand strategy.

8. SALES

1. The Importance of Sales

2. A Closer Look at Sales

3. Operational Model for Sales

In the early 1990s, when the federal government was flirting with universal healthcare and managed care was spreading across the country, many pharma companies predicted the end of large sales forces. Influence and control over prescription usage, it seemed, would shift from physicians to the government or managed care groups. Accordingly, most pharma companies decided to tighten their belts and reduce their sales forces.

Pfizer did the opposite, making an enormous bet on the importance of face-to-face interaction with doctors on driving drug sales. The company launched an aggressive plan to expand its sales force, adding thousands of representatives through its own hiring initiatives and through the acquisition of Warner-Lambert in 2000 and Pharmacia in 2003.

Today, Pfizer has assembled a worldwide selling machine with approximately 38,000 sales representatives, divided into separate sales forces, calling on primary care physicians. With approximately 11,000 sales representatives calling on physicians in the US, Pfizer has the largest US pharmaceutical sales force and a reputation for organizational selling power.

Pfizer has harnessed the power of its sales force by actively promoting its product portfolio. The sales force has enabled Pfizer to quickly launch and successfully sell its internally developed products, such as Viagra®. Moreover, the sales force has attracted partners seeking to leverage Pfizer's selling platform. Warner-Lambert, prior to its acquisition by Pfizer, used the Pfizer sales force to promote Lipitor®.

The pharma industry as a whole later reversed its course, and other pharma companies added sales representatives to their payrolls to duplicate Pfizer's selling success. Pfizer's bet paid off, and its selling machine is considered still among the most efficient and powerful in the industry, although in April 2005 Pfizer signaled that it may have to realign US sales force in response to environmental pressures.

Source: Campbell Alliance.

1. The Importance of Sales

Pharmaceutical companies rely heavily on their sales forces, or field sales forces as they are often called, to drive prescription volume and generate product sales.

The US-based pharmaceutical field sales force is roughly 100,000 strong—approximately one sales representative, or sales rep, for every nine licensed physicians, and an even lower ratio of one sales representative for every five to six practicing physicians. Sales forces, however, focus on the practicing physicians who write the most prescriptions (called high prescribers), or approximately 250,000 out of the 875,000 physicians in the US.

This standing army of highly trained professionals is the most expensive and, by consensus, highest-impact promotional weapon in the pharmaceutical company arsenal. Pharmaceutical companies make a huge investment in their field forces, spending an estimated $300,000 to recruit, train, and field each sales representative.

Even in an era of mass communication, the pharmaceutical industry remains committed to regular personal interaction with important customers. Sales reps are the human face of the pharmaceutical company to office-based physicians and their office and professional staff, hospital and clinic personnel who influence prescription choice, and pharmacists.

In visits to physician offices, clinics, hospitals, long-term care facilities, and pharmacies, sales representatives make in-depth product presentations and respond to questions about safety, efficacy, side effects, convenience, compliance, and reimbursement that, if unresolved, could pose barriers to prescribing a drug. Their ability to defuse concerns effectively can have a huge impact on product adoption. (See Figure 8.1)

8. Sales

Figure 8.1 The Role of Sales

Outreach to Potential Prescribers and Prescription Influencers

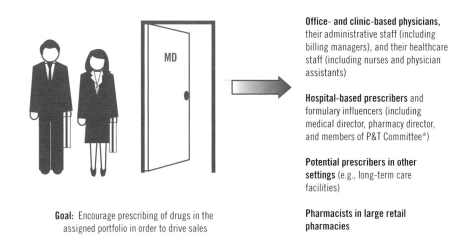

Office- and clinic-based physicians, their administrative staff (including billing managers), and their healthcare staff (including nurses and physician assistants)

Hospital-based prescribers and formulary influencers (including medical director, pharmacy director, and members of P&T Committee*)

Potential prescribers in other settings (e.g., long-term care facilities)

Pharmacists in large retail pharmacies

Goal: Encourage prescribing of drugs in the assigned portfolio in order to drive sales

*The P&T (Pharmaceutical and Therapeutics) Committee decides which drugs will be stocked by the hospital pharmacy and which of those drugs will be favored for use.

Source: Campbell Alliance.

2. A Closer Look at Sales

Sales Strategy

Sales strategy is driven by the company's portfolio strategy, which consists of the promotional plans developed by Marketing for each product.

The sales strategy defines the optimum deployment of expensive direct selling resources. Sales representatives will only be assigned to branded products with substantial historical sales or substantial sales potential. Products that are at a late stage in the life cycle and/or unimportant to the company's overall business strategy (for example, not in the therapeutic areas that the company has decided to concentrate upon) may not be promoted. (See Figure 8.2)

Figure 8.2 The Relationship of Sales and Marketing Strategies

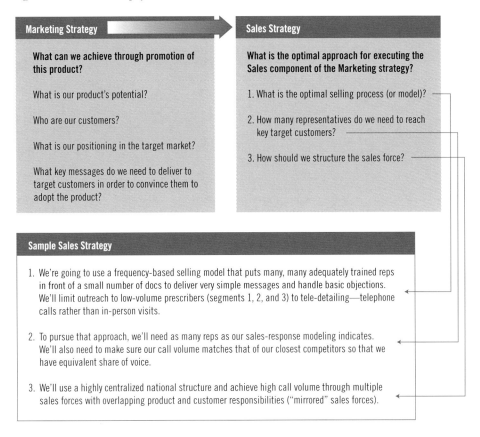

Source: Campbell Alliance.

Sales Details

The primary promotional technique is the sales presentation or "detail"—a carefully structured face-to-face interchange with target prescribers (first and foremost, physicians).

Sales representatives try to structure details around key product messages, but they must be careful to avoid a "canned" presentation. Instead, the best reps engage in an apparently free-flowing exchange regarding the disease state and physician concerns about product adoption, interposing key messages as appropriate.

During many details, the rep will discuss more than one product. The specific products to be promoted by each sales force and the order in which they will be promoted are determined by high-level Marketing and Sales executives. The terms P1, P2, and P3 are often used to refer to a product's position in a sales call. P1 is the highest-priority product and must be presented; P2 and P3 products are less important and may not be presented at all.

Sales reps also frequently leave behind free product samples to encourage physicians to try their patients on a "starter dose."

A typical sales call includes a planning, execution, and recording component, and is outlined in Figure 8.3.

Figure 8.3 A Typical Sales Call

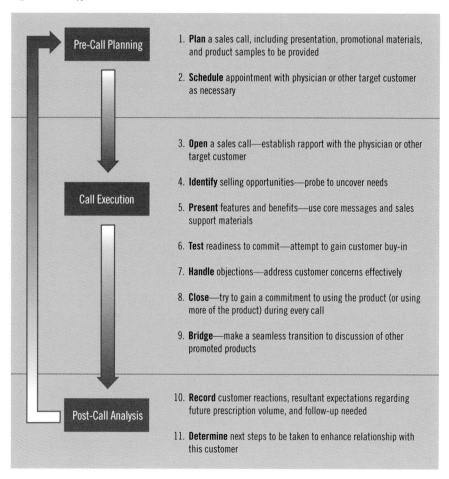

Pre-Call Planning

1. **Plan** a sales call, including presentation, promotional materials, and product samples to be provided

2. **Schedule** appointment with physician or other target customer as necessary

Call Execution

3. **Open** a sales call—establish rapport with the physician or other target customer

4. **Identify** selling opportunities—probe to uncover needs

5. **Present** features and benefits—use core messages and sales support materials

6. **Test** readiness to commit—attempt to gain customer buy-in

7. **Handle** objections—address customer concerns effectively

8. **Close**—try to gain a commitment to using the product (or using more of the product) during every call

9. **Bridge**—make a seamless transition to discussion of other promoted products

Post-Call Analysis

10. **Record** customer reactions, resultant expectations regarding future prescription volume, and follow-up needed

11. **Determine** next steps to be taken to enhance relationship with this customer

Source: Campbell Alliance.

Most companies provide representatives with sales information management systems, also known as sales force automation (SFA) systems, to help them plan and manage all field-based promotion activities. SFA systems are used to maintain call schedules and record outcomes. These systems are generally equipped with full profiles of physicians, including a description of his or her practice, prescribing behavior, and promotion history (the points of contact—conferences, lunches, and sales—with that prescriber). Most systems also have a "record signature" functionality that the sales force uses to have prescribers acknowledge free samples they receive, as required by law. Many have laptop and palmtop (PDA, or personal digital assistant) features.

Most reps are expected to record their field activity immediately after completing a call. Their input is used by Sales and Marketing management to monitor productivity and measure promotion effectiveness.

As the number of US pharmaceutical sales representatives has grown, it has become increasingly difficult for sales representatives to obtain access to physicians (particularly primary care physicians, who are targeted in many different therapeutic areas) to present product details. As a result, many sales calls last only a few minutes, and, in some cases, the representative may not see the physician at all. A sales call may be limited to a brief discussion with the office administrator.

Beyond Sales Details

Although they are arguably the most important promotional mechanism, sales details are not the only technique that Sales uses to inform potential customers about company products.

Sales representatives may also organize programs of value to the physicians in their respective territories, such as speaker programs in which other practicing physicians and respected clinical experts (KOLs) explore topics of professional interest. Many representatives have budgets for sponsoring local events such as speaker programs and lunches.

Sales Targeting

Because sales force time is an expensive and limited resource, efforts are concentrated on high-potential customers. Physicians, the most important customer segment, are prioritized based on a widely accepted practice: the assignment of decile rankings based on potential prescription volume. These assignments drive the intensity of promotion.

Typically a company starts with a targeted universe, which is a subset of all physicians in the country who have written prescriptions in the therapeutic area or for specific products of interest. Studies have shown that majority of the prescription volume is generated by a small minority of the prescribers, as shown in Figure 8.4. Sales promotion efforts are generally concentrated on this small group of high-prescribing physicians.

Figure 8.4 Prescribing Concentration Curve

Sales promotion efforts are increasingly concentrated on a small group of high-prescribing physicians

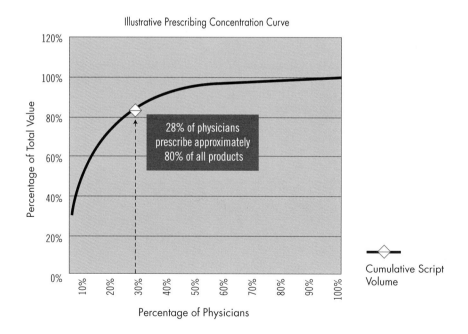

Source: Campbell Alliance.

154

The targeted universe is stratified into tenths (deciles) based on volume of prescriptions in the relevant disease state. (Some companies use fifths, or quintiles, instead.) Typically, each practice specialty is stratified separately.

Companies select the top deciles/quintiles for direct sales promotion and create target lists of prescribers to whom the sales force will promote that product or therapeutic portfolio. Occasionally, companies will have the sales force visit selected lower-decile prescribers with the perceived potential to become high-volume prescribers. (See Figure 8.5)

Figure 8.5 Division of Prescriber Universe into Deciles

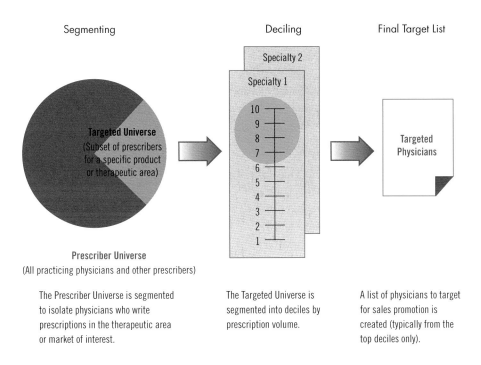

Source: Campbell Alliance.

In most markets, the prescription volume is concentrated in the top three to five deciles (and sometimes overwhelmingly in the top two). Companies can safely target these deciles exclusively and ignore lower-value physicians. The sales strategy may specify alternative, lower-cost promotions (media advertising or e-detailing, for example) for lower-value customers or prescribers.

8. Sales

Most companies will balance the incremental value of targeting physicians in a particular decile against the costs of detailing physicians in that profile. (See Figure 8.6)

Figure 8.6 Selecting Target Segments: A Balancing Act

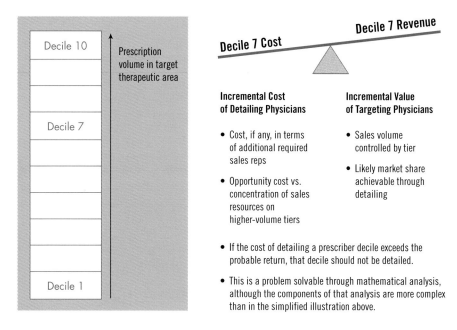

Source: Campbell Alliance.

The Plan of Action (POA)

Sales forces are guided by a POA (plan of action) generated by Marketing and Sales leaders based on the agreed–upon sales strategy. It provides explicit instructions for sales force activity, including customer targets, the content and structure of sales presentations, detailing tools, and value-added programs.

An illustrative plan of action is provided in Figure 8.7.

In addition to defining customer targets, the POA also defines frequency, meaning the number of times the rep is supposed to call on a specific customer or customer segment. For instance, a sales rep may be expected to call on each prescriber within the highest-potential physician segment—Decile 10—four times per month.

Figure 8.7 Illustrative Plan of Action

Core Components
• Core messages and detailing position for each product
• Overall reach and frequency objectives by decile and customer type (e.g., office-based physicians, hospitals)
• Breakdown of Sales support and special programs, including lunches, dinners, and symposia
• Coordination with Marketing efforts in other channels such as DTC advertising, journal advertising, and professional association meetings
• Specific territory opportunities and special instructions
• Target prescriber lists
• Promotional materials (e.g., detail pieces, samples, approved publications)

Segment	Call Frequency	Professional Guidance	Messages and Programs	
			P1 Detail—Product X	P2 Detail—Product Y
Deciles 10, 9	3x per Month	• Higher frequency for key prescribers at high target accounts.	**Messages** 1. Efficacy, safety, and dosing	**Messages** 1. Mechanism of action
Deciles 8, 7, 6	2x per Month		2. Mechanism of action	2. Efficacy, safety, and dosing
Deciles 5 and Under	1x per Month	• Productivity expectations (e.g., 8 calls per day)	3. Patient convenience	3. Epilepsy indication
			4. Pricing and reimbursement	**Programs**
		• Every prescriber at least once per month.	5. Elderly	1. Epilepsy Foundation Dinner
			Programs	
			1. Speaker programs (Neurology Board Panel)	
			2. Audioconferences	

Source: Campbell Alliance.

8. Sales

The POA specifies the order in which products will be promoted during a detail. It is accompanied by specific promotional pieces to facilitate sales efforts (e.g., samples, collateral sales aids and articles, giveaways, such as branded pens and calendars). These materials may include summaries of clinical studies.

The POA is typically recalibrated every quarter or trimester to reflect market or promotional changes.

Ideally, sales representatives executing the POA provide ongoing feedback throughout a selling cycle (quarter or trimester), to both headquarters Marketing and Sales leaders and their immediate managers (regional and district).

They offer updates on customer interaction and promotional effectiveness, as well as insights gained into competitive activities. As appropriate, these findings are incorporated into the company's POAs for the next selling cycle.

Regulatory Oversight

The content of sales messages and the sales aids used to deliver them is subject to regulation by the FDA, the Federal Trade Commission (FTC), the Department of Health and Human Services' Office of Inspector General (OIG), and other governmental entities, including the attorneys general of each state. Professional associations, such as the Pharmaceutical Research and Manufacturers of America (PhRMA), provide guidelines to pharmaceutical companies, while other associations that are unaffiliated with the pharmaceutical companies, such as the American Medical Association, provide general guidelines for physicians on interaction with company sales representatives.

Even outside publications by KOLs and industry experts are subject to regulatory control if they are used in promotion.

Sales reps are not allowed to initiate discussion of off-label product uses (that is, uses that have not been approved by the FDA). Representatives may refer queries from prescribers to the Drug Information department or to their team of medical science liaisons (MSLs), generally PhDs, PharmDs, or MDs who are competent to field clinical queries about such matters and, because they are not part of the Sales function, have no incentive to provide a biased description of clinical results in order to encourage product adoption.

MSLs, who are typically part of Medical Affairs, are expected to meet regularly with KOLs and other influential physicians to discuss a company's clinical development activities, including clinical trials and phase 4 marketing studies. They encourage leading physicians to participate in clinical trials or company-sponsored speaker programs.

Regulations safeguard the ability of prescribers to choose products in an unbiased and informed manner, by preventing such irregularities as dissemination of misleading information or financial incentives for prescribers to choose a particular brand.

Promotional materials and conversations are not the only aspects of Sales activity subject to regulation. Under the federal Prescription Drug Marketing Act (PDMA), representatives must account for all product samples in their possession and secure signatures from customers when samples are distributed.

Sales Training

Sales personnel need to be very knowledgeable about both their products and the market. All sales representatives undergo rigorous initial and on-going training to familiarize them with the company's products and customers, as well as the business and regulatory environment. In addition to substantive education, they also receive training to hone their selling skills. (See Figure 8.8)

Figure 8.8 Topics Covered During Training

Product Training	• Therapeutic area, disease state, and relevant anatomy • Relevant pharmacology • Product (details on dosing, uses, mechanism of action, differentiation from relevant competition) • Package insert • Key clinical studies and reprints • Selling environment (hospital, clinic, office) • Market dynamics and competitive environment • Reimbursement • Business ethics (e.g. promotional guidelines)
Selling Skills	• Company-specific selling skills model • Product-specific selling skills • Use of sales tools/reprints • Responses to physician objections • Role playing
Sales Tool Training	• Sale Force Automation • Territory management • Administrative functions • Sampling and sample accountability

Source: Campbell Alliance.

Sales training is a highly structured process that typically includes home-based, classroom-based, and on-the-job training (much of which is computer-guided in order to monitor progress and add convenience for the remote representatives). Graded exams, role playing, and other techniques are used to formally and informally assess performance and ensure that new representatives can credibly and reliably represent the company to its customers. Initial sales training typically lasts three to six months. (See Figure 8.9)

Figure 8.9 Overview of a Typical Initial Sales Training Program

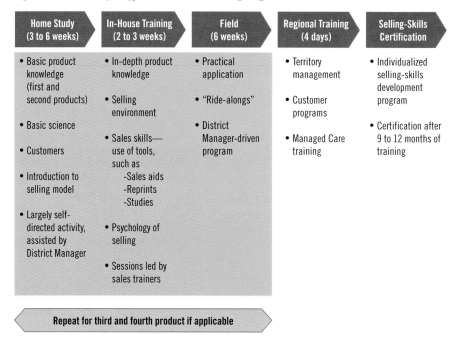

Source: Campbell Alliance.

Training is particularly intensive in preparation for a new product launch, which is considered a "make-or-break" stage for a product's success.

Sales Force Size and Structure

Pharmaceutical sales forces are sized and organized to maximize the financial return on promotion to the company's highest-potential customers, and size and structure are considered extremely important factors in their effectiveness.

Advanced modeling and analytic techniques are used to evaluate how various customers will respond to promotion and how much promotion (and how many representatives) can be justified.

A niche market has sprung up for consultants who utilitze analytics to determine the optimal configuration. They use advanced analytical techniques to define a sales force size and structure that will offer ideal coverage for a company's entire promoted portfolio.

The overall structure or design of a given company's sales force is largely a function of product mix and customer mix. Typical design models address product, geography, and key customer segments.

The Sales function within most companies uses the same geographic hierarchy: territories (the smallest), which are aggregated into districts, which in turn are rolled up into regions. A territory typically corresponds to a multiple zip code alignment. In dense areas, like major cities, a territory may contain only a single zip code—or even just part of one zip code. A company might aggregate 500 territories in 50 districts—providing a span of control of one manager to 10 representatives, a typical number for the industry—and then aggregate those districts into five to 10 regions. When a company deploys multiple sales forces for different products, the sales forces may report into a central manager at the district, regional, or national level. (See Figures 8.10 and 8.11)

Figure 8.10 The Sales Force Leadership

National Managers	• Define Sales strategy, in conjunction with Marketing and Brand Management leaders
Regional Managers (RMs)	• Hire and train DMs • Develop the administrative, management, and leadership skills of their DMs (sales force recruitment, training, and tactics) • Analyze overall regional sales performance in order to fine-tune performance planning • Provide overall leadership—getting the right people in place as DMs and maintaining morale to enhance performance
District Managers (DMs)	• Define optimal tactical approach to executing Sales strategy at the district level—how to deploy resources and attack specific kinds of accounts • Recruit, hire, and dismiss sales representatives • Analyze district sales trends (strengths, weaknesses, and opportunities) • Take a very active role in training and mentoring sales representatives to enhance productivity • Provide overall leadership—getting the right people in place as sales reps and maintaining morale to enhance performance

Source: Campbell Alliance.

8. Sales

Figure 8.11 Geographic Organization of the Sales Force

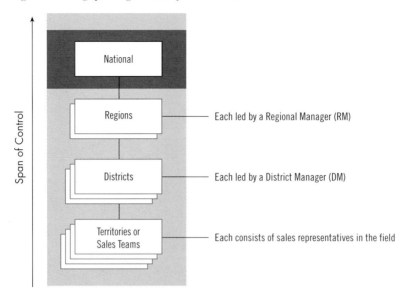

Span of Control

National

Regions ———— Each led by a Regional Manager (RM)

Districts ———— Each led by a District Manager (DM)

Territories or Sales Teams ———— Each consists of sales representatives in the field

Source: Campbell Alliance.

In many companies, the regional staff includes human resources professionals focused on recruiting and hiring sales representatives, as well as analysts devoted to analyzing local markets and performance trends.

Only an enterprise with an extremely limited and homogeneous portfolio of products could organize its Sales solely by geography. The vast majority of companies first "carve up" Sales in accord with some other organizing principle (or principles) and then subdivide the resulting organization by geography. (See Figure 8.12)

One type of sales force organization is by customer segment. (See Figure 8.13) Sales forces that visit physician offices are divided into primary care (targeting primary care physicians) and specialty (targeting the specialists that influence the therapy that is being promoted).

Most companies also have institutional sales forces that target hospitals and clinics. Generally, institutional sales forces detail hospital products or special hospital uses of products. They operate in a complex selling environment, which often involves influencing physicians who can help get the drug on formulary and those who will drive demand once the product is on formulary—pharmacists, nursing staff, and other professionals who influence drug purchasing or prescribing decisions.

Figure 8.12 Typical Options for Sales Force Organization

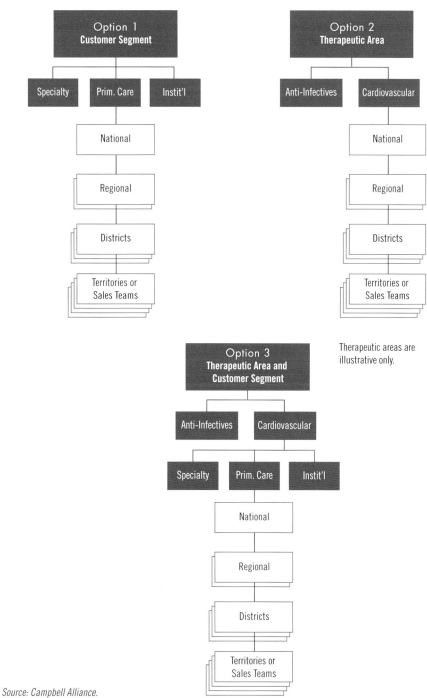

Therapeutic areas are illustrative only.

Source: Campbell Alliance.

Figure 8.13 Customer Segment Sales Forces

Primary Care	• Promote products to primary care physicians • May represent several products or therapeutic areas
Specialty	• Promote products to specialists only • Generally carry more detailed promotional materials and may distribute higher-strength samples than primary care sales reps • Often responsible for developing relationships with thought leaders for speaker programs
Institutional (Hospitals)	• Promote products to hospital administrators, hospital pharmacists, and physicians • Specifically focused on ensuring inclusion in hospital formularies and awareness among administrators, pharmacists, and physicians of special pricing and incentives available to the hospital
Managed Markets	• Work with government institutions, MCOs, GPOs (with memberships consisting of hospitals and other providers), PBMs, and often Trade (retail pharmacies and wholesalers) • Establishes contracts and relationships at the account (headquarters) level • Typically managed through the Managed Markets function

Source: Campbell Alliance.

A Managed Markets sales force, consisting of account managers, is typically administered separately. Managed Markets sales forces work with payers and large direct purchasers. Their customer targets include group purchasing organizations, integrated delivery networks, managed care organizations, and pharmacy benefit managers. They are usually organized under an account management model and report to Marketing or Managed Markets. Their role is discussed in greater detail in Chapter 9.

A sales force organized by customer segment (subdivided by geography) is most common for companies with a diverse product portfolio without a distinct therapeutic focus. Pharmaceutical companies with a rich portfolio of products in several discrete therapeutic areas (e.g., cardiovascular products, oncology products) may make therapeutic focus the primary organizing principle for their sales team. These sales forces promote the products within a given therapeutic area to all customer segments (primary care, specialists, institutional). Within these sales forces, different teams or representatives are assigned to each customer segment. As appropriate, a hybrid of these two approaches may be used.

Most large companies deploy complementary "mirrored" sales forces to increase the frequency of contact with high-value prescribers. Mirrored sales forces typically have the same list of targeted physicians to call upon and detail the same products. They may have different promotional priorities among those products or present different product indications or uses.

A company may also extend its sales force by engaging a contract sales organization (CSO)—essentially, a sales force for hire from an external vendor. In smaller companies or those with inexperienced sales forces, a CSO may be hired to provide all coverage for a high-priority product. Larger companies with substantial sales forces of their own may use a CSO to supplement the efforts of the internal sales team.

Sales forces are always managed locally (that is, by country or group of countries), so that the organization, size, and operations model can be adapted to the specifics of the marketplace. Regulations vary significantly from country to country, making it difficult to manage cross-border sales forces effectively. The US sales forces usually report to a vice president of US Sales and Marketing.

Large pharmaceutical companies have traditionally attracted the "best of the best" in the sales profession due to their range of opportunities. Nonetheless, positions are not always easy to fill with professionals experienced in the relevant therapeutic area(s). Many Sales organizations have a hiring or recruiting group attached to them so that they can aggressively seek out new reps on a continuing basis.

Large companies may screen as many as 10,000 candidates per year. New hires span a variety of backgrounds and include recent college graduates, usually with degrees in chemistry, biology, or pharmacology. People with previous pharmaceutical sales experience are generally in high demand.

Sales Force Resizing

Companies frequently fine-tune sales force size based on perceived opportunities and portfolio needs. The "right sizing" determination is influenced by such factors as the number of high-volume targets, the extent to which those targets overlap across multiple products, and the workload/productivity goals set for the sales force. Companies are often able to fine-tune the sales force effort at a local level through sales targeting and detailing.

Less frequently, pharmaceutical companies make major sizing changes such as adding a new sales force or undertaking a major expansion of an existing one. These changes are usually driven by launch of a major new product or anticipation of serious new competitive threats. Marketing collaborates with Sales leaders on such decisions.

Even more rarely, the basic structure of the sales force is radically altered. Innovations of this magnitude are usually triggered by serious concerns about previous sales performance or the ability of the existing structure to support strong performance in the future. Major changes in the product portfolio—usually brought on by acquisitions and divestitures of companies and product portfolios—can also trigger radical changes in the sales force structure.

The decision to adopt a new organizational principle may be the result of a change in internal leadership or in the marketplace. For instance, a new CEO concerned about personal accountability, may do away with mirrored sales forces that make it more difficult to assign sales credit to a single representative. Or a company whose primary therapeutic area is the focus of stepped-up cost scrutiny from managed care organizations may decide to bolster its managed care sales force.

A fundamental reorganization typically includes analysis of different sales force models (for instance, by therapeutic area, customer, or decentralized region) to determine how to achieve desired reach and frequency. Advanced evaluative techniques, such as customer response to promotion and incremental cost-benefit analysis, are used to define optimal promotion intensity and the number of resources needed to support it.

Incentive Compensation

Incentive compensation is used as a motivational tool to drive the behavior of the sales force.

In settings where the sales representatives are largely self-directed, incentive compensation helps to tie their rewards with the achievement of company objectives. In other words, companies use incentive compensation to "pay for performance."

Getting the incentive pay formula right is considered essential to driving optimum sales performance. Sales force management—that is, vice presidents of Sales in coordination with HR or Sales Operations managers and directors—establishes performance incentives for the sales representatives. A significant portion of sales force compensation is tied to sales for their products among assigned customers in their assigned geography. Incentive-based compensation commonly accounts for 20% to 25% of total pay potential, but the full range can run as low as 10% and as high as 40%.

Typically a target dollar value is set for incentive pay and allocated among the promoted products. Performance for each product is then measured against an objective consistent with the company's overall sales and promotion strategy. To encourage a team ethic, a percentage of incentives may be based on district and/or regional performance and on company performance.

Figure 8.14 shows some key considerations force sales force incentive plans.

Figure 8.14 Sales Force Incentive Plans

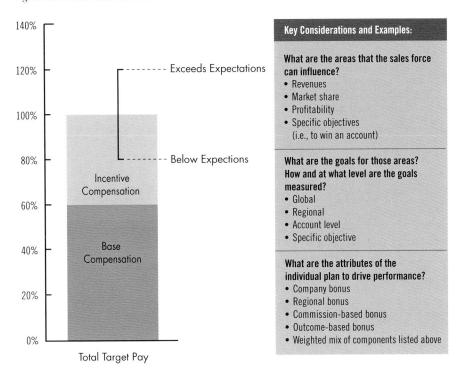

Source: Campbell Alliance.

Figure 8.15 provides an example of a sales force incentive plan based on achievement of specific objectives.

Monthly or quarterly performance reports let management and sales representatives know how their performance stacks up against incentive-pay benchmarks. These reports track the market share and/or sales volume for various products by territory, zip code, and sometimes individual. The sales team examines these reports for unexpected changes in prescriber behavior so that they can adapt their call plans if necessary.

Figure 8.15 Incentive Compensation—Example

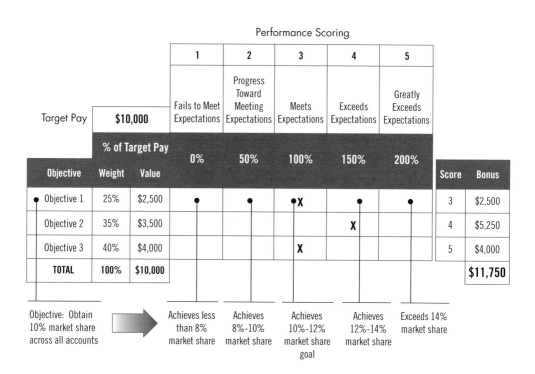

Each objective is weighted to represent a percentage of the total incentive target pay. Objectives are defined along a five-point scale that sets target performance and required criteria for achieving an incentive above and below the target on each objective. "Meets Expectations" should be challenging.

The plan will not differentiate performance if all participants can easily achieve scores in the three-to-five range.

Source: Campbell Alliance.

3. Operational Model for Sales

The sales forces are supported by headquarters groups that provide training, operational support, and analyses essential to defining organizational structure, incentive compensation, and sales performance.

Sales force training is designed to prepare well-educated professionals with the information and skills they need to understand customers, products, and regulatory issues well enough to represent the company to its customers.

Most pharmaceutical companies have an extensive support organization (Sales Operations) to communicate with representatives and ensure they have the tools, materials, and information needed to carry out their responsibilities. This support function provides promotional materials (e.g., detail pieces, samples), oversees field-based automation systems, and coordinates a fleet of company cars.

A number of important sales management functions, including Sales Analytics, report to Sales Operations. These functions define the appropriate size, structure, and alignment of the sales force; develop the incentive compensation program; and generate sales reports for each territory. A dedicated Field Communications group is available to help by sending the sales force promotion materials and other information as needed. (See Figures 8.16 and 8.17)

Figure 8.16 Operational Model for Sales

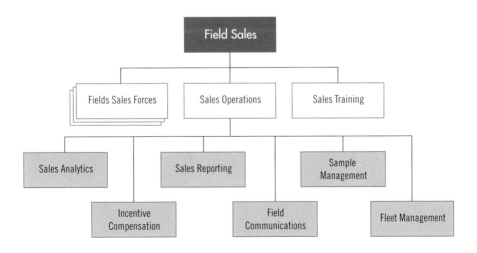

Source: Campbell Alliance.

Figure 8.17 Descriptions of Functions

Function	Role
Field Sales Forces	• Responsible for delivering direct promotion to physicians and other customers involved in drug selection • Often include local management (DMs or RMs)
Sales Training	• Responsible for initial and ongoing training for representatives and DMs
Sales Operations	
Sales Analytics	• Responsible for sales force sizing, structure, and alignment and other analytic functions, such as measuring customer response to promotion
Incentive Compensation	• Charged with development and implementation of incentive programs that align sales forces to company goals and objectives
Sales Reporting	• Responsible for performance reports that are distributed to both sales representatives and management, including analysis of performance vs. that of peers
Field Communications	• Responsible for responding to requests for promotional materials and information, as well as assistance with sales force automation (SFA) and other tools
Sample Management	• Responsible for ensuring field access to samples for distribution and ensuring compliance with PDMA regulations
Fleet Management	• Responsible for procurement and maintenance of company cars used by the sales forces

Source: Campbell Alliance.

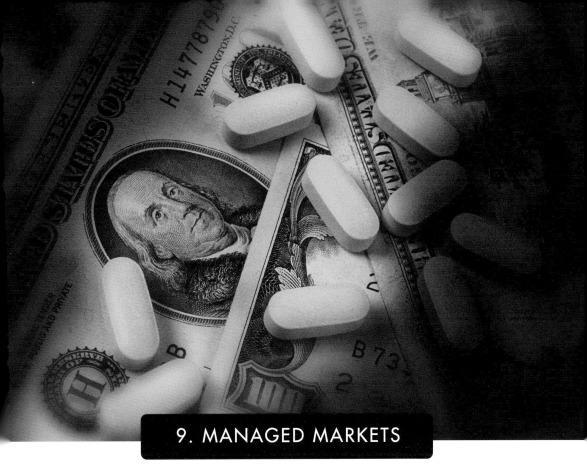

9. MANAGED MARKETS

1. The Importance of Managed Markets

2. A Closer Look at Managed Markets

3. Operational Model for Managed Markets

BUSINESS CASE: Forest Laboratories Finds Success in Crowded Markets

Forest Laboratories was a late entry in 1998 into the antidepressant market, which was one of the largest and fastest-growing pharmaceutical markets in the US. The category was full of well-established competitive products, such as Eli Lilly's Prozac®, Pfizer's Zoloft®, and GlaxoSmithKline's Paxil®. Prozac had been on the market since 1988, while Zoloft and Paxil were introduced in 1991 and 1992, respectively. The drugs, including Forest's new drug Celexa®, are known as selective serotonin reuptake inhibitors (SSRIs), which, along with selective norepinephrine reuptake inhibitors (SNRIs), were the physician-favored treatment for depression because they offered once-a-day dosing and fewer side effects than other antidepressants.

Through the efforts of its Managed Markets function, Forest successfully made the case with managed care organizations (MCOs) that Celexa was an efficacious product with a competitive price. This positioning enabled the product to obtain solid access and reimbursement from MCOs.

Thanks in part to its managed care positioning, Celexa went on to become a blockbuster drug for Forest. The drug was launched in September 1998, and by June of 1999 it represented 7.8% of new prescriptions written for SSRIs. It continued to gain share, growing to as much as 17.5% of the total prescriptions in the SSRI/SNRI market in August 2002, for approximately $1.5 billion in annual sales.

Forest is also using this strategy—offering a product that is perceived as one of the best in its class at an aggressive price—for other drugs:

- Lexapro®, Forest's replacement product for Celexa, was launched in the same crowded antidepressant market in September 2002 and has grown to 16.7% of the SSRI/SNRI market, for approximately $1 billion in annual sales.

- Forest has also been very successful in helping Sankyo Pharma launch the hypertension drug Benicar® in a very crowded class and in competition with several larger organizations. Benicar was launched in 2002 and has achieved 9.4% total prescription share within its category.

Source: Forest Laboratories.

172

1. The Importance of Managed Markets

The Managed Markets function in a pharmaceutical company is responsible for the company's relationships with its largest corporate and government accounts, which influence billions of dollars in drug usage each year. By 2006, those corporate and governmental accounts will pay for 80% of US prescription spending in aggregate.

Although the term "managed care" is sometimes used as a substitute for "managed markets," the account base includes far more than MCOs. Managed Markets serves many distinctive customer segments, including the Veterans Health Administration, the Department of Defense, state Medicaid programs, and emerging Medicare drug benefit sponsors. Some accounts—such as hospitals, staff model HMOs (e.g., Kaiser Permanente) and some large long-term care facilities—buy drugs from pharmaceutical companies and take physical possession of them, receiving discounts from the company on these drugs. Others, including pharmacy benefit managers (PBMs) and MCOs, influence drug selection through incentives and communications to prescribers and patients. Such accounts receive pricing rebates on aggregate purchases of drugs by their patients. (See Figure 9.1)

Many managed markets relationships are governed by specially negotiated contracts in which drug companies offer rebates, discounts, or special services in exchange for favorable positioning on a formulary—an MCO's list of preferred drugs, as discussed in Chapter 3, Pharma Customers—or increases in sales or market share. These contracts are constructed with detailed specifications as to terms of eligibility, rebate type and amount, formulary position, status accorded competitive products, and compliance with the contract. Ideally, improvements in sales or market share are required before the pharmaceutical company pays discounts and incentives to the managed markets account.

In addition to working with private payers, Managed Markets also oversees relationships with government customers such as Medicaid and Medicare, which for certain populations are entitled to special pricing based on statutes or regulations rather than individually negotiated contracts.

Some Managed Markets groups also manage relationships with Trade entities that supply drugs to their other customers: retail pharmacies and wholesalers. Trade and Distribution is discussed in Chapter 11, Distribution.

Figure 9.1 Managed Markets Segments

Segments	Physical Possession of Prescription Drugs
Managed Care (MCOs and MBHOs, or managed behavioral health organizations)—May cover both commercial (private) and government-funded patients	Generally no, unless they own their own pharmacies (e.g., staff-model HMOs)
PBMs—Serve indemnity as well as managed care insurers, self-funded employer groups, and government programs	Yes, if they also run a mail-order pharmacy
Employers—Purchase insurance for employees or self-insure	No
Medicaid	No
Medicare	No
Hospitals, clinics, and large long-term care facilities	Yes
Group purchasing organizations and other buying groups	No—simply negotiate terms for their members
Federal markets (Veterans Affairs, Department of Defense)	Yes—operate depots and hospitals that supply/use drugs
Trade*—Includes wholesalers, the corporate offices of retail pharmacies, specialty pharmacies	Yes—serve as the supply chain for most drugs

* Trade entities typically purchase prescription drugs in large quantities at volume discounts, and as a result, some companies include Trade in their Managed Markets coverage. However, Trade entities do not have the effect on prescription-drug demand that institutions that use drugs (e.g., hospitals and clinics) or pay for them (managed care and PBMs) do.

Source: Campbell Alliance.

2. A Closer Look at Managed Markets

The goal of Managed Markets is to achieve and maintain profitable formulary access or position across key customer segments. To achieve this goal, Managed Markets focuses its strategy on three elements:

- Selecting key accounts that are in a position to drive product demand

- Gaining formulary access or favorable reimbursement for products from those accounts

- Leveraging formulary access, favorable reimbursement, or other programs to encourage increased prescription writing and product use (also known as "pull-through") within that account through coordinated efforts with sales, hospital representatives, account managers and Marketing in the case of very large accounts

In defining the bounds of an appropriate strategy, Managed Markets works to achieve strong sales without unduly sacrificing revenue.

The Managed Markets function can be divided into three primary functions. Managed Markets Marketing determines the overall strategy for managing the company's relationships with its largest accounts. Managed Market Sales is responsible for achieving the strategic goals at key accounts and for seeking new opportunities within those accounts. Contract Management is responsible for administering the contracts and paying rebates to key accounts. (See Figure 9.2)

Figure 9.2 Overview of Managed Markets Function

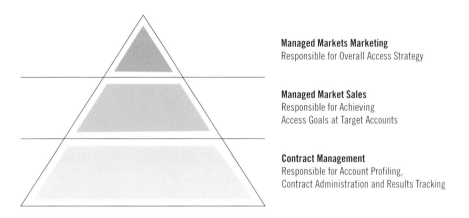

Managed Markets Marketing
Responsible for Overall Access Strategy

Managed Market Sales
Responsible for Achieving
Access Goals at Target Accounts

Contract Management
Responsible for Account Profiling,
Contract Administration and Results Tracking

Source: Campbell Alliance.

Managed Markets Marketing

Managed Markets Marketing often collaborates with Finance and Marketing to define the contracting policies that best support the company's strategy and tactics. As illustrated in Figure 9.3, the contracting policy will specify how key accounts are selected and managed, how contracts with those key accounts are developed and reviewed, which products are eligible for contract pricing, the range of discounts or rebates for those products, and a means to administer programs and measure the profitability of the accounts. A general strategy also is formulated to identify target accounts and define access objectives for particular products. Managed Markets Marketing then uses this policy to identify key accounts and to create a marketing program for each of those accounts.

Figure 9.3 Managed Markets Contracting Policy

Component	Explanation
Roles and Responsibilities	• Assigns the various roles and responsibilities for relationships with key accounts to Managed Markets, Field Sales, Legal, Finance, and Marketing
Account Management	• Describes the methodology for segmenting the accounts
Contract Eligibility	• Describes the conditions that an account must satisfy to receive favorable pricing or rebates
Contract Terms and Development	• Describes the process for developing, reviewing, and approving contracts with key accounts
Pricing and Incentives	• Determines which products are eligible for contract pricing • Determines the appropriate range of discounts, rebates, and incentives that can be offered to an individual account or on individual products
Contract Performance Profitability	• Determines the metrics for evaluating performance and profitability of a key account
Validation and Payment	• Specifies the utilization reports or other proof that an account must submit to qualify for a rebate (discounts are given on purchase invoices for those key accounts that take possession of product)
Dispute Resolution	• Specifies the guidelines for handling disputes on rebates

Source: Campbell Alliance.

Not all customer segments, and not all accounts, are of equal importance. Part of formulating the strategy is identifying the influential accounts—both in terms of size and degree of influence over prescribing patterns—that merit an investment in relationship building. (See Figure 9.4)

Some brands are so clearly superior and in such great demand among prescribers that they practically "sell themselves." In response to such demand, managed markets accounts are likely to offer access to the brand, even if the pharmaceutical company does not negotiate special pricing or offer special programs.

On the other hand, "me-too" drugs—drugs that are modified versions of existing medications—may not be covered at all, unless the pharmaceutical company's Managed Markets group makes the products more desirable through higher discounts or rebates.

Figure 9.4 Summary of Key Account Strategy

Prioritization of Accounts

- How many covered lives does the account insure?

- How much influence does the account have over drug choice?

- What do we know from past experience with this account?

Formulary Status

- Does this drug need a favored formulary status to succeed in this account?

- What formulary status is the account likely to grant?

- What formulary status do competitive products have?

- Can this drug displace or earn equal status with the currently favored drug?

Reimbursement

- No coverage

- No coverage with prior authorization requirement

- On formulary but non-preferred

- On formulary, preferred with other products

- On formulary, sole preferred drug

Source: Campbell Alliance.

Managed Markets Sales

While the centralized Managed Markets Marketing function sets general policy and strategy, Managed Market Sales applies it. Managed Markets account managers regularly visit the offices of their clients, just as Sales representatives visit physician offices, and forge long-term relationships with important corporate customers. Specifically, account managers are responsible for helping to decide whether an account is appropriate for contracting, if so, customizing the contract to the account, and then coordinating pull-through programs to generate sales once the contract is in place. (See Figure 9.5)

Within the range of options consistent with Managed Markets Marketing strategy, account managers may determine what discounts and rebates or programs are appropriate for each account.

With the assistance of Contract Management, account managers maintain detailed account profiles with information critical to understanding both how important the account is and what approaches will be useful in trying to obtain access for the drug and utilization. (See Figure 9.6)

Contracts may include terms or conditions needed to earn rebates, such as eligibility, formulary status accorded competing products, or specific

Figure 9.5 Account Management

Managed Markets Marketing sets general policy, but Managed Markets Sales
is responsible for applying the general policy to individual accounts.

Account Strategy	Contracting and Programs	Pull-Through Coordination
• Develop strategies for securing the relationship • Contribute to decisions regarding whether to offer contractual price concessions	• Negotiate contracts and pricing for selected customers, adhering to pricing policy set by company • The contract will include terms or conditions for earning rebates, such as specific interventions to be performed, total sales, or market share • Work with the account on an ongoing basis to develop programs to improve market share	• Coordinate pull-through programs with Sales and Marketing in order to translate favorable reimbursement and access positioning into actual product purchases

Source: Campbell Alliance.

interventions to encourage pull-through. Alternatively, the company may simply stipulate performance expectations (e.g., market share performance) and work with the account on an ongoing basis to develop programs to improve market share. Although contracts may cover a company's entire portfolio, pricing is specified individually for each product.

Rebates and discounts are pivotal ingredients in building managed markets relationships, but they are not the only ones. Managed Markets also promotes the merits of the product, such as its efficacy, safety, economic, and compliance advantages, over those of alternative therapies.

With internal approval from the company, account managers can offer other programs to add value to the account, including those that encourage pull-through or programs to educate physicians on disease management. These value-added programs, which are usually tailored to the customer, are offered to encourage the use of the company's products and are designed to support the customer's clinical or business objectives.

For example, a company that sells anti-hypertensives may work with an MCO to develop an educational program to inform MCO members about the symptoms of hypertension and what to do if they experience them.

Figure 9.6 Illustrative Account Profile (simplified)

Account: Campbell Pharmacy Management   **Claims Processor:**   Self
              1 Pharmacy Way
              Morristown, New Jersey   **Mail Pharmacy:**   Self

Account Type: ☐ PBM   ☐ Carrier   ☐ HMO   ☐ Hospital System   ☐ Long Term Care

Alliances/Ownership: Independent
Book of Business: Size—30 million lives (20 million managed)

Employer Group	HMO	Carrier	Medicaid	Consumer Card	Unmanaged
50%	20%	0%	0%	10%	20%

Interventions Used

Formulary: ☐ Open   ☐ Two Tier   ☐ Three Tier   ☐ Client-specific

Therapeutic Substitution: *Via mail pharmacy*
Generic Substitution: *Via mail pharmacy*
Prior Authorization: *HMO clients only*
NDC Lockouts: *Rarely*
Drug Utilization Review: *Yes*
Pharmacy Incentives: *No*

Other Comments: *Strategic imperative to secure more HMO lives and impose tighter controls over employer book of business. Historically, this account has moved market share by 1% to 2% (in a competitive market) through therapeutic interchange programs.*

Source: Campbell Alliance.

Alternatively, an MCO or PBM can send mailings to physicians that suggest the use of specific anti-hypertensive drugs in certain circumstances, subject to FDA regulations. (See Figure 9.7)

Contract Management

The terms of Managed Markets contracts can be extremely complex. Because discount and rebate levels are often tied to sales volume or market share, Managed Markets needs to monitor a very large volume of prescriptions and purchases in order to track a customer's sales performance for each covered product and provide the appropriate discounts and rebates in exchange.

Managed Markets typically maintains dedicated operations and business systems groups to handle the task of administering all contracts with their ac-

Figure 9.7 Making the Case for Desired Access

Account manager defines access goal for each priority account

Account manager "makes the case" to important accounts for granting the desired access

Tactics

Promote drug's intrinsic merits
- Make presentations to convince account leaders of product benefits
- Build demand among participating physicians by having sales force aggressively detail product
- Publish and disseminate compelling clinical and pharmacoeconomic studies

Overcome worries about overuse
- Create an appropriate-use program that educates prescribers on limits of endorsed utilization

Help client manage patient health
- Create an educational program that account can disseminate to patients with the disease, in order to encourage patients to comply with recommended regimen

Provide discounts and rebates
- Negotiate contracts that offer discounts and rebates on the product

Negotiating contracts that offer discounts and rebates is only one option for pursuing desired reimbursement and access status.

If possible, Managed Markets would like to achieve the desired positioning without sacrificing revenue per sale.

If discounts and rebates are necessary, Managed Markets strives to improve profitability by minimizing rebates and/or tying their payment to specific performance milestones.

Source: Campbell Alliance.

counts. These groups, which are often referred to as Contract Management, make certain that contracts comply with company policy and that customers comply with the terms of their contracts.

Disputes over pricing and eligibility occur, and dispute resolution is another important Contract Management responsibility. (See Figure 9.8)

Contracted discounts and rebates may be absolute (that is, have a fixed price per product purchased or dispensed), performance-based (the amount of rebates and/or discounts are tied to the impact on product market share or sales

Figure 9.8 Template for a Managed Markets Contract

Section	Typical Content
General	• Contracting entities and contacts • Effective dates and renewal clause • Dispute resolution and termination • Terms of eligibility, including requirement that purchases be for the customer's "own use" to prevent resale of discounted product • Indemnification for product misuse • Audit rights (for company and customer) • Confidentiality
Contracted Products	• Contracted products and their identification codes • Competitive products (for market share contracts) • Formulary position of contracted and competitive products • Other promotional requirements (including restrictions on competitor promotions)
Pricing	• Price (average wholesale price or wholesaler acquisition cost) • Rebate or discount calculations • Payment terms • Administrative and/or late fees (if applicable) • Special pricing guarantees (e.g., Medicaid best price protection or a "most favored nation" clause specifying no corporate customer will receive a lower rebate or discount)
Attachments	• List of eligible members or health plans • Sample runs of pricing calculations • Sample reports

Source: Campbell Alliance.

volume), or both. In the performance-based case, customers receive a small per-unit rebate and are also eligible for an additional rebate based on market share performance.

In setting pricing for accounts, Managed Markets has a legal obligation to offer government customers such as Medicaid and the Veterans Health Administration equally, if not more, advantageous terms as private-sector customers. Contract Management also oversees compliance with these regulations.

It is critical for Managed Markets to track contract impact as well as contract compliance, because the concessions they make in the hopes of generating increased sales represent a huge commitment by the pharmaceutical company. Contract Management tracks volume and market share performance for each account and product and compares these to the performance metrics specified in the contract. Typical performance metrics include in-plan market share growth, unit utilization, comparison with national or local market share, or comparison against some benchmark, such as national averages and/or prior period performance.

Some companies hold periodic formal reviews with their accounts to promote customer satisfaction, assess contract performance, and seek new opportunities to collaborate and grow the business relationship. This is typically the responsibility of the account manager working with Contract Management.

Collaboration With Sales to Drive Pull-Through and Utilization

Managed Markets ideally works hand-in-hand with Sales to ensure that the company gets maximum value from its managed markets contracts and programs—that is, realizes its goal of increased product sales and market share. Managed Markets (in conjunction with Marketing) must develop clear and compelling messages about product access and value-added programs that Sales can incorporate into selling efforts.

For instance, it is important that sales reps be able to respond knowledgeably to a physician query about their product's status on the formulary of payers important to the physician's patients. Some physicians may be interested in programs to increase the likelihood that patients will adhere to a complex drug regimen. Sales representatives must also be trained in how to overcome physician objections if a product is disadvantaged on important formularies. (See Figure 9.9)

Figure 9.9 Bringing the Sale Home

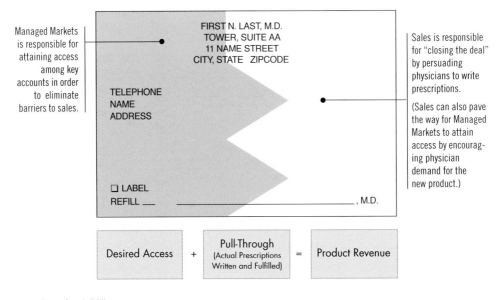

Source: Campbell Alliance.

3. Operational Model for Managed Markets

Managed Markets is a distinctly US-based function and, in global pharmaceutical companies, typically reports to the president of US Operations or the vice president or senior vice president of US Sales and Marketing.

As discussed above, Managed Markets typically includes Managed Markets Marketing, Managed Market Sales, and Contract Management. Trade Relations may be included within the function. Managed Markets works closely with Marketing and Sales, as well as with Legal and Finance, to ensure that contracts comply with pricing regulations and that the company's profit objectives are not compromised by overly aggressive pricing agreements.

Although pharma companies may have hundreds or thousands of contracts with major accounts, the Managed Markets function is typically handled by a relatively small number of individuals. A small company may have only five individuals working in Managed Markets, while a large company may have close to a hundred.

The creation of a dedicated Managed Markets function dates back to the 1980s, when the rise of managed care began in the US. (See Figures 9.10 and 9.11)

Figure 9.10 Operational Model for Managed Markets

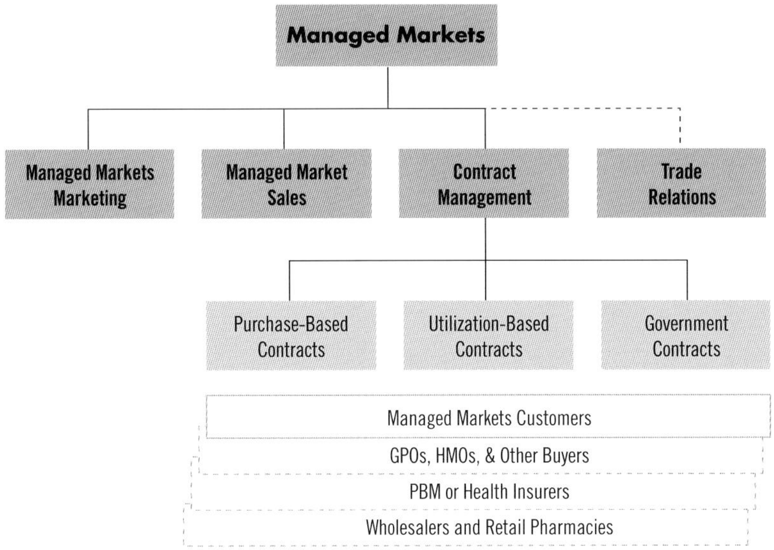

Source: Campbell Alliance.

Figure 9.11 Descriptions of Functions

Function	Description
Managed Markets Marketing	• Develops strategies and programs used to promote products to managed markets customers • Works with Account Managers to develop programs for customers, such as patient educational or compliance programs
Managed Market Sales	• Responsible for managing the company's relationships with major accounts-some of which are large enough to warrant the assignment of a dedicated, senior professional • Typically have selling backgrounds • Has broad responsibilities for contract negotiation, account performance, and profitability • Has input on rebates and discounts—but does not have unilateral authority to commit a large contract on behalf of the company • Works with Sales management to focus sales force on pull-through efforts
Contract Management	• Responsible for administering discounts and rebates, and eligibility for large accounts • Often has direct contact with accounts • Generally organized by type of contract (utilization-based or purchase-based) • Has a dedicated subgroup to handle government contracts and invoices, and price calculations
Trade Relations	• Responsible for relationships with trade partners, i.e., drug wholesalers and retail pharmacies • Typically handle prime vendor agreements with wholesalers and any special programs or performance incentives put into place with retail pharmacies

Source: Campbell Alliance.

10. MANUFACTURING OPERATIONS

1. The Importance of Manufacturing Operations

2. A Closer Look at Manufacturing Operations

3. Operational Model for Manufacturing Operations

1. The Importance of Manufacturing Operations

Manufacturing Process Development

Pharmaceutical companies that have discovered a promising drug candidate need to develop a robust, reproducible, and cost-effective manufacturing process for the drug.

They rely on Manufacturing Operations to manufacture the drug in a form that can be easily administered to trial subjects and patients and to package the product for mass distribution. For blockbuster drugs, ramping up to produce large quantities of each marketed product makes it possible for hundreds of thousands, or even millions, of people to have access to an effective drug treatment. Although niche products' production volume is much lower, many of these drugs face the same manufacturing hurdles.

Drug manufacturing is a complex, carefully regulated production process. There is a relatively limited number of manufacturing facilities. At these facilities, there are frequent manufacturing interruptions and product shortages owing to daunting challenges inherent in manufacturing pharmaceutical products.

Given the nature of the product, the stakes are also high. A batch that is not up to specified quality standards can be ineffective or even dangerous. This creates a need for stringent quality systems to prevent ineffective or dangerous drugs from being released to vthe market.

Labeling, Packaging, and Distribution

Manufacturing Operations also handles the labeling, packaging, and storage of packaged drugs and their distribution for clinical trials and to drug wholesalers and other customers who "buy direct" from pharmaceutical companies. Clinical trials are discussed in Chapter 5, Clinical Development, and distribution to wholesalers and trade is discussed in Chapter 11, Distribution.

Supply Chain Management

To make large-scale manufacturing and distribution possible, Manufacturing Operations needs to develop and manage a large network of facilities. The function charged with planning for and coordinating these resources is known as Supply Chain Management. This management function also includes raw material procurement. In an outsourcing environment, responsibility for procuring raw materials and components is distributed among the contractors. (See Figure 10.1)

Figure 10.1 Operations

Manufacturing, Distribution, and Supply Chain Management

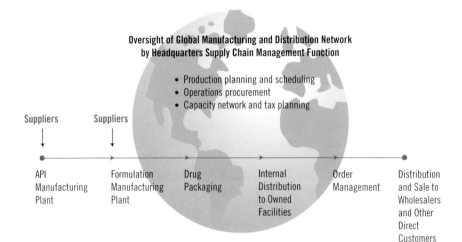

**Oversight of Global Manufacturing and Distribution Network
by Headquarters Supply Chain Management Function**

- Production planning and scheduling
- Operations procurement
- Capacity network and tax planning

Suppliers   Suppliers

API
Manufacturing
Plant

Formulation
Manufacturing
Plant

Drug
Packaging

Internal
Distribution
to Owned
Facilities

Order
Management

Distribution
and Sale to
Wholesalers
and Other
Direct
Customers

Source: Campbell Alliance.

Leaders in Supply Chain Management at large pharmaceutical companies oversee a global manufacturing and distribution network. To decide how to allocate resources across countries and regions—and how large a pool of aggregate resources is required—supply chain managers must be adept at:

- Business forecasting—Translating company sales forecasts into demand for units of product

- Production and capacity planning—Creating a roadmap for keeping pace with anticipated demand for various drugs

- Supply procurement—Obtaining the necessary materials for production and packaging

- Internal distribution logistics—Managing drugs' journey from manufacturing plants to internal storage centers

2. A Closer Look at Manufacturing Operations Activities

Chapter 2, "What Is a Drug?", introduced the concept that a marketed drug product consists of an API (active pharmaceutical ingredient) integrated into a formulation that facilitates administration and ensures stability of the drug product. Manufacturing processes are first developed during preclinical development and are gradually "scaled up" to commercial levels as clinical development progresses. Commercial manufacturing is the production of a drug in quantities sufficient for market demand. Scale-up to this point typically occurs prior to or during phase 3 clinical trials. Manufacturing Operations oversees manufacture of the API and the drug product, as well as the packaging, labeling, and distribution of the drug product. (See Figure 10.2)

Figure 10.2 Development and Scale-Up of Manufacturing Operations

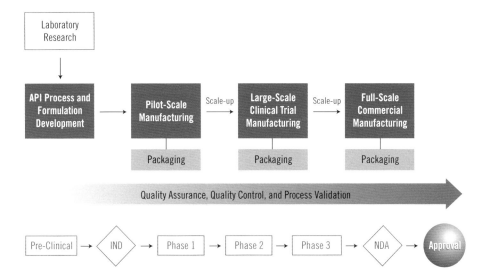

Source: Campbell Alliance.

Manufacturing Process Development

A company that is seeking permission to begin clinical trials must include in the Investigational New Drug Application, or IND, submitted to the FDA a description of the process for producing the API, full analytical characterization of the API, a description of the process for manufacturing the drug product, a description of the analytical test methods used for release testing, and documentation establishing the stability of both. It could be said that while Development defines the process of bringing a new drug to market, Manufacturing implements that process.

API Manufacturing Process

The API manufacturing process, which is usually patented, synthesizes the API through chemical or microbial means and isolates the product from contaminants by purification.

The manufacturing process is governed by master batch records, formulation records, and standard operating procedures (SOPs) designed to produce consistent, reproducible product batches. The batch record will specify conditions, such as time, temperature, and pH that need to be observed and recorded during production. The batch record will also document compliance with the defined manufacturing process and SOPs. The batch record is discussed in greater detail under Quality Systems in this chapter.

The API process may include special safety or product-handling features. Environmental protection, cleaning procedures, and techniques to control risks such as explosion and flammability may be incorporated into the chemical processing step. Worker and environmental safety are important issues that are always addressed in manufacturing. Facilities that use flammable or explosive solvents are required to perform this work in explosion-proof facilities. These requirements are common for the chemical industry at large and are overseen by the US Occupational Safety and Health Administration (OSHA). Cleaning is a separate issue that pertains to quality and purity of subsequent batches made in that same equipment.

Drug Product Manufacturing Process

Like API manufacturing, drug product manufacturing is governed by a master batch record and SOPs and documented in a batch record. The drug product batch record is separate and independent from the API batch record. Formulation is one component of drug product manufacturing and includes tableting, encapsulation, or lyophilization (removal of water content to enhance drug stability). Typically, formulations are patented, as are drug delivery systems. Unlike API manufacturing processes, drug product manufacturing processes are fairly straightforward and typically not patented. The drug product may be solid, semisolid, or liquid. (See Figure 10.3)

Figure 10.3 Physical Forms Drugs Can Take

Solid dosage forms	Tablets, capsules, powders, and granules
Semi-solid dosage forms	Creams, ointments, gels, suppositories
Liquid dosage forms	Solutions, syrups, suspensions, drops, nasal sprays
Sterile liquids	Eye drops, injectable perenterals

Source: Campbell Alliance.

An important consideration in drug product manufacturing is ensuring that the API is uniformly distributed. Typically, different dosage strengths of the drug product require varying amounts of API but a constant proportion of excipients (the substances that are present in defined concentrations to control pH and appearance, as well as to ensure proper quality characteristics and solubility).

Some drugs are administered via alternate delivery mechanisms such as a transdermal patch or inhaler. In these situations, it is critical for the delivery system to dispense the intended drug dosage consistently. When these systems are used, the company developing the new product usually partners with a drug delivery company to co-manufacture the product.

Pilot Plants

As noted in Chapter 5, Clinical Development, the manufacturing process for a drug is initially designed in process development, where researchers develop a small-scale manufacturing process that is repeatable and that generates a product of appropriate quality and purity. A process is designed with the intention that it be scalable and cost-effective. The manufacturing process is then transferred to pilot manufacturing facilities, where the process is scaled up to approximately one-tenth the predicted commercial scale; that is typically adequate for producing sufficient quantities of the drug for preclinical, phase 1, and phase 2 clinical trials. API process development and drug product formulation development occur throughout the drug development process, but are typically complete prior to initiating pivotal phase 3 clinical trials.

Pilot plants are typically separate from large-scale plants (although they may be in the same building). In addition, some facilities only have pilot or small-scale capabilities, and others only have large-scale or commercial operations. A pilot facility could become a commercial plant if approved for that purpose by the FDA.

Due to differences in the competencies and equipment involved, API manufacturing is performed in different facilities from those used for drug product manufacturing. The processes involved in API manufacturing and drug product manufacturing tend to be completely different and have different requirements. Producing an API involves highly specialized chemical and biological production processes and technologies, while producing a drug product involves precise control over content uniformity, as well as control of microbial and other forms of contamination. (See Figure 10.4)

Figure 10.4 API and Formulation Manufacturing

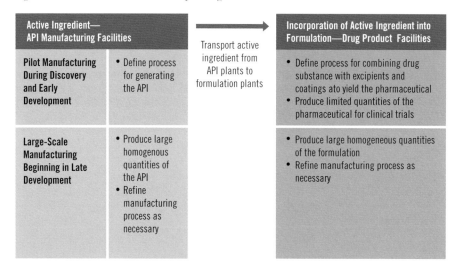

Source: Campbell Alliance.

Commercial Manufacturing

Manufacturing processes created during preclinical development are gradually scaled up to commercial levels as clinical development progresses. Commercial manufacturing is the production of a drug in quantities sufficient for market demand. Scale-up to this point typically occurs prior to phase 3 clinical trials.

Following refinements made during clinical development, the manufacturing process and product information is provided in a final form in the New Drug Application (NDA) or the Biologics License Application (BLA). The application provides a complete description of the manufacturing process, including in-process controls and critical process parameters, removal of process- and product-related impurities and contaminants, and validation of the process. The product is fully characterized by a range of analytical methodologies, and quality is determined and defined by analytical testing and the ability to meet predefined specifications. Specifications are required throughout development, but defined limits or ranges are not determined until later in development, when an adequate number of batches have been made to determine the capabilities of the process. Testing criteria typically get tighter as the development progresses.

Pharmaceutical companies use a hybrid of process manufacturing techniques. A single product can be generated through a series of chemical reactions, mixing techniques, and discrete manufacturing steps in which individual components are created separately and then assembled. This manufacturing approach is comparable to the production of cars and consumer electronics in that both the API and drug product manufacturing processes are continuous, but each process has a distinct completion point. In addition, the processes are designed to have discrete intermediate stopping points at which process intermediates can be held and stored, and pooling of resources can potentially be performed at different points.

Quality Systems

Developing a process for producing drug batches of consistent quality, purity, and safety is a tremendously involved and complicated undertaking. To ensure that drug products used by consumers and trial subjects meet quality standards, the FDA and the industry have developed detailed regulations known as Good Manufacturing Practices (GMPs). GMP regulations describe the manufacturing systems (processes, methods and procedures, controls, information systems, equipment, and facilities) required to produce safe and effective drug and bio-pharmaceutical products.

Pharmaceutical companies implement two major quality systems to ensure quality. Quality Assurance (QA) ensures the quality of the process by validating compliance to GMP; Quality Control (QC) ensures the quality of the product by testing and evaluating the manufactured product to ensure quality, purity, and safety.

Process Quality

Before a drug product can be commercialized, the process used to manufacture the drug must be validated. Any facility may be registered with the FDA, but registration alone does not imply regulatory compliance or quality. Validation demonstrates and documents that a process is reproducible and meets defined criteria. QA must verify and validate through audits and documentation that manufacturing systems repeatedly produce outcomes conforming to process and product specifications filed in the NDA. In order to validate the plant, a company must provide the results of at least three consecutive validation runs demonstrating that the process specifications filed in the NDA reproducibly yield a product that meets specifications.

The FDA will approve a defined and specifically validated process as part of the product approval process and will approve a facility to manufacture a new product by conducting a Pre-Approval Inspection (PAI). During this inspection, FDA inspectors review all aspects of the facility, process, and analytical validation, as well as documentation, training, and all aspects of GMP. There are situations in which a product-specific PAI is not performed. For example, if the FDA is already familiar with a manufacturing facility and process because the facility is using a similar process to make another marketed drug, then it may choose to forego inspection. However, the FDA reviews processes and facilities periodically (generally, every two years) and whenever the manufacturing process is altered.

There are three different levels of response and notification for changes in the manufacturing process:

- Minor changes are reported in an annual report filed with the FDA

- Moderate changes require FDA notification but do not require formal review and approval. This is known as a CBE-30, or Change Being Effected that will be implemented in 30 days.

- Major changes require full FDA review and approval before they can be implemented.

Failure to follow the change control procedures is a major GMP violation and can result in severe penalties such as a non-approvable letter for an NDA, or a warning letter or consent decree for a marketed product.

Even after processes have been validated, the pharmaceutical company closely monitors its manufacturing quality by regularly checking on adherence to agreed-upon processes and evaluating the drugs produced through those processes.

QA also reviews batch records (see Figure 10.5), which document manufacturing and packaging processes and results, to verify that each batch is created following the master batch record and the production process approved by the FDA.

Batch Records

A batch record is a specific set of instructions for manufacturing a pharmaceutical product and is used to control API and drug product manufacturing. It typically references SOPs needed to create the product and provides areas for written approval by critical stakeholders in the manufacturing process, including Manufacturing, Quality Assurance- and Quality Control.

Rigorous controls are in force for documenting processes and for making any changes in standard processes for a specific production run. Deviations to the process are investigated by Quality Assurance and are documented in deviation reports.

FDA inspectors scrutinize batch records to ensure that the manufacturing process is properly documented and that procedures were followed during the performance of a manufacturing run.

Figure 10.5 Batch Record Components

Component	Description
Batch Information	• Includes product to be made, size of batch, product date, lot/control information, and authorization
Formulation Records	• Describe ingredients and ingredient weights needed to formulate a product batch
Drug Product Release Testing	• Defines the anticipated characteristics of the drug product; for example, the release specifications for a tablet will describe the correct size, shape, weight, and color, while release specifications for a syrup formulation will describe the correct color, viscosity, and volume
Manufacturing Procedure	• Describes equipment needed, process steps (such as mixing), and quality checks to be performed during manufacturing; also defines step sequence and timing

Source: Campbell Alliance.

Product Quality

QC tests raw materials, in-process samples, and final products to ensure that the production process yields a product of appropriate quality, purity, and safety. During the manufacturing process, testing is performed at specified intervals. Prior to the release of product into distribution, testing is performed on a replicate sample from a batch or on a randomly selected product from the beginning, middle, and end of a drug product manufacturing run.

QC analytical tests confirm that the product meets the specifications in the IND or NDA. (See Figure 10.6) Samples from each batch are tested for conformity to specifications. QC testing is considered part of the manufacturing process, and test results are included in the documents reviewed by QA.

Figure 10.6 Quality Control Analytical Tests

Test	Assay	Objective
Quality	Appearance	• Verify the color, clarity, shape, scoring, trademarks, and other unique visual characteristics
	pH	• Confirm that a solution has been properly formulated and buffered
	Excipient content	• Confirm that excipient concentrations meet specfications
	Content uniformity	• Confirm that the batch is homogenous based a statistical sampling of the batch.
	Dissolution	• Test how quickly solid or lyophilized dosage form dissolves. Minor differences in processing parameters could have an impact on dissolution that would be undetectable by other means
Identity	Mass spectrometry	• Confirm identity by mass
	SDS-PAGE	• Confirm identity by comparison of product banding patterns to reference material
	HPLC	• Confirm identity based on chromatographic retention time
Potency/ Strength	UV	• Verify strength or concentration of proteins
	HPLC	• Verify strength or concentration of all products
	Bioassay	• Verify product potency or bioactivity
Purity	SDS-PAGE	• Confirm purity by comparison of product banding pattern relative to reference material
	HPLC	• Confirm purity by several chromatographic methods, including reversed phase, ion exchange, and size exclusion HPLC
Safety	Sterility	• Confirm sterility per USP for parenterals
	Bioburden	• Confirm bioburden per USP for non-sterile products
	Particulates	• Confirm particulate count per USP for parenterals

Source: Campbell Alliance.

Each production batch must be tested by QC and approved by QA before the product can be sold. QA and QC review, which are required for every batch run of a product, are time-consuming and labor-intensive. However, quality oversight is both a GMP requirement and a sound business practice. Great efficiency—and consistently strong quality findings—are essential if manufacturing productivity goals are to be met and product shortages averted.

External Regulation of Quality

External regulation of quality plays a significant role in pharmaceutical manufacturing. In addition to issuing documentation and process standards guidance, the FDA conducts regular reviews of manufacturing plants and batch records to identify any quality issues.

If an inspected facility fails to meet FDA standards, it can be shut down until problems are corrected. Regulatory shutdowns of manufacturing facilities can lead to product stockouts—a situation in which a pharmaceutical company cannot keep up with demand and therefore loses sales to competitive products. Even worse, critical drug shortages can occur, which is the FDA's primary concern in situations where there are no competing products.

Product Packaging

Clinical and commercial manufacturing conclude with product packaging. Like manufacturing, product packaging is scaled up throughout clinical development. (See Figure 10.7)

Packaging serves multiple purposes:

- Protecting the product from contaminants and environmental factors affecting shelf life

- Identifiably branding of the package in the eyes of customers

- Labeling the product in accord with FDA standards

- Tracking the product through numeric codes

There are three "layers" of product packaging.

Primary Packaging

Primary packaging actually touches the product and protects it from contact with contaminants. It includes bottles and caps, blister packs (cellophane-backed packages in which individual tablets or gel caps are encased in plas-

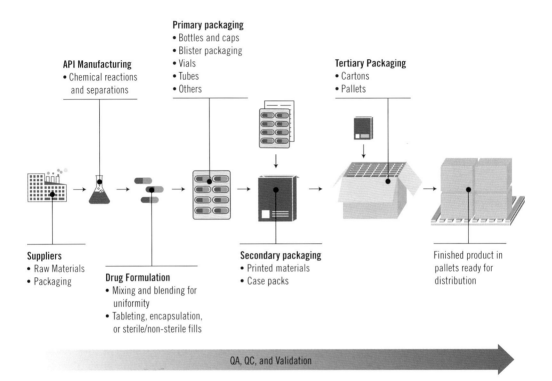

Figure 10.7 A Review of Manufacturing and Packaging

API Manufacturing
• Chemical reactions and separations

Primary packaging
• Bottles and caps
• Blister packaging
• Vials
• Tubes
• Others

Tertiary Packaging
• Cartons
• Pallets

Suppliers
• Raw Materials
• Packaging

Drug Formulation
• Mixing and blending for uniformity
• Tableting, encapsulation, or sterile/non-sterile fills

Secondary packaging
• Printed materials
• Case packs

Finished product in pallets ready for distribution

QA, QC, and Validation

Source: Campbell Alliance.

tic pouches), and unit-dose packaging (individually wrapped single doses frequently used in hospitals). The nature of primary packaging may affect a product's shelf life and, therefore, is selected to protect from light, humidity, and microbial or other contamination; planned primary packaging must therefore be described in an NDA. A change in primary packaging requires a refiling with the FDA.

Secondary Packaging

Secondary packaging includes boxes or cartons that hold one or more primary packages, and printed material that goes either in the package (the package insert—the folded-up sheet of paper that contains detailed information on the product) or on the box or bottle (for example, the use instructions on the back of a bottle of aspirin).

Secondary packaging during clinical development is typically handled specifically by a Contract Research Organization (CRO) that does much of the work by hand because of the diverse requirements for clinical trials.

Manufacturing Operations must be equipped to respond to changes in labeling (e.g., when the FDA-approved uses for a brand increase or new risks are discovered) and to alter the expiration date and lot number as new product batches are produced.

Label accountability is a critical quality function. Quality also ensures that the right product is getting the right label.

Tertiary Packaging

Tertiary packaging is the preparation of cases, cartons and pallets for shipping and distribution to customers.

Once the product has been packaged, it is ready for distribution.

Supply Chain Management

Supply Chain Management is responsible for developing the global production network and ensuring its ability to satisfy product demand.

Supply Chain Management shoulders three primary responsibilities: to ensure adequate overall capacity through network planning and outsourcing, to establish operational performance targets, and to manage procurement from suppliers of raw materials and services.

Capacity Planning

Supply Chain Management is responsible for ensuring that capacity is in place to support anticipated demand for a product or a portfolio of products. Because demand for a pharmaceutical product is subject to large fluctuations across the product's life cycle, a forecast typically looks ahead no more than five years. Such forecasts are developed for each product (including various formulations) based on input regarding brand outlook, the sales environment in each country in which the product is or will be sold, and the impact of new competing products (pipeline forecasts).

If Supply Chain Management anticipates that its current network will not keep pace with demand, it will propose investment in additional plants and technology or it will seek outsourcing partners.

Demand forecasts drive some decisions regarding the size and placement of manufacturing facilities, but tax and cost considerations also play a role. For example, companies may consider locating facilities in jurisdictions that have low corporate tax rates or offer tax incentives.

Long-term capacity planning is especially critical, and difficult, when new products are being launched. Most companies will try to validate processes and register equipment at existing plants to produce new products.

Supply Chain Management may also analyze the potential to outsource manufacturing or packaging responsibilities, depending on the internal capabilities of the company and its overall business strategy.

Outsourcing by large pharmaceutical companies is usually driven by capacity constraints or a decision to preserve the resources that would be required to build and maintain a particular manufacturing operation. Outsourcing by smaller pharmaceutical or biotech companies is driven usually by a business model that focuses on outsourcing as the way to minimize outlays for capital equipment and facilities.

Production Targets for Plants

Based on its understanding of market demand, Supply Chain Management is responsible for establishing more detailed business goals for Manufacturing Operations—productivity and financial objectives—and coordinating the activities of suppliers, plants, and distribution centers to achieve them.

Production forecasts are often developed for every product and assigned to plants that are registered to produce the product in question, based on available capacity. Because the cost of incremental production is low compared with lost revenue on sales missed due to drug shortages, pharmaceutical manufacturers regularly strive to produce volumes that exceed projected demand.

Typically, pharmaceutical manufacturers have every incentive to produce in excess of anticipated demand to avoid stockouts—that is, insufficient product on hand to meet customer requirements. This incentive is particularly marked because the rigors of drug quality control make it difficult to gear up production to meet unexpected needs—although, as the Cipro example at the opening of this chapter demonstrates, it is possible.

Companies sometimes redeploy inventory across distribution centers to accommodate high demand in a particular region.

Procurement

To maximize their purchasing power through discounts based on volume, most pharmaceutical companies centralize sourcing of raw materials. Typically, Procurement establishes global pricing contracts with suppliers, and local purchasing organizations within the company procure materials or services in accordance with these contracts. In other cases, for example when materials are needed in a specific locale, procurement will simply identify preferred suppliers and allow local purchasing leaders to negotiate with them.

Procurement for manufacturing purposes requires considerable foresight, because the company must use raw materials from the suppliers that it specified in the product NDA. Procurement tries to influence supplier selection during clinical development in favor of vendors from which the company already obtains other supplies. Concentrating purchases among a small group of proven suppliers makes the supply chain easier to manage and enhances purchasing leverage.

Procurement is intent on cost control from a big-picture perspective—not only the cost of the materials themselves but the impact of late or poor-quality materials on productivity and sales (e.g., rejected materials, operations downtime, product recalls). Pharmaceutical companies will often pay more to purchase materials from a supplier with a solid reputation for quality in order to avoid downstream issues such as recalls.

Pivotal Role of IT in Supporting Manufacturing

Information Technology, or IT, support is essential for effective management of the manufacturing process and distribution networks. Manufacturing IT is one of the few IT functions within a pharmaceutical company that manages large-scale information systems used for business transaction processing. Manufacturing relies on advanced information systems to support supply chain management and product manufacturing. These systems guide the manufacturing process and support compliance with GMPs and other regulatory requirements. They are used to plan, track, and measure the results of Manufacturing Operations.

A separate system, which facilitates order management, customer service, and distribution, may be managed independently of the manufacturing systems. The systems are generally well integrated, and are designed to comply with the regulatory requirements for manufacturing and product handling.

The major IT issue in manufacturing is computer validation and electronic records, as required by the FDA under its 21 CFR Part 11 regulations. These regulations are intended to permit the widest possible use of electronic records in the drug manufacturing process. (See Figures 10.8 and 10.9)

Figure 10.8 Overview of Operations Systems

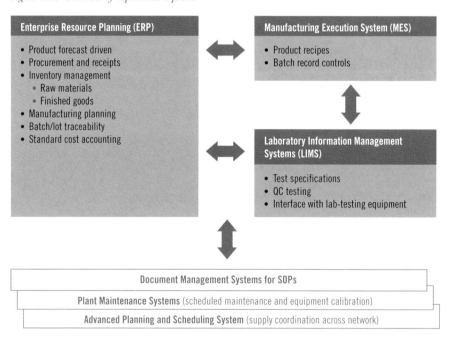

Source: Campbell Alliance.

Figure 10.9 Description of Operations Systems

System	Description
Enterprise Resource Planning systems (ERP)	• Translate production forecasts into requirements for raw material purchases, inventory maintenance, and manufacturing planning • Provide standard financial features (product costing, accounts receivable, and accounts payable) for use in calculating production costs • Provide batch traceability features so that company can link together the production chain—from the raw materials used to generate a product batch to the distribution centers where those batches are housed—as required by GMPs
Manufacturing Execution Systems (MES)	• Guide the manufacturing process based on the established product recipe and create the batch record, which contains details such as weight and dispensing data for raw materials, adjustments to ensure that the potency of the active ingredient is as specified, and equipment cleaning information • Facilitate, through batch records, periodic FDA audits • Link to the document management systems for SOPs
Laboratory Information Management Systems (LIMS)	• Support QC testing of the product • Contain tests specifications and track test results • Generally interface directly with laboratory testing equipment
Document Management Systems (DMS)	• Manage the document life cycles for SOPs, product specifications, and other operation documents • Provide rigorous controls over changes to approved documents • Ensure GMP and Part 11 compliance
Plant Maintenance Systems	• Schedule and track maintenance and recalibration of plant equipment • Help companies comply with GMP documentation requirements for equipment upkeep and alteration
Advanced Planning & Scheduling (APS)	• Forecasts demand and plan supply across an entire operations network

Source: Campbell Alliance.

10. Manufacturing Operations

3. Operational Model for Manufacturing Operations

Oversight of the manufacturing network and overall procurement management are typically centralized. Because a global perspective on network investments is essential, Supply Chain Management and Commercial Manufacturing are typically headquarters functions, which report up to a senior Manufacturing Operations executive.

The Procurement component of Supply Chain Management is highly specialized and regulated. As a result, it is usually managed separately from general corporate procurement, which purchases services and materials for day-to-day business operations, such as office supplies.

Manufacturing Operations IT typically reports to a global IT leader, but the staff will be assigned to work with country- or market-specific Manufacturing Operations teams on a full-time basis. Some IT professionals may report to country or market leaders, especially if they support systems involving order management and customer service.

Quality Management must be maintained as a separate function in order to promote independent judgment.

Quality Management may report directly to the COO or CEO. (See Figures 10.10 and 10.11)

API Manufacturing may be performed in dedicated plants located in sites around the world. API and drug product facilities are typically multi-product facilities. (Antibiotics, for example, are an exception and must be manufactured in separate, dedicated facilities to avoid cross-contamination.)

Manufacturing Operations for drug products are often organized geographically by region (for example, the Americas or Europe).

Most companies have distribution centers all over the world, and local market affiliates generally decide how much product (in correct local packaging) will be maintained in inventory. Each country typically manages its own distribution centers, with local market leaders placing internal "orders" to Manufacturing for product as needed.

For the US, which is generally the largest market, most companies try to operate distribution centers that have access to either the East or West Coasts to supply wholesalers and direct customers in all 50 states.

Figure 10.10 Operational Model for Manufacturing Operations

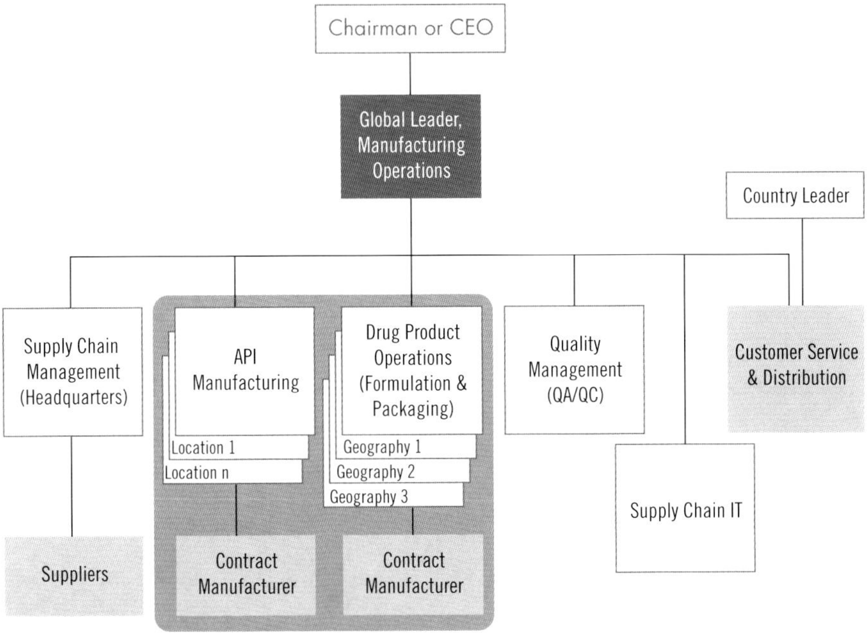

Source: Campbell Alliance.

Figure 10.11 Descriptions of Functions

Function	Description
Supply Chain Management	• Plans short- and long-term capacity and manages relationships with suppliers • Usually controls product movement between plants and distribution centers
API Manufacturing	• Produces APIs
Drug Product Operations	• Produces drug products and performs packaging and labeling
Quality Management	• Provides QA oversight and QC testing throughout the manufacturing process
Supply Chain IT	• Provides IT support for supply chain management and commercial manufacturing
Customer Service & Distribution	• Within country markets, handles order management (sales, receivables, returns) and customer service for all direct purchasing customers

Source: Campbell Alliance.

Outsourcing

Because drug manufacturing is so difficult to do well and the fixed costs associated with maintaining plants are so high, pharmaceutical companies frequently outsource manufacturing activities to contract manufacturing organizations (CMOs). Outsourcing is very common for small companies and biotech companies, and its use varies across big pharma.

If "owned" capacity registered to make the product in a given country is insufficient to meet demand in that country, a company might contract with a CMO for extra capacity.

Packaging is sometimes outsourced to ease efforts to address local regulations and differences in native languages and approved labels.

Many companies also outsource an internal distribution network to move product from plants to regional warehouses or distribution centers. (See Figure 10.12)

Figure 10.12 Role of Commercial Manufacturing Organizations

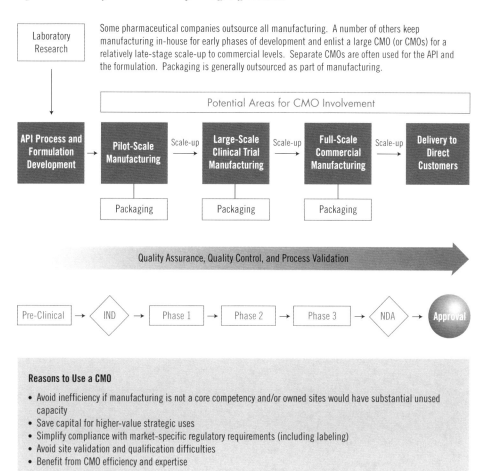

Some pharmaceutical companies outsource all manufacturing. A number of others keep manufacturing in-house for early phases of development and enlist a large CMO (or CMOs) for a relatively late-stage scale-up to commercial levels. Separate CMOs are often used for the API and the formulation. Packaging is generally outsourced as part of manufacturing.

Reasons to Use a CMO

- Avoid inefficiency if manufacturing is not a core competency and/or owned sites would have substantial unused capacity
- Save capital for higher-value strategic uses
- Simplify compliance with market-specific regulatory requirements (including labeling)
- Avoid site validation and qualification difficulties
- Benefit from CMO efficiency and expertise

Source: Campbell Alliance.

10. Manufacturing Operations

207

11. DISTRIBUTION

1. The Importance of Distribution

2. A Closer Look at Distribution

3. Operational Model for Distribution

The US subsidiary of a worldwide pharmaceutical company was preparing for a February 2004 launch of its new dermatology product. The company had products in several major categories in the US, including immunology, cardiovascular and anti-infectives, but it would be entering the dermatology category for the first time.

Fortunately, the market conditions for the new product were favorable. There had been no major advances in treatment of the disease state for over 30 years, and both physicians and patients were leery of the existing standard because of possible side effects. The nearest direct competitor was a year or two away from commercialization. As the company refined its commercial launch plans, its Distribution function became increasingly involved. Prior to commercial launch, the product would need to be launched into the various trade channels that would eventually supply product to patients.

Distribution crafted a trade launch plan, including a budget, to move its product onto store shelves. Approximately six months prior to estimated product approval and subsequent launch, Distribution began to prepare the trade channel for the product launch. The company's objective was to ship product to 100% of the wholesale channel and to reach 65% of the retail channel. To attract wholesale participation, Distribution offered discounts and allowances, as well as favorable timing on payments. To attract retail participation, Distribution offered favorable stocking terms and programs, in addition to a concerted communications effort to notify major retail outlets of the new product offering.

In January 2004, the company shipped $15 million of product to wholesalers in preparation for the February product launch. Within 70 days, 65% of the product had moved into retail stores. By the end of the first year, sales were 10% higher than planned. The company attributes its success to a combination of factors:

- A new treatment entity in an underserved market
- A reasonable launch program, fully budgeted
- Dedicated sales team calling on a targeted specialty

Source: Campbell Alliance.

1. The Importance of Distribution

Distribution is designed to move a high-value and compact product efficiently through a complex customer network. Getting a drug product to the patients who need it in a timely manner without inducing either gluts or shortages is not easy.

The catalog of drugs available in the US consists of 11,000 drugs (of which 2,800 are FDA-approved prescription drugs) produced by about 500 manufacturers.

To further complicate matters, patients receive those products through a complex network of commercial sources, including approximately 37,700 independent and chain pharmacies, 62,300 clinics, 9,500 hospital pharmacies in the 6,000 US hospitals, and 14,700 mass merchandisers and supermarkets in the US. (See Figure 11.1)

Figure 11.1 Network of Patient Access Points

Selected Patient Access Points	Number in US
Chain Pharmacies	19,800
Independent Pharmacies	17,900
Hospital Pharmacies	10,000
Food and Mass Merchandisers (primarily over-the-counter drugs)	14,700
Mail Order and Internet Pharmacies	370
Home Health Care	5,400
Clinics	62,300
Other (includes HMOs, PBMs and specialty pharmacies)	1,200

Source: IMS Health, IMS National Prescription Audit Plus™, 2004.

As if the various access points in the customer network were not already complex enough, the drugs are subject to extensive controls and regulations to ensure product safety: products must be stored in adherence to the manufacturer's specifications; narcotics and other drugs with the potential for abuse must be stored, monitored, and sold in adherence with regulations for controlled substances; vaccines and antidotes are required in sufficient quantities to prevent outbreaks of disease; and expired or faulty products must be removed from commerce and destroyed or reclaimed.

The distribution channels provide the critical link between pharmaceutical companies and the myriad locations where drug products are dispensed. Pharmaceutical companies also rely on distribution channels, particularly wholesalers, to handle the customer service function for their products. (See Figure 11.2)

11. Distribution

Figure 11.2 Overview of Pharmaceutical Distribution System

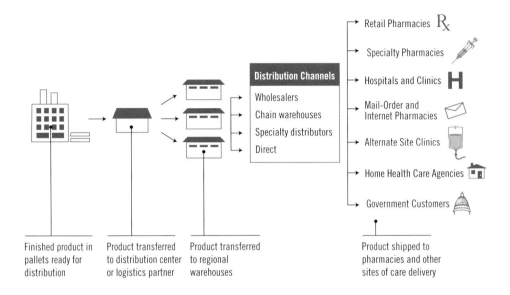

Source: Campbell Alliance.

2. A Closer Look at Distribution Activities

Pharmaceutical companies distribute most of their product to end users through three primary channels—drug wholesalers, chain warehouses, and specialty distributors. These channels then distribute product to retail pharmacies, hospital pharmacies, mail-order pharmacies, physician offices, alternate site clinics, home health care providers and, at times, directly to patients. (See Figure 11.3)

Primary Channels

Drug Wholesalers

Wholesalers play a dominant role in the distribution system—approximately 80% of all prescription drugs sold in the US go through them. Wholesalers provide a cost-effective way for pharmaceutical companies to deliver and sell their prescription products. They buy large volumes of product from pharmaceutical companies for sale and distribution to the various distribution endpoints across the US. This function allows pharmaceutical companies to

Figure 11.3 The Role of Drug Wholesalers in the Pharmaceutical Supply Chain

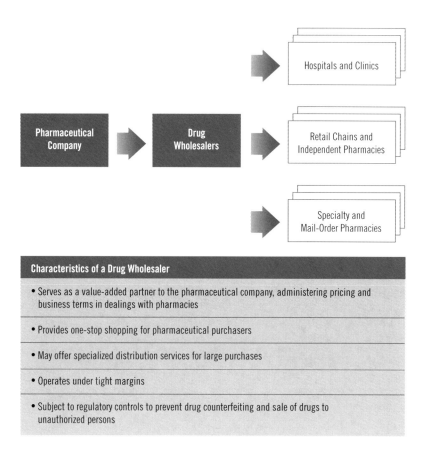

reduce their costs by shipping large volumes to a small number of centrally lo-cated warehouses instead of shipping small volumes to every pharmacy across the US. Likewise, the drug dispensers—pharmacies, for example—are able to purchase a wide variety of products from a single source in usable quantities, eliminating the need to contract with each pharmaceutical company or to receive large inventories of product.

Wholesalers deliver product to drug dispensers five to six days per week throughout the year. Further, wholesalers are able to deliver product to 90% of drug dispensers within 24 hours via a system of over 275 warehouse and shipping locations across the US.

11. Distribution

213

As intermediaries, drug wholesalers are positioned to provide additional value-added services to both drug manufacturers and to drug dispensers. For example, wholesalers monitor demand for pharmaceutical companies to ensure adequate product availability in the marketplace and often handle routine customer service issues. They also administer pharmaceutical companies' pricing and business terms in dealings with drug dispensers. In addition, they package or repackage products (a service to both manufacturers and dispensers); provide point-of-sale computer systems that help drug dispensers process prescriptions, submit reimbursement claims, and detect drug interactions; and extend credit to drug dispensers.

Wholesalers purchase products from pharmaceutical companies at the wholesale acquisition cost, or WAC, and make a profit by reselling products to buyers at a mark-up. Under certain circumstances, wholesalers sell a product to a buyer at a price lower than its WAC for that product. For example, a hospital or buying group may have negotiated a contract with a pharmaceutical company that specifies a special price on a product, but the hospital still purchases its products through a wholesaler. In cases like that, the wholesaler will submit a request to the pharmaceutical company for the difference in price. This request is called a chargeback and is a routine occurrence. Each year, pharmaceutical companies process millions of chargeback requests and remit hundreds of millions of dollars in chargeback payments to wholesalers.

Chain Warehouses

Chain stores typically distribute their drug inventory to their own retail stores through a centralized warehouse or series of warehouses. Most chains purchase their top-selling pharmaceutical products directly from the manufacturer at a volume discount. Other products are acquired as needed from wholesalers. The chain drug warehouses tend to have very good distribution capabilities for oral products, both solid and liquid, and limited distribution capabilities for controlled substances and injectables.

Specialty Distributors

Certain distributors have focused on a niche within the market and fill a gap left by traditional drug wholesalers, physician offices, and clinics. These specialty distributors typically provide products and services that require special product handling or special associated services. For example, a specialty distributor may specialize in products that need to be refrigerated or frozen, or in controlled drugs that require secure storage. These specialty distributors typically distribute products directly to physicians' offices, alternate site clinics, and hospitals.

In addition to their distribution services, specialty distributors can also offer large telemarketing capabilities that can be used to contact provider offices, checks product inventory levels, and provide additional promotion to their customers.

Manufacturers often provide special incentives to specialty distributors for sales-related activities because of their niche in the market. As a result, prices are sometimes below WAC with more flexible payment terms.

Patient Access Points

Specialty Pharmacies

Typically, specialty pharmacies deal with patients in therapeutic groups that require high-cost, injectable medications (chronic diseases such as HIV and Crohn's, for example). The pharmacies may manage programs at the request of the manufacturer. As part of the programs, the pharmacy may keep extensive lists of physicians and patient data, and, as licensed pharmacies, they can provide educational services, patient intervention programs, and counseling to physicians or patients. The pharmacies distribute product direct to a primary provider, home health agency or directly to the patient.

Specialty pharmacies typically receive their product from wholesalers or directly from the manufacturer.

Retail Pharmacies (Chain and Independent)

Most patients purchase their drugs from their local retail pharmacy. Retail pharmacies typically receive their drug inventories from drug wholesalers or, in the case of chain pharmacies, their chain warehouses.

These pharmacies fill prescriptions written by physicians or other prescribers, with substitution for products available as generics. Retail pharmacies usually dispense only a 30- to 60-day supply of medication, which allows them to keep low inventory levels, to monitor prescription usage in repeat customers, and to generate additional business when customers return for refills. Products offered by pharmacies tend to be in standard and familiar packaging, including tablets, inhalers, capsules, liquids, creams and ointments, and suppositories.

Hospital Pharmacies

Hospital pharmacies typically provide medications for patients under their care, whether the patients are being treated as inpatients or through outpatient clinics. The hospital pharmacies usually negotiate discounts with pharmaceu-

11. Distribution

tical companies, either directly or through group purchasing organizations. However, hospital pharmacies tend to rely on wholesalers for inventory. Inpatients typically receive unit-dosed products, while outpatients typically receive products in standard pharmacy sizes.

Mail Order and Internet Pharmacies

Mail order and Internet pharmacies provide bulk prescription fulfillment to patients, usually for chronic illnesses. These pharmacies typically receive their drug inventories from wholesalers or directly from the manufacturer in the largest commercial sizes available. These pharmacies then ship a 60- to 90-day supply of product to customers at a volume discount.

Many pharmacy benefit managers and managed care organizations utilize mail order and Internet pharmacies to dispense medication to their patients with chronic conditions.

Physician Offices

Physician offices typically carry a limited supply of inventory, including product samples left by pharmaceutical company representatives and vaccines or other injectables that need to be administered in physician offices.

Physicians tend to keep small quantities of vaccines and other injectables in inventory, preferring to replenish their supply frequently from specialty distributors or medical/surgical suppliers.

Alternate Site Clinics

Some alternate site clinics—such as emergency medical centers, dialysis centers, long-term care facilities, and outpatient clinics—tend to purchase their products through wholesalers, although many join group purchasing organizations for better prices. Products sold to these clinics are packaged generally in unit doses.

Home Health Care Agencies

Home health care agencies typically acquire products from local specialty pharmacies, since most products are purchased for specific patients under the direction of their physician. The agencies tend to assist patients with complex drug administration, such as injectable medications and tube feedings.

Direct Purchase Systems

Even though most customers purchase through wholesalers, pharmaceutical company order management and customer service operations are usually designed to allow customers to buy products directly if they prefer.

Important components of direct–purchase systems include capabilities for:

- Determining customer eligibility to make direct purchases (based on such factors as credit verification and verification of DEA permission to take possession of controlled substances)

- Processing and billing for orders, taking into account regulatory guidelines on pricing for that type of customer and any special contract price that has been negotiated

- Managing product movement—including shipping, returns, and product expiration

In addition to supporting business transactions, the customer service information systems usually track direct and indirect sales and have sophisticated interfaces with wholesalers for purposes of order processing and information sharing about customers, products, and prices.

Launching Products into Distribution

A key consideration in new product launches is getting product physically onto shelves or into the hands of patients. Working alongside Sales, Marketing, and Manufacturing Operations, Distribution creates a plan of distribution for a new product that addresses:

- The preferred method of distribution for the product

- Preferred pricing

- Product size, SKU, method of administration, storage requirements, and shipping methods

- Initial order quantities

- Fulfillment of orders

11. Distribution

3. Operational Model for Distribution

Logistics and Customer Service Functions

The Logistics and Customer Service functions are typically aligned with country or market leaders because customer mix, distribution networks, and product distribution requirements vary considerably from market to market.

Most companies have distribution centers all over the world. Local market operations generally decide how much product (in proper local packaging) will be maintained in their local inventory. In the US, most companies maintain sufficient distribution to deliver product across the continental US within 24 hours. With airborne and truck-based shipping alternatives available, many companies are able to achieve their distribution needs with a single distribution center located near a major shipping hub or two distribution centers (one to reach each coast).

Responsibility for managing the pricing relationships with the trade channels typically falls under Managed Markets, or, at times, the Sales function. The Trade Relations group will negotiate and monitor pricing contracts with direct purchasers, including wholesalers and group purchasing organizations. (See Figures 11.4 and 11.5)

Outsourcing—Third Party Logistics Partners

Some companies, usually start-up companies, contract with a third-party logistics partner to provide the required warehousing services and infrastructure. Among other services, the logistics supplier typically provides:

- Customer service
- Order fulfillment
- Inventory management
- Chargeback processing
- Returns
- Product tracking
- Accounts receivable
- Transportation management

The logistics partners also provide technology links between the pharmaceutical company client and major drug wholesalers and distributors to support the contracted services.

Figure 11.4 Operational Model for Distribution

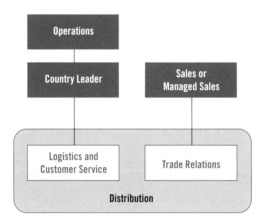

Figure 11.5 Description of Functions

Function	Description
Logistics and Customer Service	• Within country markets, handles order management (sales, order fulfillment and shipping, receivables, and product returns) for all direct purchasing customers
Trade Relations	• Frequently located within the Managed Markets group, negotiates pricing contracts with group purchasing organizations, wholesalers, and other trade organizations

11. Distribution

AFTERWORD

As you conclude your first reading of *Understanding Pharma*, I wanted to offer a few words about the journey you've taken.

I hope *Understanding Pharma* conveyed a strong sense of the pharmaceutical industry's complexity. As the pharma and biotech sector confronts a challenging regulatory and market environment, that complexity is only likely to increase

I hope we also managed to communicate the complexity associated with the complexity of a pharmaceutical or biotech company. People with vastly different backgrounds and roles must collaborate across functions to keep the enterprise on track.

You are one of those people. If you come away with only one message, it should be that your work makes a very significant contribution to your company's success. In some cases those contributions are very visible. Other equally critical roles have lower profiles. But there are no unimportant functions in pharma—only activities that are a mystery to people in other parts of the company. This book was written to dispel some of that mystery.

In any career, knowledge is power. No doubt, you have acquired and will continue to acquire a very sophisticated understanding of the function in which you work. Familiarity with other parts of the company enterprise will position you to work much more effectively with your colleagues each and every day and ultimately to serve a broader leadership role.

If this was your first reading of *Understanding Pharma*, I hope, and trust, that it won't be the last. I think you will find the book a valuable resource to turn to again and again for an overall industry perspective and practical function-specific information.

12. APPENDIX

1. Overview

2. Financial Management and Control

3. Human Resources

4. Information Technology

5. Legal

6. Other Corporate Functions

1. Overview

Like all major corporations, pharmaceutical companies have corporate functions such as Finance, Human Resources, Information Technology and Legal. These groups are largely responsible for ensuring management and financial control over operations and are instrumental in helping different functional areas carry out their day-to-day responsibilities. Corporate functions for pharmaceutical companies look and operate similarly to their peers in other industries, but they do have some unique characteristics. This chapter briefly discusses those characteristics.

2. Financial Management and Control

Financial Management and Control in the pharmaceutical industry is similar to that of other industries, but some accounting practices are unique to the pharmaceutical business.

Financial Management

Financial Management (Finance) for pharmaceutical companies is similar to the function in other industries, and it includes standard functions for financial planning, budgeting, recording transactions to ledgers, and reporting results internally and to stockholders. As in any major corporation, finance and accounting practices for pharmaceutical companies are guided by generally-accepted accounting principles (GAAP) along with Securities and Exchange Commission (SEC) guidelines for external reporting.

Most companies use a standard profit and loss (P&L) format to manage and report financials. Gross revenues (or gross sales) represent the total amount of revenue generated by the company. Net revenues are reported after deducting product returns, chargebacks, and rebates from gross sales. Gross profits are reported after deducting manufacturing costs (cost of goods sold, or COGS). R&D costs, selling, general and administrative costs (SG&A), and accounting for alliances with other companies are deducted from gross margins to calculate operating income. Finally, costs related to debt financing, taxes, and special items, such as exceptional costs related to mergers, are subtracted from gross profits to calculate net income (also called "the bottom line").

Accounting for alliances varies from deal to deal based on the structure of the deal and its terms. For example, royalty or licensing income from out-licensing deals would typically be reported as revenue, while a royalty or licensing expense from an in-licensing deal would be reported under COGS. Other deals may involve investments in the partner company or in joint ventures; in those cases, the accounting treatment can become more intricate.

While sub-ledgers (Accounts Payable, Accounts Receivable, Payroll, and others) in pharma companies are much like they are in other companies, some accounting practices are designed to record business transactions that are unique to the business.

The following are two such examples.

- Revenues are recorded when product is shipped to wholesalers or direct customers. Rebates, chargebacks, and product returns are recorded as adjustments to revenue.

- R&D investments are expensed as incurred, as opposed to appearing on the balance sheet as an asset.

Internal Audit

Most companies maintain Internal Audit teams that typically review all operations that can have a material or significant impact on a company's financials (in other words, all the operations that are described in this book). These teams are responsible for verifying the company's controls over business operations and record keeping systems, and they are often responsible for verifying controls on record keeping at customers, suppliers, and business partners. Internal auditors are independent, usually reporting to the chief financial officer (CFO). Their responsibilities are global, and they complement the efforts of Legal, Regulatory/Medical Affairs, Quality Management, and the CRAs that audit sites of clinical trials. (See Figure 12.1)

Operational Model for Financial Management And Control

As in any company, Finance is led by the company's CFO, who usually reports to the CEO or Chairman and sits on the company's board of directors and audit committee. Corporate Finance personnel are usually deployed throughout a company's operations and are often dedicated to R&D, Operations, and each affiliate (within a geographically based company). Corporate Finance personnel may be assigned to national or regional sales teams, as well as to brand teams. The remaining functions typically reside within Corporate.

Figure 12.1 Areas Typically Tested by Internal Audit

Area	Focus of Testing
General Operations	Transaction processing and controls for all operations that can materially affect financials, such as order management, contract administration, and procurement
Sales Force	Compliance with Prescription Drug Marketing Act (PDMA) regulations to prevent fraud and abuse
Pricing	Compliance with government pricing guarantees (Medicaid and Veterans Health Administration hospitals)
Wholesalers	Product handling, returns, and expirations, as well as contract pricing and eligibility
Hospitals and Clinics	Compliance with resale restrictions on product sold to hospitals and clinics
Pharmacy Benefit Managers and HMOs	Compliance with contracts (for example, monitoring formulary position)

Source: Campbell Alliance.

Figure 12.2 shows a typical organizational model for Financial Management and Control, while Figure 12.3 describes the key functions.

Figure 12.2 Operational Model for Financial Management and Control

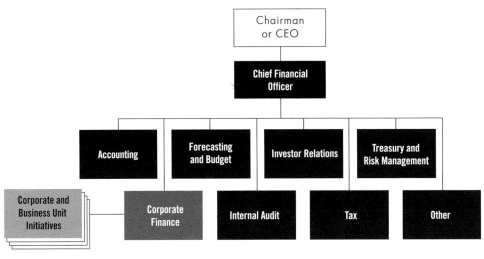

Source: Campbell Alliance.

Figure 12.3 Description of Functions of Finance Management and Control

Function	Description
Accounting	• Collect and analyze company financial information for monthly, quarterly and yearly reports to local and global management and investors
Corporate Finance	• Provide analysis for corporate and business unit initiatives • Review financing alternatives • Advise management on strategic mergers and acquisitions
Forecasting and Budgeting	• Prepare and analyze company-wide operating and capital forecasts and budgets
Internal Audit	• Review company operations to verify the company's controls over business operations and record-keeping systems • Verify controls on record-keeping systems of customers, suppliers, and business partners • Identify opportunities to improve processes
Investor Relations	• Manage communication between the company and its shareholders • May report directly to the CEO
Tax	• Coordinate and manage the company's tax planning
Treasury and Risk Management	• Manage the company's cash reserves to ensure adequate cash on hand to fund operations while generating interest on savings and investments • Manage accounts payable (including payroll) and accounts receivable • Manage the company's financial risk through financial instruments and insurance

Other	• A company may often include other functions within its Finance department:
	  • Portfolio Management (for a company with significant investment in other companies)
	  • Procurement/Purchasing
	  • Real Estate Management (for a company with significant investment in real estate)
	  • Travel

Source: Campbell Alliance.

3. Human Resources

Like any other corporate function, Human Resources, or HR, plays a critical role in the company's success. While companies will vary in their implementation of the HR function, HR typically is responsible for obtaining and maintaining an effective workforce for the company's strategic and day-to-day operations. In short, HR's mission is to recruit, develop and retain the talent necessary for the pharmaceutical company to operate successfully, as shown in Figure 12.4.

12. Appendix

Figure 12.4 HR Overview

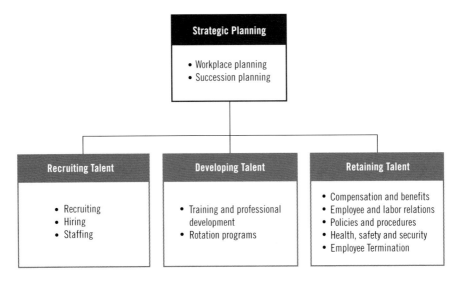

Source: Campbell Alliance.

The responsibilities of HR departments within pharmaceutical companies are fairly consistent with those of HR departments within other industries. Most differences are the result of the complexity of the pharmaceutical industry, coupled with the global nature of the business. The HR department must serve a company functioning within an industry that includes science and medicine, bulk manufacturing and packaging, logistics, marketing and sales, customer support, and significant government regulation. Accordingly, pharmaceutical companies require a very broad set of skills and competencies to operate. For example, roles within a pharmaceutical company include scientists, microbiologists, lawyers, physicians, plant engineers, administrative assistants, accountants, and market researchers. Human Resources must recruit, develop and retain talent across those varying roles.

Operational Model for Human Resources

HR generally reports to an executive vice president or chief human resources officer, who in turn, reports directly to the CEO.

HR staff is usually centralized, but because of its role and responsibility across the company, HR often is divided into smaller, more manageable groups assigned to particular divisions or business units and may be co-located with the businesses that they support. For example, some pharmaceutical companies use separate HR teams to support the commercial business (including Marketing, Sales, Managed Markets and Corporate), Research and Development, and Manufacturing Operations. See Figures 12.5 and 12.6 for a typical operational model for Human Resources and a description of its key functions.

Figure 12.5 Operational Model for Human Resources

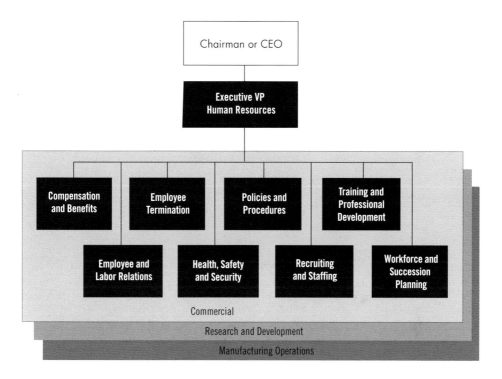

Source: Campbell Alliance.

Individuals within HR tend to be either HR generalists, with roles spanning across the entire department, or HR specialists, with roles focused on specific functions such as savings plan analyst or training manager.

HR often uses external agencies for support, including outside lawyers for assistance with employment and labor law, or external recruiting firms and temporary staffing agencies for assistance with staffing and recruiting. Also, many pharmaceutical companies outsource certain aspects of Human Resources, including the payroll aspect of Compensation and Benefits and many aspects of Training and Professional Development.

Figure 12.6 Description of Functions of Human Resources

Function	Description
Compensation and Benefits	• Evaluate, maintain and negotiate the compensation and benefits offered to employees • Recognize and reward individual, team and company-wide performance • Work with Accounting to administer the company Payroll
Employee and Labor Relations	• Serve as a liaison between employees and management to communicate issues such as employment concerns, employee satisfaction, and company-wide change • Negotiate with and maintain relations with employee labor unions where applicable
Employee Termination	• Terminate employees, when appropriate, in a dignified professional manner that retains goodwill and limits legal exposure
Health, Safety and Security	• Evaluate and maintain a safe and secure working environment • Administer Occupational Safety and Health Administration (OSHA) guidelines to foster a safer workplace
Policies and Procedures	• Develop, implement, and maintain policies and procedures that create a fair, effective and professional workplace
Recruiting and Staffing	• Design and implement a recruiting and staffing strategy to bring the required talent to the company
Training and Professional Development	• Design and implement training and professional development programs to prepare employees for their roles and responsibilities, to help employees transition to new roles and responsibilities, and to cultivate talent within the company • Work with Sales to create and maintain an effective sales force
Workforce and Succession Planning	• Work with the company's business units to identify short- and long-term goals and forecast the skills and labor required to achieve those goals • Often determine whether to meet needs internally or to outsource services • Identify current and future key positions within the company and then develop processes to recruit or develop candidates to fill those positions

Source: Campbell Alliance.

4. Information Technology

Information Technology (IT) delivers advanced information systems used for scientific, clinical, and analytical applications.

IT supports every function of a pharmaceutical company. Unlike some other industries, in which IT is largely responsible for systems that support internal business processes, a pharmaceutical company's IT group is additionally challenged to provide specialized systems that support scientific, clinical, and analytical processes that are used for drug discovery, clinical development, and market analysis. In addition, pharmaceutical companies' systems are often critical to ensuring their compliance with regulations.

Clinical Systems

Clinical systems are designed to collect data from trial sites and support the preparation of new drug application (NDA) submissions. Systems for clinical development must be able to accept information from sites all over the world and stage the information for analysis and reporting. Once the data have been collected and scrubbed (the industry term for making the data anonymous), specialized, large-scale systems are used to develop statistical summaries. In addition, as information is collected and documents are organized for NDA submissions, highly controlled document management systems are used to track documents and changes in a manner that complies with FDA electronic document handling and control regulations.

Commercial Systems

Commercial systems integrate and deploy information about promotional activity and customer behavior. Most companies today have Sales Force Automation (SFA) systems, which are used by their sales forces to access information about their customers' prescribing or usage behavior.

Most companies are strategically expanding the features of SFA systems to provide large-scale Customer Relationship Management (CRM) solutions to track all aspects of a company's relationship with important customers. This effort ideally involves collecting Clinical Development, Medical Affairs, and Sales activity and other internal information, and linking it with vendor-supplied data about customer and market behavior. This information can provide the basis for territory alignment and for sales force size and structure. Great care is taken to comply with applicable federal legislation and state privacy laws.

Operations Systems

Operations and Corporate functions often rely on transaction-based Enterprise Resource Planning (ERP) systems that are designed to help the company meet regulatory requirements.

Operations systems, including Manufacturing, Distribution, and Customer Service, are largely transaction-oriented and similar to many other companies. Except for the quality and regulatory features, these systems are similar to those used by other process manufacturing companies.

Corporate systems for accounting, finance and HR are similar to those used in other industries, but are adapted to the special needs of the pharmaceutical industry.

For integrated Operations and Corporate systems, many companies have adapted standard ERP packages which have integrated functionality that can be enhanced to provide the features needed for quality and regulatory control. (See Figure 12.7)

Figure 12.7 Features of Pharmaceutical Information Systems

Functional Area	Typical Features
Discovery	• Specialized simulation tools, databases, and technologies to support scientific experimentation and test many user-controlled applications
Development	• Large-scale data management and statistical analysis systems to collect and analyze results of clinical trials • Controlled document management systems to track documents and changes involved in FDA filings • Project management systems to monitor clinical development resources and spending
Manufacturing Operations	• Large-scale transaction systems for Enterprise Resource Planning (ERP), which are linked to systems that control and monitor production
Marketing	• Analytically oriented data warehouses and tools that are used for customer segmentation and market analysis • Customer profiles and behavior information obtained from vendors, combined with promotion information received from sales and other channels
Sales	• Electronic territory management systems (ETMS) to support field sales activities, including call planning, call recording and sample accountability • PDAs, tablets, and other remote technologies to simplify sales presentations
Managed Markets	• Large-scale systems used to administer pricing and contract eligibility, including government pricing • Account management tools, including account performance reporting
Distribution	• Order management and customer service systems to control order processing, pricing, customer billing, and product distribution to wholesalers and pharmacies
Corporate	• General systems for accounting, financial reporting, HR and other administrative functions • May be integrated with ERP

Source: Campbell Alliance.

IT Operations

In addition to providing specialized business applications, IT ensures the availability, capacity, and connectivity of systems and technology on a global basis. IT also establishes and maintains global standards for technology and communications to ensure global connectivity.

Operational Model for Information Technology

IT typically reports to the company's chief information officer (CIO), and some companies have separate CIOs for systems that support R&D. The CIO typically reports to the CEO, and, in some companies, the CIO sits on the company's board of directors.

IT staff members are deployed throughout the business, and IT professionals are usually dedicated to and often co-located with the business teams that they support. R&D, Operations, and Corporate teams tend to be managed globally; Sales, Marketing, Managed Markets, and Order Management systems tend to be supported by teams that are assigned to local affiliates. In addition to the business application teams, IT typically has groups that support Operations, Communications and overall IT Strategy. Figures 12.8 and 12.9 depicts a typical operational model for IT and descriptions of key functions.

Figure 12.8 Operational Model for Information Technology

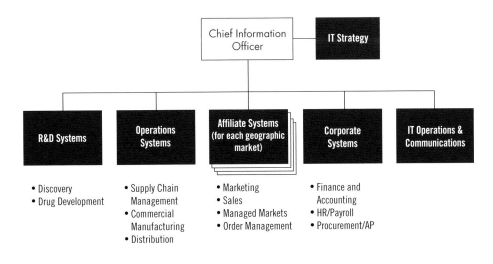

Source: Campbell Alliance.

Figure 12.9 Description of Functions of Information Technology

Functional Area	Description
IT Strategy	• Planning for emerging technologies and changes in business application architecture
R&D	• Simulation, clinical data management, and statistical systems that support discovery and drug development • May report to separate R&D IT leader
Operations	• Global systems that support supply chain management and commercial manufacturing operations
Affiliate	• Marketing, Sales and the systems that are typically controlled by geographically based affiliates • Local systems may be built on global standards and platforms, especially for order management and ETMS
Corporate	• Standard Accounting, Finance, HR and other systems that support corporate functions • Usually managed globally
IT Operations	• Day-to-day management of data centers and networks

Source: Campbell Alliance.

As discussed throughout this book, as competition intensifies, many companies are beginning to specialize in therapeutic areas and to develop therapies that target smaller populations. These changes, combined with the results of research on the human genome, are expected to have a significant impact on companies' operations and IT infrastructure.

5. Legal and Compliance

Legal helps line management navigate issues involving pricing, intellectual property (IP), and regulatory compliance.

Legal

Most pharmaceutical companies maintain a staff of attorneys and paralegals to help line management navigate through the many legal and regulatory issues that affect the business. Pricing, fraud and abuse, IP management—

which includes securing and protecting patents and other intellectual property for innovation—and regulatory compliance all fall within the purview of the legal staff. Additionally, any matters involving legal action by or against the company and business transactions conducted on behalf of the company (such as licensing products or collaborating with third-party research organizations) also involve the legal staff. Legal also helps a company manage its relationships with the FDA and other regulators.

The company's general counsel, who is always an attorney, leads the legal staff. Most companies also rely on the advice of outside counsel to provide expertise in specific legal issues or jurisdictions as the need arises, and there are law firms that specialize in issues or law affecting health care generally and the pharmaceutical industry specifically.

Compliance

A separate Compliance team enforces a company's ethical code of conduct. Most companies also have a compliance officer (or chief compliance officer), who may report to the general counsel or directly to the company's CEO (and sometimes to both). The compliance officer concentrates on a variety of matters, including compliance with laws and regulations, sales and marketing practices, ethics, anti-trust matters, conflicts of interest, and confidentiality. The compliance officer may also have responsibility for close coordination with Manufacturing, R&D, and Regulatory Affairs to help manage a company's overall compliance risk exposure.

The compliance officer often collaborates with the Legal staff to handle issues such as fraud and abuse associated with selling practices. Compliance programs also often involve staff training.

Government Affairs

Government Affairs supports lobbying efforts at the state and federal levels. These teams work to ensure that the company is fully aware of legislative proposals and their potential impact on the company.

Operational Model for Legal and Compliance

A company's legal staff may range in size from a few attorneys to over 100 attorneys and paralegals. Attorneys tend to be organized by area of specialty, such as regulatory, IP, general corporate and litigation. Some attorneys may be co-located with operations teams, especially IP attorneys who work closely with Discovery and Development teams to secure patents and protect the company's innovations. The general counsel almost always reports to the company's CEO. (See Figure 12.10 and Figure 12.11)

Figure 12.10 Operational Model for Legal and Compliance

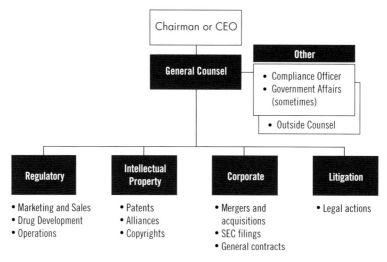

Source: Campbell Alliance.

Figure 12.11 Description of Functions of Legal and Compliance

Functions	Description
Regulatory	• Work with line functions and operations to ensure regulatory compliance involving Sales and Marketing, R&D, and Operations
Intellectual Property	• Work with R&D and others to protect company assets (innovation) and secure patents • Work on alliances and copyrights for promotional materials
Corporate	• Provide general legal support for mergers and acquisitions, SEC filings and contracts
Litigation	• Deal with court actions

Source: Campbell Alliance

6. Other Corporate Functions

Other Corporate Functions operate similarly to their peers in other industries. Pharmaceutical companies have functions for Corporate Communications, Public Relations, Procurement, and other areas that are essential to the successful operation of the business. The functions are guided by the unique characteristics of the business but operate in much the same way as in other industries. Their size and responsibilities are commensurate with the size and scale of the company, and many are global in scope.

INDEX

A

Abbreviated new drug applications (ANDAs), 118

Absorption (ADME testing), 21, 23

Access restrictions, drug classification based on, 27–30

Acquisitions, 113, 118

Active pharmaceutical ingredients (APIs), 19–20

    in generic drugs, 27

    manufacturing of, 190, 192, 204

    patented entities as, 71

    strength of, 20, 21

Acute care products, 26

Adherence to treatment, 47–49

ADME testing, 21, 23

Administrative infrastructure, 10–12

ADRs. *See* Adverse drug reactions

Advanced Planning & Scheduling (APS), 203

Adverse drug reactions (ADRs), 98

Adverse events (AEs), 98, 99

Advertising, direct-to-consumer, 49

AEs. *See* Adverse events

Agonists, 20

Alliances, 107, 109

Alternate site clinics, 216

American Medical Association (AMA), 6–7, 44, 158

ANDAs. *See* Abbreviated new drug applications

Antagonists, 20

APIs. *See* Active pharmaceutical ingredients

APS. *See* Advanced Planning & Scheduling

Average wholesale price (AWP), 138

B

Batch records, 195

BD. *See* Business Development

Behind-the-counter drugs, 30

Bias, protection against, 92–93

Big Pharma, external relationships/ partnerships of, 11–14

Biochemical effects of drugs, 22

Bioequivalence, 27

Biologic "large molecule" ingredients, 19, 20

Biologics Licensing Application (BLA), 76, 85, 193

Biotechnology companies (biotechs), 12, 107

BLA. *See* Biologics Licensing Application

"Black box" warnings, 31

Blockbuster drugs, 27, 187

Blood and blood products, 20

Branded messages, 128–129

Branded products, 26
    competition among, 35–36
    generics, 26
    high-demand, 186
    management of (*See* Marketing)
    prescription, 26–27

Brand teams, 146

Budget, marketing, 135

Business Development (BD), 11, 106–120
    approvals, 110–112, 118
    assessing opportunities, 112
    core competencies for, 119, 120
    defining strategy, 109–110
    and Discovery, 73
    and Drug Development, 102
    identifying opportunities, 110, 111
    importance of, 106–109
    and Marketing, 127
    monitoring deals, 119
    negotiating deals, 112–117
    operational model for, 119–120
    and out-licensing, 143
    overview of, 109
    procedure for, 108

C

Capacity planning, 199–200

Care settings
    drug classification based on, 24–26
    spectrum of, 3

Case report form (CRF), 97–100

CBER. *See* Center for Biologics Evaluation and Research

CDER. *See* Center for Drug Evaluation and Research

Center for Biologics Evaluation and Research (CBER), 5

Center for Drug Evaluation and Research (CDER), 5, 85

Chain warehouses, distribution via, 214

Channels
    communication, 129–131
    distribution, 211–215
    promotional, 124

Chargeback, 214

Chemical "small molecule" ingredients, 19

Chronic care products, 26

Classification of drugs, 23–30
    based on access restrictions, 27–30
    based on care setting, 26
    based on duration of use, 26
    based on market potential, 27
    based on novelty, 26–27
    based on target customer, 24, 25
    based on therapeutic categories, 24, 25

Clinical development
    average number of trials, 79
    clinical trials, 91–100
    cost of, 80
    Phase 1, 83–84

Phase 2, 84

Phase 3, 85

Phase 4, 90

phases of, 82–85, 90

timeline of, 78

Clinical research associates (CRAs), 94, 95, 98

Clinical research organizations. *See* Contract research organizations

Clinical systems, 231

CMOs. *See* Contract manufacturing organizations

Coatings, 22

Co-commercialization, 114

Combinatorial chemistry, 68

Commercialization, 113, 114

Commercial manufacturing, 192–193

Communication channels, 129–131

Competition, 35–36

Compliance
    as function, 235–236
    persistence vs., 47, 48

Compliance officers, 7, 235

Comprehensive commercial plan, 127, 128

Computer-aided drug design, 8

Computer validation, 202

Concessionary pricing, 54. *See also* Rebates

Consumers, 47–49
    demand influenced by, 39
    in driving product use, 47, 48
    key characteristics of, 48

Contract Management, 175, 177, 179–182, 184

Contract manufacturing organizations (CMOs), 14, 206

Contract packaging organizations (CPOs), 14

Contract research organizations (CROs), 94, 95, 98, 99, 101, 103–104, 199

Contract sales organization (CSOs), 14, 165

Contract terms, 115–117

Controlled substances, 27–29

Corporate Communications, 234

Corporate infrastructure, 10–12

Corporate systems, 230

Cosmetics, 18

Cost management, 7–8

Cost structure (drugs), 34, 35

CPOs. *See* Contract packaging organizations

CRAs. *See* Clinical research associates

CRF. *See* Case report form

CROs. *See* Contract research organizations

CSOs. *See* Contract sales organization

Customers, 38–59
    consumers and patients, 47–49
    government as, 40, 41
    influences among, 38
    major groups of, 38–42
    payers and pharmacy benefit managers, 50–55
    pharmacies and pharmacists, 54, 56–59
    physicians and other prescribers, 42–47
    price breaks to, 138, 139
    "Trade," 135

Customer Service, 218

D

Data Management, 10

Data vendors, 132

DAW. *See* Dispense as written

DDMAC. *See* Division of Drug Marketing, Advertising, and Communications

DEA. *See* Drug Enforcement Administration

Deals. *See* Business Development

Deal value, 116–117

Deciles, 155, 156

Delivery methods, 21, 191

Demand
  forecasting, 200
  influencing, 38–40, 42, 50

Department of Defense (DOD), 173
  as customer, 41
  pricing for, 139

Department of Justice (DOJ), 118

Deployment, logistics of, 137

Details, sales, 151–153

Development. *See also* Business Development; Drug Development
  deals occurring during, 113–114
  Marketing role during, 126–128

Devices, 18

Diagnostics, 2

Dietary supplements, 19

Direct purchase systems, 216–217

Direct-to-consumer (DTC)
  advertising, 49
  promotion, 124

Discounts, 178

Discovery, 33, 62–74
  deals occurring during, 113
  disease and target selection, 65–66
  duration of, 79
  importance of, 62–65
  lead identification, 66–69
  lead optimization, 70–71
  lead series, 70
  Marketing role during, 126–128
  operational model for, 73–74
  patient protection, 71–72
  process of, 65
  transition to Development, 72–73

Dispense as written (DAW), 44, 45

Dispersing agents, 22

Distribution, 210–219
  in ADME testing, 21, 23
  direct purchase systems, 216–217
  importance of, 210–212
  launching products into, 217
  in manufacturing, 187
  operational model for, 218–219
  patient access points, 215–216
  primary channels for, 212–215

Districts, sales, 161–162

Divestiture, 113

Division of Drug Marketing, Advertising, and Communications (DDMAC), 129

Document Management Systems (DMS), 203

DOD. *See* Department of Defense

DOJ. *See* Department of Justice

Dosage ranges, 23

Dosing regimens, 30

Double-blind studies, 92, 93

Drivers of product use
    consumers, 47, 48
    pharmacists, 56
    prescribers, 43

Drug Development, 33, 76–104
    application for marketing product, 85–89
    clinical trials, 91–100
    conduct of studies, 94–95, 97–99
    duration of, 79
    incremental approach to, 8
    operational model for, 100–104
    Phase 1 trials, 83–84
    Phase 2 trials, 84
    Phase 3 trials, 85
    Phase 4 studies, 90
    phases of, 77, 78, 82–85, 90
    preclinical, 80–82
    risk in, 4
    success rate for, 7, 78
    transition from Discovery to, 72–73

Drug Enforcement Administration (DEA), 5, 44, 58

Drug formularies, 51, 53–54

Drugs, 18–36. *See also specific topics*
    active pharmaceutical ingredients in, 19–20
    ADME testing of, 21
    classification of, 23–30
    costs of, 7
    definition of, 18–19
    formulation of, 20–22
    generic, 8 (*See also* Generic drugs)
    lifestyle-enhancement, 4
    and managed care, 7
    manufacturing process for, 190–192
    means of discovering, 67 (*See also* Discovery)
    mechanism of action for, 20, 21
    pharmacodynamics, 22–23
    pharmacokinetics, 21
    physical forms of, 191
    product life cycle for, 32–36
    in US market, 30–32

Drug utilization review (DUR), 59

Drug wholesalers, 39

DTC. *See* Direct-to-consumer

Durable medical equipment, 2

DUR. *See* Drug utilization review

Duration of use, drug classification based on, 24–26

E

Electronic records, 202

Employers, as payers, 38

Enterprise Resource Planning (ERP), 203

Ethical issues, gray areas in, 7

Excipients, 20, 22

Excretion (ADME testing), 21, 23

External relationships, 11–14

F

FDA. *See* Food and Drug Administration

Federal Food, Drug and Cosmetic Act (FFDCA), 18

Federal Trade Commission (FTC), 5, 118, 158

FFDCA. *See* Federal Food, Drug and Cosmetic Act

Field Communications group, 169

Financial Management and Control, 224–227

Financial projections, 135

Food and Drug Administration (FDA), 5, 6, 18–20
    approval of drugs by, 30
    and clinical development process, 77
    consumer advertising oversight by, 49
    Division of Drug Marketing, Advertising, and Communications (DDMAC), 129
    Good Clinical Practices, 94
    Good Manufacturing Practices, 193–194
    IND applications to, 81
    market exclusivity granted by, 33
    and NDA approval process, 85–90
    NDC number assignment by, 31
    NME/NCE testing requirements of, 83
    promotional claims monitoring by, 129
    promotion restrictions by, 42
    and SAE reporting, 98, 99
    sales regulation by, 158
    and validation of processes, 194

Formularies, drug, 51, 53–54

Formulation of drugs, 20–22, 190–191

Franchise model, 145

Frequency (sales calls), 156

FTC. *See* Federal Trade Commission

Full-service pharmaceutical companies
    business development in, 10
    corporate and administrative infrastructure for, 10–12
    external relationships/partnerships of, 11–14

major activities of, 9–10
    structure of, 8–14

G

GCP. *See* Good Clinical Practices

Gene-based targeting, 69

Generic drugs, 8, 27
    ANDAs for, 118
    excipients and reactions to, 22
    name used for sales of, 26
    and product life cycles, 33
    substitution of, 59

Generic erosion, 34

Genomics, 69

Geographic leadership, 11, 12

Global Marketing, 144

Global organizations, 11

Global pharmaceutical industry, 14–15

GMPs. *See* Good Manufacturing Practices

Good Clinical Practices (GCP), 94, 98

Good Manufacturing Practices (GMPs), 193–194, 197

Government, as customer group, 40, 41

Government Affairs, 235

GPOs. *See* Group Purchasing Organizations

Group-model HMO pharmacies, 58

Group Purchasing Organizations (GPOs), 139

Growth stage, 34, 141–142

H

Hart-Scott-Rodino Antitrust Improvements Act of 1976, 118

Healthcare
> costs of, 7–8
> role of pharmaceuticals in, 2–3
> spectrum of settings for, 3
> tax dollars for, 40

Health insurance system, 7

Health maintenance organizations (HMOs)
> pharmacies/pharmacists in, 58

Hepatitis C, 122

HER2, 62

High prescribers, 149, 154

High-throughput screening, 68

HMOs. *See* Health maintenance organizations

Home health care agencies, 216

Hospital-based care products, 26

Hospital pharmacies, 56, 57, 215–216

HR. *See* Human Resources

Human epidermal growth factor receptor 2 (HER2), 62

Human Resources (HR), 227–230

I

Inactive ingredients, 20

Incentive compensation (sales), 166–168

Incremental approach (drug development), 8

IND application. *See* Investigational New Drug application

Indemnity plans, as payers, 40

Indications, new, 143

Influence, points of, 42

Information technology (IT), 201–204, 234–230

In-licensing, 108, 113, 115

Innovation, 8, 9. *See also* Discovery
> overview of, 9
> profit as driver of, 4

Institutional pharmacies, 56, 58

Institutional review board (IRB), 91, 92

Institutional sales forces, 162

Insurers, as customers, 38

Internal audits, 225, 226

Internet pharmacies, 57, 216

Interventions, 51

Investigational New Drug (IND) application, 77, 81, 82

In vitro testing, 63, 64, 70, 71

In vivo testing, 64, 70, 71

IRB. *See* Institutional review board

Isomers, 34, 35

IT. *See* Information technology

J

Japan, global pharmaceutical sales in, 15

K

Key communication channels, 129–131

Key opinion leaders (KOLs), 45, 133, 158

KOLs. *See* Key opinion leaders.

L

Labeling
    accountability in, 199
    in manufacturing, 187
    NDC, 31

Laboratory Information Management Systems (LIMS), 203

"Large molecule" ingredients, 19

Launching products, 217

Launch stage, 34, 137, 140–141

Lead compounds, 63
    identification of, 66–69
    optimization of, 70–71
    series of, 70

Legal, 232–234
    and Discovery, 73
    and Drug Development, 102
    as "watchdog" department, 7

Licensing
    Biologics Licensing Application, 76, 85
    in-licensing, 108, 113, 115
    opportunities for, 110, 111
    out-licensing, 73, 108, 113–115, 143
    partnerships for, 108
    of prescribers, 44
    state license boards, 44

Life cycle. *See* Product life cycle

Lifestyle enhancement drugs, 4

LIMS (Laboratory Information Management Systems), 203

Line extensions, 143

Logistics, 218

M

Mail-order pharmacies, 57, 216

Managed care, controls imposed by, 7

Managed care organizations (MCOs), 38, 40, 73
    educational programs for, 178-179
    as payers, 50
    pharmacies/pharmacists in, 59
    reliance on PBMs by, 52–53

Managed Markets, 173–184
    account management, 177–180
    collaboration with sales, 182
    contract administration, 179–182
    goal of, 174–175
    importance of, 173–174
    marketing for, 175–177
    operational model for, 183–184
    primary functions in, 175
    and promotional strategy, 135
    sales force for, 164, 175, 177–180, 184

Managed Markets Marketing, 175–177

Managed Markets Sales, 175, 177–180, 184

Manufacturing and Operations, 9–11

Manufacturing Execution Systems (MES), 203

Manufacturing Operations, 186–207
    commercial manufacturing, 192–193
    development and scale-up of, 189

importance of, 186–188

IT support in, 201–203

labeling, packaging, and distribution, 187

manufacturing process development, 186–187, 190–192

operational model for, 204–207

product packaging, 197–199

quality systems, 193–197

Supply Chain Management, 187–188, 199–201

Manufacturing processes

    development of, 186–187, 190–192

    validation of, 194–195

Market exclusivity, 33, 36

Marketing, 122–146

    and Discovery, 73

    during discovery and development stage, 126–128

    and Drug Development, 102

    financial projections, 135

    Global, 144

    during growth stage, 141–142

    importance of, 122–125

    key communication channels, 129–131

    during launch stage, 137, 140–141

    local, 144

    long-term product data-generation plan, 124

    during maturity stage, 142–143

    message plan, 128–129

    organizational model for, 143–146

    patient targeting, 133–135

    payer targeting, 135, 136

    prescriber targeting, 132–133

    priorities in, 123

    and product life cycle stages, 126

product performance monitoring, 125

product pricing, 138–139

promotional mix, 135–137

promotional strategy, 123–124

regional, 144

sales targeting, 132

strategies for, 39

Marketing and Sales, 9–11

Market potential, drug classification based on, 27

Markets, managed. See Managed markets

Market share performance, 141

Maturity stage, 34, 142–143

MCOs. See Managed care organizations

Mechanisms of action, 20, 21

Medicaid, 41, 138, 139, 173

Medical Affairs, 10, 103

Medical devices, 2, 18

Medical directors, 94, 95

Medical science liaisons (MSLs), 103, 158

Medical supplies, 2

Medicare, 40, 41, 173

Medicare Prescription Drug, Improvement, and Modernization Act of 2003, 40, 118

Medicines. See Drugs

Mergers, 118

MES (Manufacturing Execution Systems), 203

Message platform, 123, 128–129

Metabolism (ADME testing), 21, 23

"Me-too" drugs, 176

Mirrored sales forces, 164–165

246

Molecular modeling, 68, 69

MSLs. *See* Medical science liaisons

Multisource products, 26

N

National Drug Code (NDC), 31

NCE. *See* New chemical entity

NDAs. *See* New Drug Applications

NDC (National Drug Code), 31

Negotiating deals, 112–117

New chemical entity (NCE), 71, 72, 83

New Drug Applications (NDAs), 85–90
    classification of, 87–88
    clinical trials prior to, 79
    major components of, 86
    and Phase 3 trials, 85
    and process quality, 194
    review process for, 88

New molecular entity (NME), 71, 72, 83

NME. *See* New molecular entity

Non-clinical studies, 82

Non-professional promotions, 130

North America, global pharmaceutical sales in, 15

Novelty, drug classification based on, 26–27

Nursing home pharmacies, 58

Nutraceuticals, 19

O

Occupational Safety and Health Administration (OSHA), 190

Office-based care products, 26

Office of the Inspector General (OIG), 5, 158

Off-label uses of products, 30, 158

OIG. *See* Office of the Inspector General

"Open label" trials, 90

Operational model
    for Business Development, 119–120
    for Discovery, 73–74
    for Distribution, 218–219
    for Drug Development, 100–104
    for Financial Management and Control, 225–227
    for Human Resources, 228–229
    for Information Technology, 233, 234
    for Legal and Compliance, 235–236
    for Managed Markets, 183–184
    for Manufacturing Operations, 204–207
    for Sales, 168–170

Operations systems, 231, 232

Opportunities
    assessment of, 110–112
    segmentation based on, 132

Oral delivery method, 21

Organizational model, for Marketing and brand management, 143–146

"Orphan" drugs, 27

OSHA. *See* Occupational Safety and Health Administration

OTC medications. *See* Over-the-counter medications

Out-licensing, 73, 108, 113–115, 143

Outsourcing
    of clinical development, 103–104
    of distribution, 218–219
    drivers of, 200
    of manufacturing, 206
    relationships in, 13–14

Over-the-counter (OTC) medications,
28–29

P

P1/P2/P3, 152

Package inserts (PIs), 31–32, 86–87

Packaging, product, 187, 197–199

PAI (Pre-Approval Inspection), 194

Parenteral delivery method, 21

Partnerships, 11–14, 107–110

Patents, 8, 32
    for isomers, 35
    protecting, 71–72
    window of protection by, 32–34

Patient access points, 215–216

Patients, 47–49
    as customers, 38
    monitoring of, 3
    pharmacy profiles of, 59
    as target customers, 133–135

Payers, 38, 50–55
    demand influenced by, 39
    formulary evaluation criteria of, 53
    pricing for, 139
    strategies for winning over, 8
    as target customers, 135, 136

Payments, deal, 117

PBMs. *See* Pharmacy benefit managers

PCPs. *See* Primary care physicians

PDMA. *See* Prescription Drug Marketing
Act

PDUFA. *See* Prescription Drug User Fee
Act of 1997

Performance monitoring, 141

Persistence (in product use), 47, 48

Pharmaceutical companies
    Big Pharma, 11–14
    differentiation by, 46
    external, as source of intellectual
    property, 107
    full-service, 8–14
    and managed care, 7
    negative perception of, 8
    points of influence for, 42
    regulatory control framework for, 6–7

Pharmaceutical industry
    cost management in, 7–8
    full-service pharmaceutical
    companies, 8–14
    impact of, 4
    innovation in, 8, 9
    regulatory framework for, 5–7
    role of, 2
    worldwide scope of, 14–15

Pharmaceutical Research and
Manufacturers of America (PhRMA),
6, 158

Pharmaceuticals
    decision-making process for, 40, 42
    in healthcare, 2
    indications for, 30

Pharmacies, 39, 54, 56–59
    classes of trade, 56

classifications of, 54, 56

pricing for, 138, 139

in supply chain, 40

Pharmacists, 54, 56–59

care management/counseling by, 40

in driving product selection/use, 56

role of, 58–59

in supply chain, 40

Pharmacodynamics, 22–23

Pharmacogenomics, 69

Pharmacokinetics, 21

Pharmacy and therapeutics (P&T) committees, 51, 53

Pharmacy benefit managers (PBMs), 40, 51–54

PhRMA. *See* Pharmaceutical Research and Manufacturers of America

Physician offices, drug inventory of, 216

Physicians, 42–47

as customers, 38

demand influenced by, 39

drugs prescribed by, 30

high prescribers, 149, 154

number of, 45

sales reps' access to, 153

Physiological effects of drugs, 22

Pilot plants, 191–192

PIs. *See* package inserts; *also* principal investigators

Placebo groups, 93

Plan of Action (POA), 137, 156–158

Plant maintenance systems, 203

POA. *See* Plan of Action

POC. *See* Proof of concept

Points of influence, 42

Positioning, 123

Pre-approval inspection (PAI), 194

Precautions (on labels), 31

Preclinical development, 77, 78, 80–82

Pre-launch stage, marketing during, 128–137

Premerger Notification Program, 118

Prescribers, 42–47

classifications of, 45

defined, 42

in driving product use, 43

high prescribers, 149

key characteristics of, 43

licensing and professional guidelines for, 44

segmentation of, 132–133

as target customers, 132–133

Prescription Drug Marketing Act (PDMA), 159

Prescription drugs, 28

effective patent life for, 34

Medicare benefits for, 40

OTC forms of, 29

Prescription Drug User Fee Act of 1997 (PDUFA), 88

Prescriptions, written, 44–45

Presentations, sales, 151–153

Pricing, 138–139

for government, 40

for Managed Markets, 177–179

for position on formulary, 54

Primary care physicians (PCPs), 45, 153

Primary care products, 25

Primary packaging, 197–198

Principal investigators (PIs), 94, 95, 97

Printing inks, 22

Procurement, 201, 236

Production forecasts, 200

Production targets, 200

Product life cycle, 32–36. *See also specific stages*
    deals during stages of, 113–115
    marketing objectives during, 126

Products
    extending life of, 143
    packaging of, 187, 197–199
    performance monitoring for, 125
    quality of, 196–197

Professional promotions, 130

Profit margins, 34

Project managers, 94, 95

Promotional claims, language for, 32

Promotional mix, 124, 135–137

Promotions. *See also* Marketing
    channels for, 129–130
    to consumers, 49
    to prescribers, 46, 47
    professional vs. non-professional, 130
    strategy for, 123–124, 128, 135
    total US spending on, 124

Proof of concept (POC), 84

Protein-based targeting, 69

P&T committees. *See* Pharmacy and therapeutics committees

Public Relations, 236

Q

QA. *See* Quality Assurance

QC. *See* Quality Control

Quality Assurance (QA), 103, 193–195, 197

Quality Control (QC), 193, 196, 197

Quality Management, 204

Quality of life, 4

Quality systems, 193–197
    external regulation of, 197
    or processes, 194–195
    for products, 196–197

R

Randomization, 93

R&D. *See* Research and Development

Rebates, 54, 178

Reformulations, 143

Regional Marketing units, 144

Regions, sales, 161–162

Regulation. *See also specific laws*
    of clinical investigations, 94
    framework of, 5–7
    of quality, 197
    of sales, 158–159

Regulatory Affairs, 7, 10, 102–103

Regulatory functions, business units responsible for, 11

Research and Development (R&D), 9–11
    and BD function, 119
    Discovery in, 63

Research-based pharmaceutical companies, 8, 13. *See also* Full-service pharmaceutical companies

Retail pharmacies, 54, 56, 57, 135, 215

Revenues
  for brands vs. generics, 27, 28
  at expiration of patents, 35
  generic erosion of, 34
  monitoring of, 140, 141
  pharmaceutical, 14

S

SAEs. *See* Serious adverse events

Sales, 148–170
  forecasts of, 125, 128
  global, 15
  importance of, 148–150
  incentive compensation for, 166–168
  Managed Markets collaboration with, 182
  Marketing role in, 125
  operational model for, 168–170
  peak, 34
  plan of action for, 156–158
  to prescribers, 46
  regulatory oversight of, 158–159
  resizing of sales force, 165–166
  sales force, 149
  sales presentation (detail), 151–153
  size/structure of sales force, 160–165
  strategy for, 150–151
  targeting, 154–156
  training in, 159–160

Sales calls, 152, 153

Sales force
  incentive plans for, 166–168

investment in, 149
mirrored, 164–165
resizing of, 165–166
size/structure of, 160–165
in US, 149

Sales force automation (SFA) systems, 153, 231

Sales Operations, 169

Samples, product, 45, 152

Scale-up, 77, 189, 192

Schedules (controlled substances), 27–29

Secondary packaging, 198–199

Segmentation, 136
  of patients, 133, 134
  of prescribers, 132–133, 155
  for sales, 155
  for sales force organization, 162, 164

Selective norepinephrine reuptake inhibitors (SNRIs), 172

Selective serotonin reuptake inhibitors (SSRIs), 172

Serious adverse events (SAEs), 98, 99

SFA systems. *See* Sales force automation systems

Side effects, 22

Single blinding, 93

Single-source products, 26

Site management organizations (SMOs), 104

"Small molecule" ingredients, 19

SMOs. *See* site management organizations

SNRIs *See* selective norepinephrine reuptake inhibitors

Specialists (physicians), 45–46

Specialty care products, 25

Specialty distributors, 214–215

Specialty pharmacies, 56–57, 215

SSRIs. *See* selective serotonin reuptake inhibitors

Staff-model HMO pharmacies, 58

State boards of pharmacy, 44

State license boards, 44

Steroids, 20

Strategies
    brand, 146
    business development, 109–110
    for managed markets, 174–175
    marketing, 39, 151
    promotional, 123–124, 128, 135
    sales, 150–151
    for winning over payers, 8

Strength, drug, 20, 21

Study protocols, 91, 92, 98

Suppliers, 12, 13

Supply chain management, 187–188, 199–201

T

Target customers
    drug classification based on, 24–26
    patients as, 133–135
    payers as, 135, 136
    prescribers as, 132–133
    sales to, 132, 154–156

Target product profile, 66

Target selection (Discovery), 63, 65–66

Territories, sales, 161–162

Tertiary packaging, 199

Therapeutic categories, drug classification based on, 24, 25

Therapeutic model, 145

Therapeutic window, 23

Tiered co-pays, 54

TNF. *See* tumor necrosis factor

Tobacco products, 19

Toxicity, 22–23

"Trade" customers, 39, 135, 173, 174

Trade Relations, 183, 184, 218

Training, sales, 159–160

Transdermal delivery method, 21

Trials. *See* Clinical development

Tumor necrosis factor (TNF), 76

U

Unbranded messages, 128, 129

United States Patent and Trademark Office (USPTO), 32

United States (US)
    distribution centers in, 204
    drugs marketed in, 30–32
    pharmaceutical revenues in, 14

USPTO. *See* United States Patent and Trademark Office

Utilization management programs, 54, 55

V

Vaccines, 20

Value-added programs, 178–179

Vendors, 12, 14
>data, 132
>full-service CROs, 104

Veterans Healthcare Administration (VHA), 41, 173

VHA. *See* Veterans Healthcare Administartion

Virtual development model, 103

W

WAC. *See* Wholesale acquisition cost

Warehouses, chain, 214

Warnings (on labels), 31

"Watchdog" departments, 7

Wellness, drugs promoting, 2

Western Europe, global pharmaceutical sales in, 15

Wholesale acquisition cost (WAC), 138, 214

Wholesalers, 39, 135
>pricing for, 139
>as primary distribution channel, 212–214